The Multimedia Workshop

Macromedia Director

Matthew Holtz

Wadsworth Publishing Company
I(T)P™ An International Thomson Publishing Company

Belmont • Albany • Bonn • Boston • Cincinnati • Detroit • London • Madrid • Melbourne
Mexico City • New York • Paris • San Francisco • Singapore • Tokyo • Toronto • Washington

Technology Publisher: Kathy Shields
Assistant Editor: Tamara Huggins
Production: Stacey C. Sawyer, Sawyer & Williams
Production Services Coordinator: Gary Mcdonald
Print Buyer: Karen Hunt
Permissions Editor: Peggy Meehan
Designer: Gary Palmatier
Copy Editor: Patterson Lamb
Technical Illustrator: Fog Press
Cover: Cloyce Wall; photo by David Bishop
Signing Representative: Dwayne Coy
Compositor: Fog Press
Printer: The Johnson & Hardin Company

This book is printed on acid-free recycled paper

Printed in the United States of America
1 2 3 4 5 6 7 8 9 10—01 00 99 98 97 96

For more information, contact Wadsworth Publishing Company:

Wadsworth Publishing Company
10 Davis Drive
Belmont, California 94002, USA

International Thomson Publishing Europe
Berkshire House 168-173
High Holborn
London, WC1V 7AA, England

Thomas Nelson Australia
102 Dodds Street
South Melbourne 3205
Victoria, Australia

Nelson Canada
1120 Birchmount Road
Scarborough, Ontario
Canada M1K 5G4

International Thomson Editores
Campos Eliseos 385, Piso 7
Col. Polanco
11560 México D.F. México

International Thomson Publishing GmbH
Königswinterer Strasse 418
53227 Bonn, Germany

International Thomson Publishing Asia
221 Henderson Road
#05-10 Henderson Building
Singapore 0315

International Thomson Publishing Japan
Hirakawacho Kyowa Building, 3F
2-2-1 Hirakawacho
Chiyoda-ku, Tokyo 102, Japan

ISBN: 0-534-31073-7

Library of Congress Cataloging-in-Publication Data

Holtz, Matthew.
The multimedia workshop : macromedia director / Matthew Holtz.
p. cm.
Includes index.
ISBN 0-534-31073-7
1. Multimedia systems. 2. Macromedia director. I. Title.
QA76.575.H668 1995
006.6—dc20 95-20204
CIP

Contents

Preface

Purpose

The Multimedia Workshop comprises a series of texts about multimedia applications and related software. Each book in the series focuses on one particular software package. By using one or more texts in the series, you will become familiar with multimedia software and gain experience in creating your own applications. Each book provides beginning/intermediate levels of understanding for the software covered.

Prerequisites

These books presume that users have some experience with the Windows operating environment. However, reviews of Windows procedures are provided as they are used.

Approach

The Multimedia Workshop uses a practical approach. Its texts begin with the basics and emphasize what you need to know in today's multimedia environment. Comprehension is stressed rather than memorization; however, when memorization is necessary, the texts offer some memory aids.

Saving and Submitting Your Work

Follow your instructor's directions on where to store your work—for example, on a floppy disk or in a directory on a hard disk. Be sure to make backups of your work. Your instructor will tell you whether to submit your work on disk or in printed form or both.

Chapter Organization

Each chapter begins with a list of chapter objectives that tell you what you will learn in the chapter.

The main section of each chapter covers a software-specific multimedia topic. Coverage includes discussion, examples, hands-on exercises, organized lists, illustrations, and notes. In addition, all new terms are defined when the terms are introduced.

The end-of-chapter material includes a list of key terms covered in the chapter, as well as review questions to test your understanding.

Projects

Projects also appear at the end of each chapter. They review the material learned in the chapter and help you apply it in new ways. Some projects require only that you recall what you have learned, others that you expand on chapter material, and still others that you do research. Projects may require the creation of disk files or printed output; your instructor will let you know if you need to submit the material for evaluation.

Notes

A variety of notes cover points that are tangential to the section topic. These notes are signaled by a "catch word" that appears at the beginning of each note to alert you to the note's purpose or topic. Examples are "Careful," "Troubleshooting," "Reminder," "Preview," and "Note." Notes are identified by an arrow like the one at left.

Appendix/Glossary/Index

Each book in the Multimedia Workshop series has an appendix that consists of an alphabetical listing of procedures, along with the steps needed to accomplish them. Each book also includes a glossary with definitions of terms used in the text, along with the chapter where each term is discussed. In addition, there is also a comprehensive index at the end of each book.

Second Color

The book design uses a second color to direct your attention to the hands-on exercises. This color is also used in the art to indicate areas that are under discussion.

Chronological Coaching

Throughout this series, command sequences are presented in the order in which they are performed. I call this approach *chronological coaching*; it makes the sequences logical to follow and hence easier to learn. For example, other manuals might say something like "Change the Directories option by using the Save As command on the File menu." Instead, we would say "Use the File menu's Save command to change the Directories option." Thus steps are clearly laid out in the logical order in which they must be executed.

Command and Other Conventions

Commands on the various menus are presented with "hot keys" indicated as they appear on the screen. Thus underlined letters in commands on the screen are underlined when referenced in text, and so on. However, ellipses (. . .), which indicate that a command leads to a menu, are generally omitted in text because what occurs after the command is usually under discussion anyway. Also, to distinguish them from general text, commands and options have initial capital letters, even when they are lowercase on the screen.

Defaults will generally be used (for example, c:\ to indicate the hard drive). Your instructor will tell you if your defaults differ.

Technologies

You will use the software under discussion to create a variety of files on disk. You may also make use of sample files provided with the software. You might examine sample files to determine how they are constructed and at times incorporate them into your own work. If you have the equipment, you can also make use of video and audio.

Practical Tips

Preview each chapter by looking at the figures. Check the table of contents as well, to preview the headings in the chapter.

Take your time in following the steps so that you don't accidentally skip or incorrectly execute a key step. Although I have tried to anticipate what you could do wrong, it's not possible to foresee all possibilities. Errors may not be immediately evident and could come back to haunt you long after you create them, making troubleshooting difficult.

Save your work regularly. Always save before leaving your computer or when something else requires your attention. Also, save before trying something new or complicated. That way, should you make an error that is immediately evident, you can retrieve the saved version of the file.

Be sure to check your results against the figures as you work. That way, you'll know right away if you make an error, and you'll know what to do to correct it.

Also, as you proceed, make sure that you *understand* each step; just pressing keys and clicking a mouse are not enough to teach you a skill. Review each section as you complete it. Make sure that you know you could do again what you just did; if not, review again until you can.

To the Instructor

Books in the Multimedia Workshop series cover authoring systems, programming, word processing, animation, audio production, and other topics. They can be used as texts in courses on multimedia or in parts of a generalized PC course.

Each book provides an introductory overview of an authoring program, or uses other programs alone or as a supplement to one or more authoring programs. By combining a variety of books—for example, on animation, audio, word processing, and authoring—students can acquire the skills to create complex projects from start to finish.

An instructor's manual (on disk) is available. It provides a detailed outline of the book, answers to the review questions, tips and troubleshooting, and quiz questions with answers. It also tells you how to prepare the computers for student use (for example, by protecting certain files against alteration) and to purge student files once the students are finished with the computer.

Acknowledgments

Special thanks go to the following for assistance in putting this book together: Myles Jacob Loyar; George Bergquist, Kathy Shields, Tamara Huggins, Stacey C. Sawyer, and all the other fine people at Wadsworth or associated with them; Timothy Holtz; Reverend John P. Schlegel, S. J. and the University of San Francisco; Bobby Winston and the San Francisco Shakespeare Festival; Jonathan Cooper, Michael Nadile, and Gerald Beaugez; and Eugene Brott.

I am especially grateful to IBM for the generous use of their fine equipment. Their technical support is just great.

Reviewers were Steve Jackson, Boise State University; Donald L. Jordan, Lamar University; and Brian Scarbeau, Beacon College.

Starting to Create with Director

THIS CHAPTER WILL TEACH YOU HOW TO

- **Start up Director**
- **Use the main tools of Director**
- **Design and save a movie**
- **Select, resize, and move objects**
- **Quit Director and use various icons in the Macromedia group**

WHAT IS DIRECTOR?

Director is a product of Macromedia Incorporated, located in San Francisco, California. It is a multimedia authoring program. By using Director, you—the ***author***—can create ***movies*** (also called *titles* or *applications* or *files*) with which others—the ***users***—interact on the computer to gain information and knowledge.

Director is but one of numerous authoring programs that operate on IBM personal computers and compatible machines under the Windows operating environment. Other popular authoring programs (and the companies that manufacture them) include Authorware (also from Macromedia), Multimedia ToolBook (Asymetrix), IconAuthor (Aimtech), Multimedia Viewer (Microsoft), and Multimedia Explorer (Autodesk). Each has its own unique approach for creating multimedia applications.

To create a multimedia application with Director you can combine a variety of media, such as text, animation, still graphics, sound, and video. Movies are controlled by a sophisticated grid system that coordinates all that occurs on the IBM at any given time.

THE MACROMEDIA PROGRAM GROUP

Follow these steps to start up Director.

Turn on your computer.

If Windows starts up automatically with your computer, you can skip the next step.

Type WIN to start Windows, and press the Enter key.

To start up Director, normally you first use the following steps to activate the Macromedia Director program group. If either the program group or the Director icon is already on your screen, these steps will not be necessary to start Director.

Open the Window menu.

If Macromedia appears on the menu, select it. Otherwise, select More Windows and use the resulting scroll box to select Macromedia.

The Macromedia program group appears (Figure 1.1). In this program group, there are four program items. You'll use only one item now (and generally, as well). At the end of this chapter, we'll look at the others.

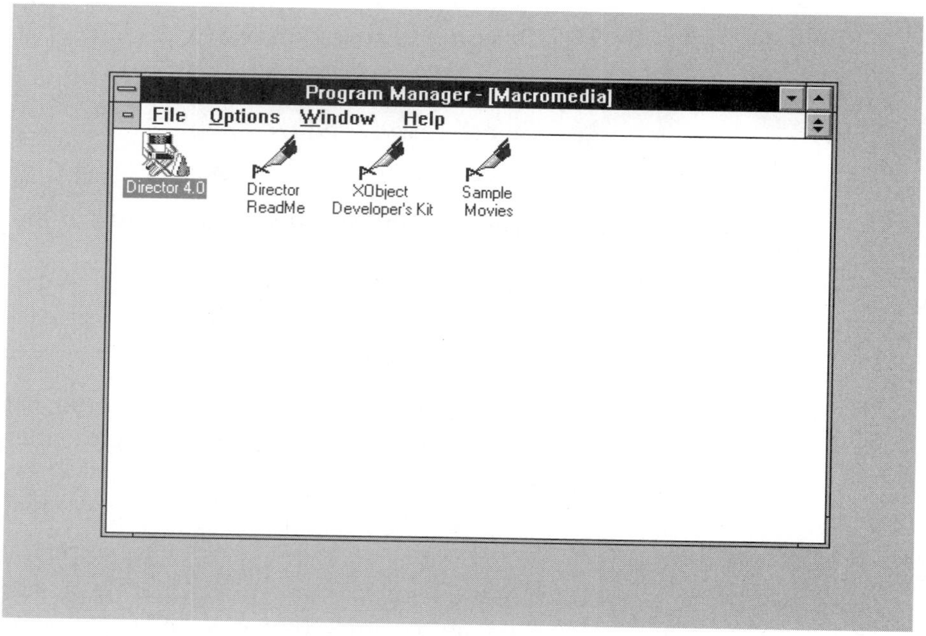

1.1 Macromedia program group with Director 4.0 icon

STARTING DIRECTOR

Start Director by selecting the **Director 4.0** program item (shown in color in Figure 1.1).

The Director window opens. The Director splash screen (Figure 1.2) appears briefly, showing the Director and Macromedia logos and the user and copyright information.

1.2 Director's splash screen

Once the splash screen goes away, Director will normally present you with several additional windows of its own, as shown in Figure 1.3. The arrangement shown in this figure is the initial setup that occurs when Director is installed. However, these windows, as well as other windows and related items, can be turned on and off. Director records the resulting arrangement on exiting. Thus, if others have been using your installed copy of Director, the screen you initially see may differ from that which you find here. As we proceed in this chapter, we'll discuss how to display and remove such items from the screen; for the moment, ignore any discrepancies between your computer and the figures.

THE MAIN WINDOWS

This view of Director has several areas of interest that we'll examine now. As we take this tour, we'll discuss various Director operations.

Windows Tools

Let's begin examining the Director screen by quickly reviewing its Windows-related tools (shown in color in Figure 1.3). You should be generally familiar with these items from an understanding of Windows, but there are some

1.3

Director's main windows with Windows-related tools

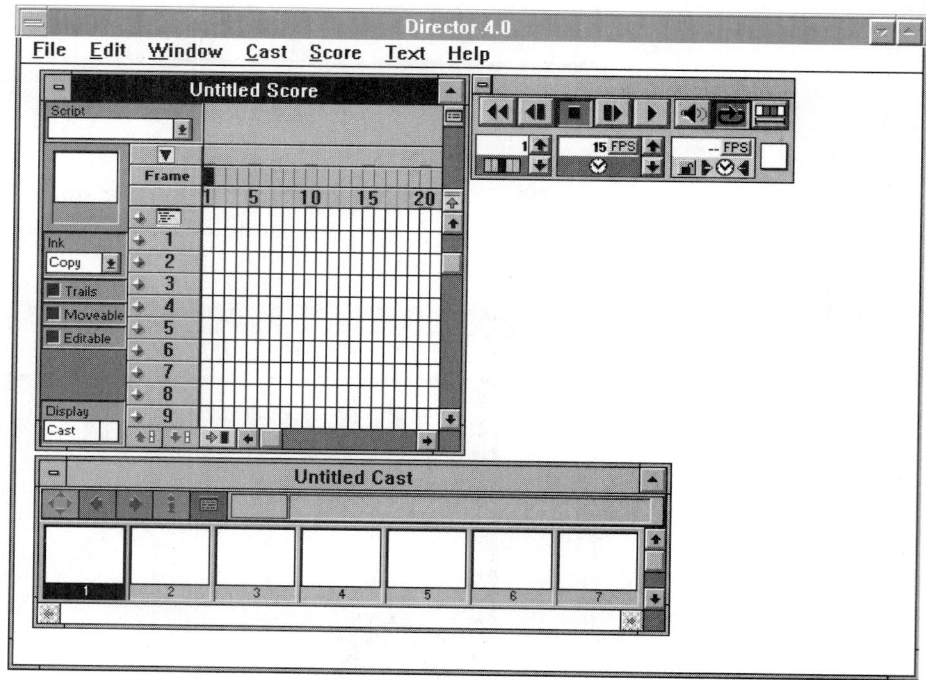

points relating to Director that need to be made. From left to right these tools are as follows:

- **Control-menu box** Contains items to change the size and position of the current window—that is, the Director window. It also allows you to close the Director window or to switch to another window.
- **Title bar** Simply displays the name "Director" and the name of the loaded file. This allows you to distinguish this window from others that are running when two or more are displayed simultaneously.
- **Minimize button** Shrinks the Director window to the size of an icon (which you can then double-click or use the Ctrl-Esc Task List or Alt-Tab to restore).
- **Maximize button** Expands the Director window so it occupies the entire screen. Except for the Control-menu box, maximizing causes all Windows-related tools to disappear, including the Title bar.

Use of the Maximize button can cause consternation since there is no Restore button for restoring the screen, as there normally is with Windows programs. Instead, you must use the Control-menu box to restore. Practice doing so as follows:

> Click the **Maximize** button or double-click the Title bar or use the Control-menu box's Maximize command.

The Director window maximizes and the Title bar and other items disappear. Borders around the window also disappear.

> Click the **Control-menu box** (or press Alt+Spacebar) and select **Restore**.

The Title bar and other items reappear.

Important: In some cases, even the Menu bar and Control-menu box will disappear. When this happens you can still display a menu by pointing the mouse at the very top edge of the screen, where the menu item would normally appear, and clicking. Alternatively, you can press Alt+Spacebar or point at the top-left corner of the screen to click. This displays the Control-menu box, from which you can then select Restore, making the menus available.

Displaying Menus

Below these Windows tools is Director's Menu bar (shown in color in Figure 1.4). The Menu bar displays the menus, and this figure also labels the fundamental windows we'll be examining.

As you proceed with this list, click each menu name in turn so that you can see its commands (as shown in Figure 1.5).

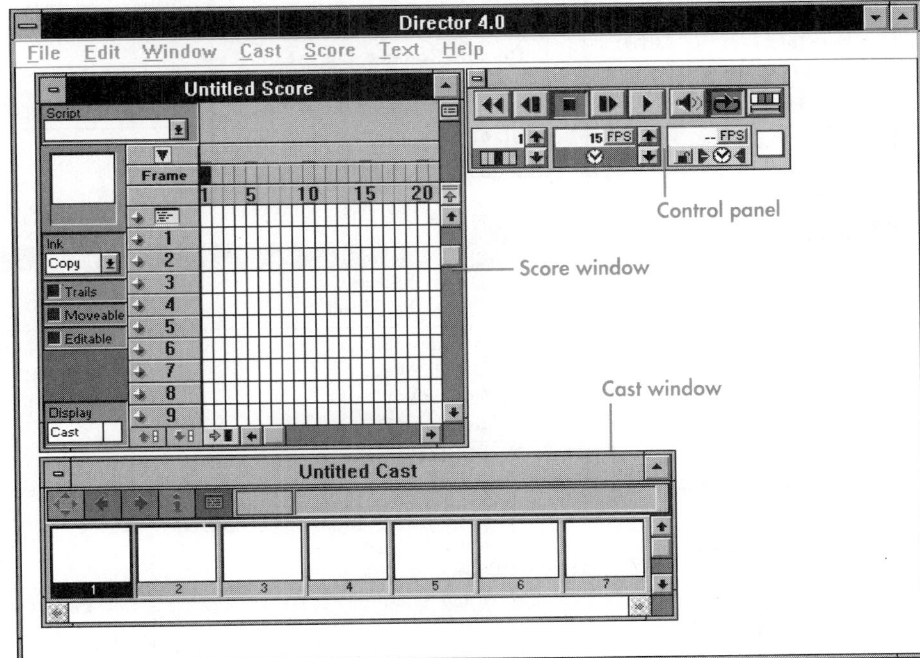

1.4
Director's Menu bar and labeled windows

The first three menus are similar in some ways to menus of other programs that run under Windows.

- **File** Opens, saves, and otherwise manipulates movies and other files. Its menu items are also used to print part or all the movie in various formats, customize movie and Director settings, and exit Director.
- **Edit** Allows you to cut, copy, and paste items and to undo such edits that you make in error. Additionally, some of the items on this menu correspond to controls in the ***Control Panel***, a set of VCR-type buttons and other controls used to play and otherwise operate movies. This correspondence is shown in Figure 1.6, which also labels items on the Control Panel that do not have a corresponding item on this menu.
- **Window** Primarily, this menu allows you to display and remove Director's various windows from the screen. Figure 1.7 shows Director's windows. Most are easily identified by names, generally on their Title bar; two without Title bar names have labels added in the figure. A check mark before an item on the Window menu means that the corresponding window is turned on (although that window could be hidden by one

1.5 Director's menus

Main Menus

File
- New — Ctrl+N
- Open... — Ctrl+O
- Close Window — Ctrl+W
- Save — Ctrl+S
- Save and Compact
- Save As...
- Revert
- Import... — Ctrl+J
- Export...
- Update Movies...
- Create Projector...
- Movie Info... — Ctrl+U
- Preferences...
- Print Setup...
- Print...
- Exit — Ctrl+Q

Edit
- Undo — Ctrl+Z
- Cut — Ctrl+X
- Copy — Ctrl+C
- Paste Bitmap — Ctrl+V
- Clear
- Select All — Ctrl+A
- Play — Ctrl+P
- Stop — Ctrl+.
- Rewind — Ctrl+R
- Step Backward
- Step Forward
- Disable Sounds — Ctrl+~
- Loop — Ctrl+L
- Selected Frames Only — Ctrl+\
- Disable Lingo
- Lock Frame Durations

Window
- Stage — Ctrl+1
- Control Panel — Ctrl+2
- Cast — Ctrl+3
- Score — Ctrl+4
- Paint — Ctrl+5
- Text — Ctrl+6
- Tools — Ctrl+7
- Color Palettes — Ctrl+8
- Digital Video — Ctrl+9
- Script — Ctrl+0
- Message — Ctrl+M
- Tweak
- Markers
- Duplicate Window

Cast
- Cast Member Info... — Ctrl+I
- Open Script — Ctrl+'
- Edit Cast Member
- Convert to Bitmap
- Transform Bitmap...
- Align Bitmaps
- Cast to Time
- Duplicate Cast Member — Ctrl+D
- Find Cast Members... — Ctrl+;
- Sort Cast Members...
- Cast Window Options...

Score
- Sprite Info... — Ctrl+K
- Delete Sprites
- Set Sprite Blend...
- Set Tempo...
- Set Palette...
- Set Transition...
- Set Sound...
- Insert Frame — Ctrl+]
- Delete Frame — Ctrl+[
- In-Between Linear — Ctrl+B
- In-Between Special...
- Space to Time...
- Paste Relative
- Reverse Sequence
- Switch Cast Members — Ctrl+E
- Auto Animate ▸
- Score Window Options...

Text
- Font
- Size
- Style
- Alignment
- Border
- Margin
- Box Shadow
- Text Shadow
- Find/Change... — Ctrl+F
- Find Again — Ctrl+G
- Change Again — Ctrl+T
- Find Selection — Ctrl+H
- Find Handler... — Ctrl+:
- Comment — Ctrl+>
- Uncomment — Ctrl+<
- Recompile Script
- Recompile All Scripts

Help
- Contents...
- Keys...
- How to Use Help...
- About Director...

Additional, Window-Specific Menus

Paint
- Hide Paint Tools
- Show Rulers
- Zoom In — Ctrl++
- Zoom Out — Ctrl+-
- Tiles...
- Patterns...
- Brush Shapes...
- Air Brushes...
- Gradients...
- Paint Window Options...

Effects
- Invert Colors
- Flip Horizontal
- Flip Vertical
- Trace Edges
- Fill
- Darken
- Lighten
- Smooth
- Switch Colors
- Rotate Left
- Rotate Right
- Free Rotate
- Perspective
- Slant
- Distort
- Auto Distort...
- Repeat Effect — Ctrl+Y

Palette
- Duplicate Palette...
- Reserve Colors...
- Invert Selection
- Set Color...
- Blend Colors
- Rotate Colors
- Reverse Color Order
- Sort Colors...
- Select Used Colors...

Lingo
- Operators ▸
- A B ▸
- C ▸
- D ▸
- E ▸
- F ▸
- G H ▸
- I K ▸
- L ▸
- M ▸
- N O ▸
- P ▸
- Q R ▸
- S ▸
- T ▸
- U V W X Z ▸

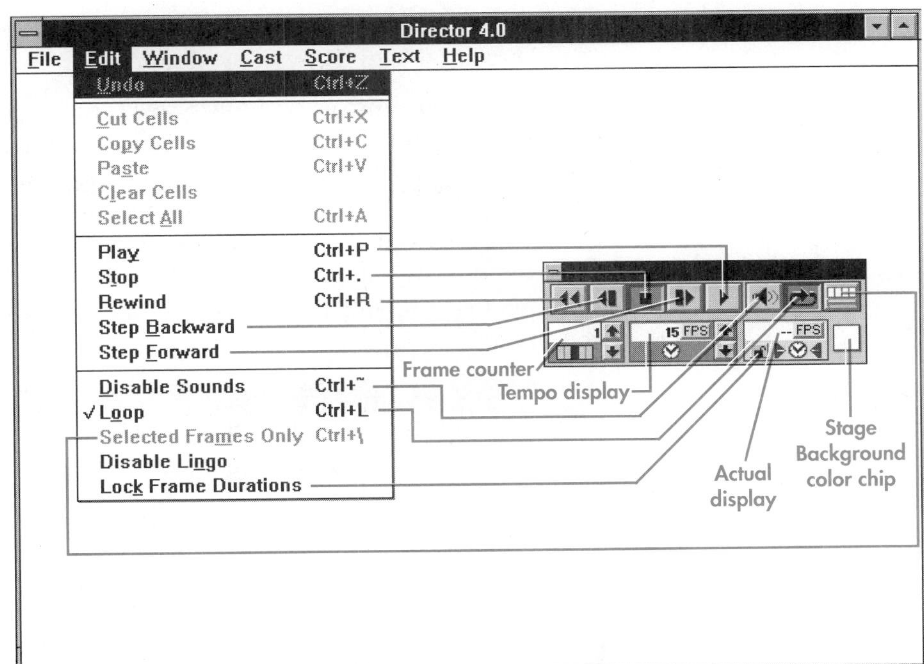

1.6 Edit menu and Control Panel

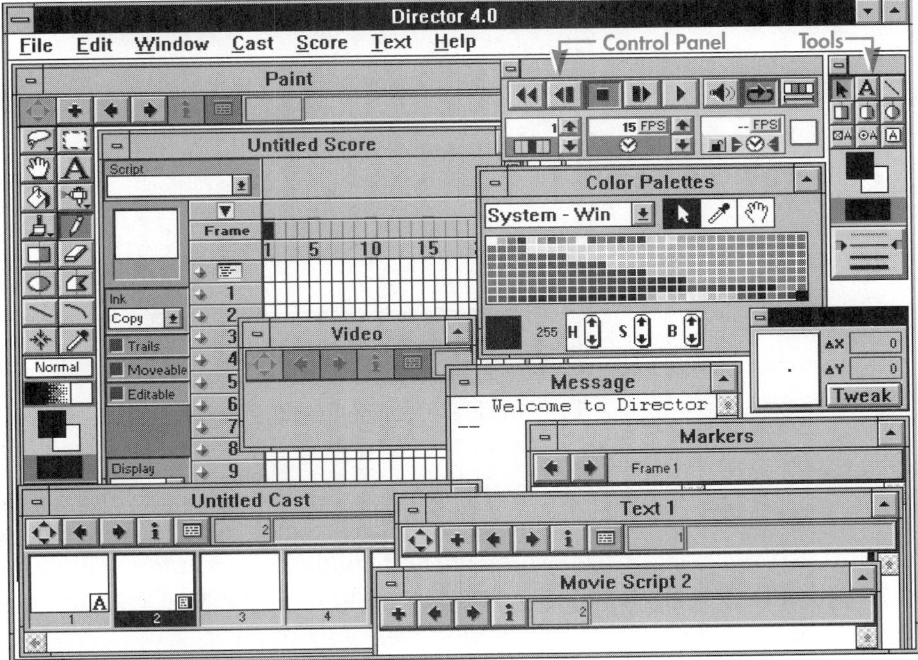

1.7 Director's windows

or more windows that cover it). Selecting an item (except Stage, discussed below, and Duplicate Window, discussed in Chapter 6) without a check mark causes one of three actions to occur.

1. If the window is not turned on, Director displays it, on top of any other displayed windows, and activates it (gives it the focus).
2. If the window is already turned on but is not activated (does not have the focus), Director activates it, bringing it to the top (in front) of other windows if necessary.

3. If the window is turned on and is the active window (has the focus), Director makes the window disappear.

Additionally, turning on Window, Stage turns off all displayed windows, leaving what appears to be essentially a blank screen (Figure 1.8). This is the ***stage***, the main area of Director that shows the movie as it is played or displays the current frame of the movie when the movie is stopped. Turning off the stage causes the menus that disappeared to reappear. You can also take away an activated window by using File, Close Window (or Ctrl+W). You can also close all windows (leaving only the stage) by holding down the Alt key as you use this command.

1.8
Stage

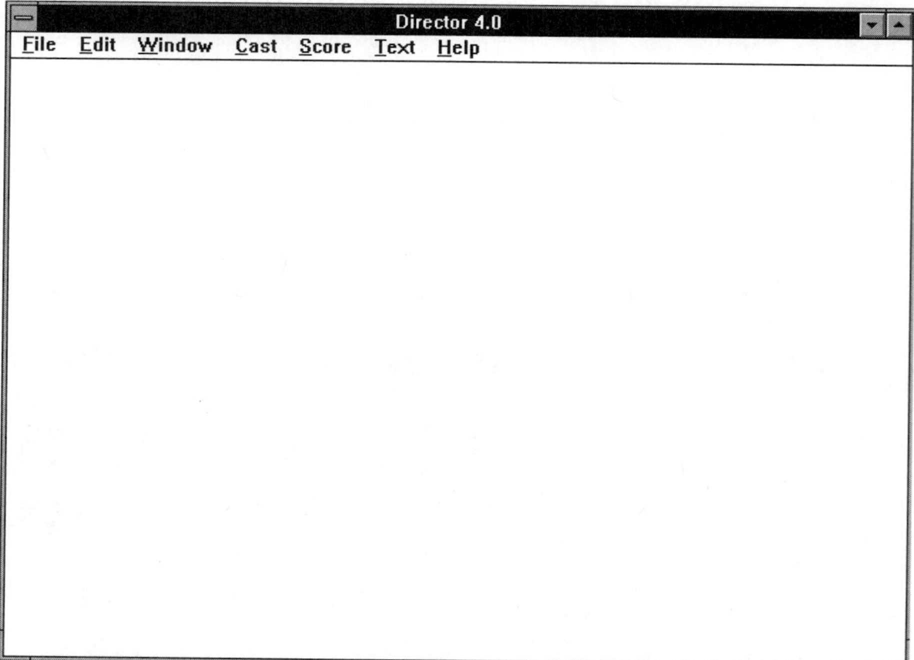

Experiment with turning the various windows on and off.

Finish with only the following windows turned on: Control Panel, Cast, Score.

- **Cast** Items on this menu operate on ***cast members***: graphics and other items, including sounds, text, movies, palettes, and others that are the fundamental building blocks for making a movie. Cast members appear in the Cast window (see Figure 1.4), where each is assigned a number and optionally a name.

As an example, Figure 1.9 shows the Cast window, maximized, for the \director\samplmov\tour\tour.dir movie, included with Director. (When saved, Director movies are automatically assigned the DIR extension.) Items on this menu allow you to find a cast member, get information about it, duplicate it, and make changes in it, and to customize the Cast window. This menu also provides a way to move copies of cast members to the next Director component we'll examine, the score.

- **Score** The *score* is the grid-type structure that Director uses to organize a movie. Items called ***sprites*** that appear on the stage are placed in cells that govern their behavior over time, frame by frame in the movie. A

1.9
Cast window

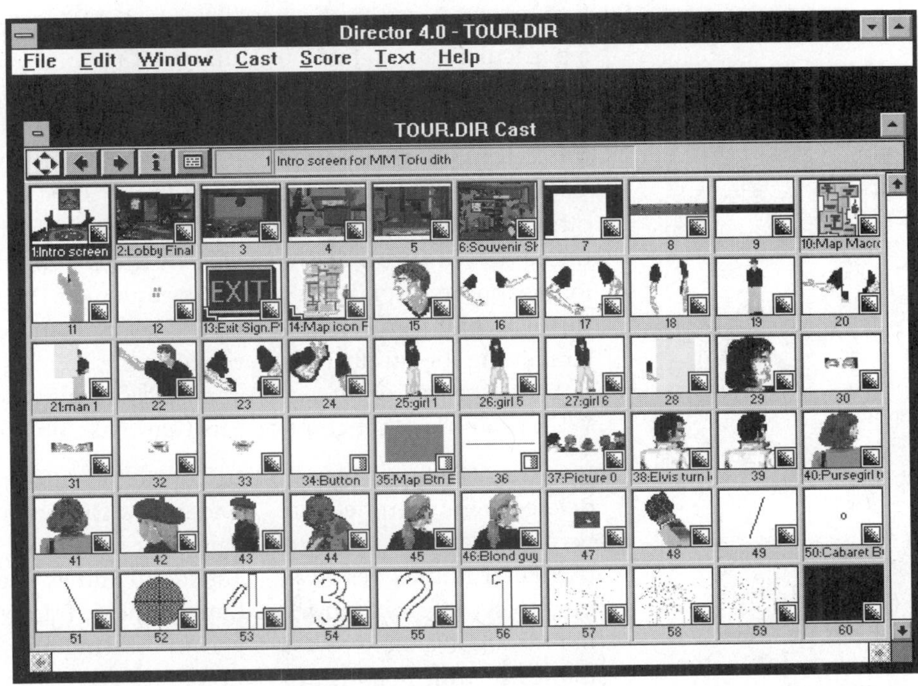

sprite is a copy of a cast member that contains additional information as well, such as the sprite's position on the stage.

Figure 1.10 shows a part of the score for the same sample movie whose cast you saw in Figure 1.9. In the score, progression of the movie is represented by the columns from left to right. Each column is one frame in the movie, and frames are identified by frame numbers at the tops of the columns. Each row, from top to bottom, is called a ***channel***; channels are numbered along the left edge. The first six channels are specially designated for effects (Tempo, Palettes, Transitions, Sounds 1 and 2, and Script); the numbered channels, also called *Sprite channels*, are available for general use.

1.10
Score window

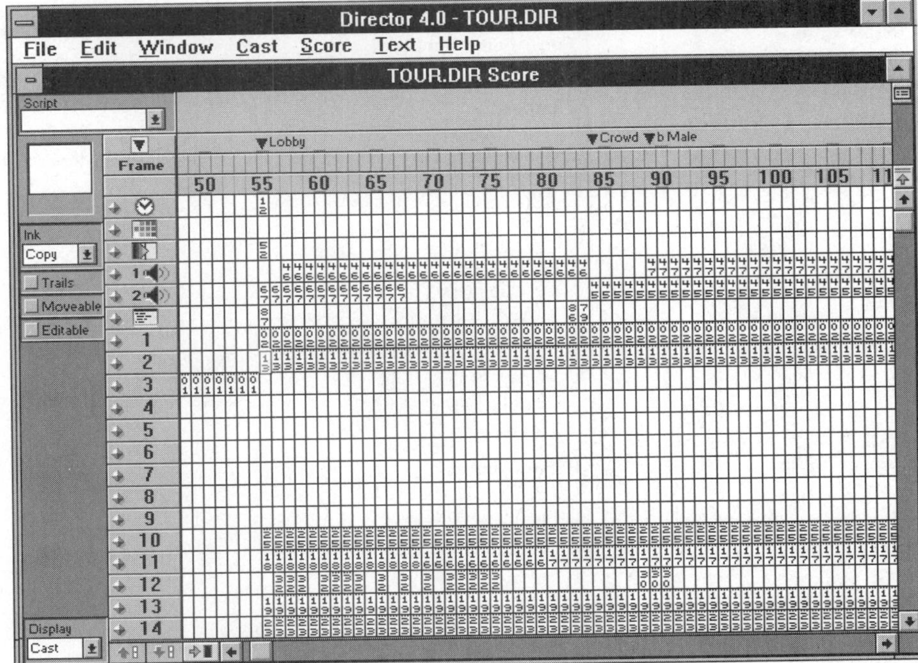

A number within a ***cell*** (position where a frame and channel intersect) refers to a particular cast member by number. It means that the cast member has been assigned to the cell, thus creating a sprite that appears on the stage at a particular time. Take, for example, the cell in color in Figure 1.10. It shows that this cell has been assigned cast number 13, which is the Exit sign (see Figure 1.9). Thus the Exit sign appears in frame 55 of the movie, along with all the other cast members that appear at the same time (that is, those also assigned to frame 55 but in other channels). In the movie, this is the moment when a lobby appears, and this is notated by a marker (▼) labeled "Lobby" toward the top. The Exit sign remains on the screen, as indicated by the stream of cells containing the number 13 that follows this cell in successive frames of channel 2. You'll see this occur as you play this sample movie, which we'll do shortly. We'll examine other components that make up the score as we use them.

Items on the Score menu allow you to get information about sprites and to delete them when necessary. (Deleting a sprite does not delete the cast member used to create it; only the particular sprite that appears on the stage in the particular frame goes away.) This menu allows you to make sprites fade in or out, to set effects, and to add and remove frames. A whole variety of commands are available to assist you in creating and manipulating sprites automatically, thus making animations easier to create. We'll create an animation toward the end of this chapter. Finally, you can use this menu to customize the score itself.

- **Text** Allows you to apply a variety of effects to text, such as changing fonts. Also allows you to search for text and lets you work with scripts, programming created with Director's programming language, Lingo.
- **Help** Provides information on the use of Director. The *Contents* command leads to a listing of the menus (Figure 1.11); if you want to find out about an item on one of the menus, select this command and then select the appropriate menu. The *Keys* command allows you to see the keyboard shortcuts for various menu commands (along with and in addi-

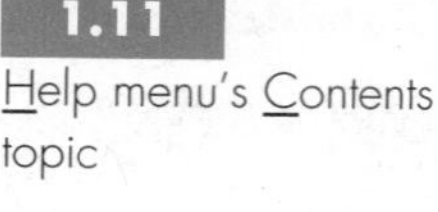

Help menu's Contents topic

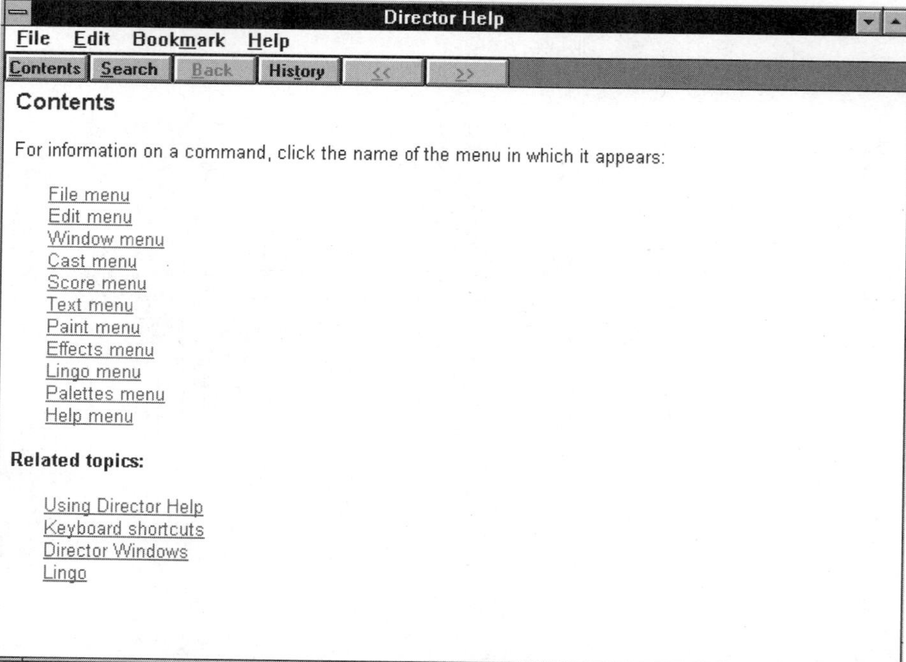

tion to the shortcuts that appear on the actual menus themselves). Help operates as it does in other Windows programs; if you're not familiar with how Help systems operate, be sure to examine *How to Use Help*. *About Director* provides information on how your copy of Director is handling memory, as well as program credits.

You can also get help information about windows and most dialog boxes. To do that, you press Ctrl+? (the Ctrl key with the ?/ key). The mouse cursor changes into a plus sign with a question mark to the right and below (+?) when it is over an area for which there is information. If you click at that point you'll get information about the window or dialog box you are pointing at. Alternatively, you can press and hold the Alt and Shift keys simultaneously (+? appears) and, still holding the keys, click. This technique works on dialog boxes as well.

Most dialog boxes have a Help button. Click it and you'll get help information about that dialog box (Figure 1.11).

Pressing the F1 key when no menus or dialog boxes are showing displays the Help contents.

- **Additional menus** Finally, there are four menus that appear only when specific windows are open and activated, as follows:

  Paint window: Paint menu and Effects menu
  Color Palettes window: Palette menu
  Script window: Lingo menu

  These menu names appear on the Menu bar between the Text and Help names; they disappear once the corresponding window is taken away or deactivated.

  Use the **Window** menu (or equivalent method) to display each of these three windows in turn, observing the Menu bar as you do.

Tip: When you're using these specific windows, it's important to remember that these menus exist. Otherwise, it's easy to search fruitlessly for features in the windows when they are actually available via the Menu bar. We'll look at the special menus as we work with their corresponding windows.

PLAYING A MOVIE

Now may be a good time to view the sample movie whose cast (Figure 1.9) and score (Figure 1.10) we examined earlier. This movie provides a "tour" of Macromedia and demonstrates some things you can do with Director. It is less helpful in providing an actual understanding of how to use the program, but it does provide an introduction to Director's main elements: cast, paint, score, stage, and Lingo.

Begin by taking away all menus as follows.

If you have any menus showing, open the **Window** menu and choose **Stage** (or press Ctrl+1) to take them away.

The result is an empty stage like the one you saw back in Figure 1.8.

Open the **File** menu and select **Open** (or press Ctrl+O).

The dialog box in Figure 1.12 appears.

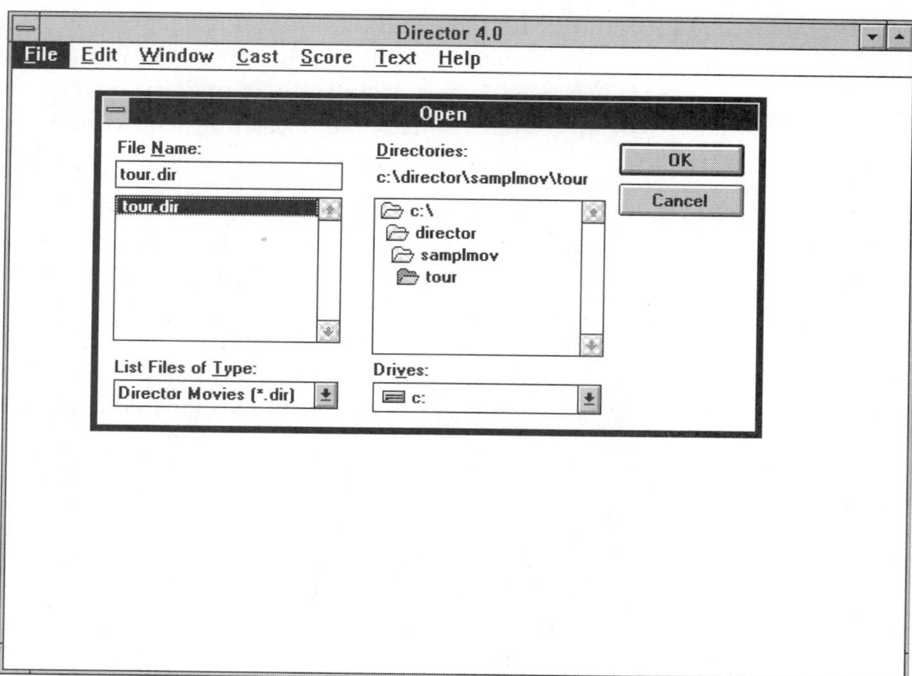

1.12 File menu's Open dialog box

Navigate to the **c:\director\samplmov\tour\tour.dir** file as shown in the figure.

Click the **OK** button or press the Enter key or double-click the file name to open the movie.

The screen shown in Figure 1.13, proclaiming, "Your guided tour will begin momentarily," appears. Don't believe it. It seems that the movie was designed to repeat itself, apparently for use in a public area, pausing at this screen before each reshowing. However, you must start it playing the first time.

1.13 TOUR.DIR movie

Troubleshooting: If the screen shown in Figure 1.13 doesn't appear, someone may have saved the movie in a position other than at the beginning. If so, rewind the movie to the beginning by opening the Edit menu and choosing Rewind or by pressing Ctrl+R.

With the introductory screen in place and no menus showing, open the **Edit** menu and select **Play** or press Ctrl+P.

When the movie starts to repeat, open the **Edit** menu and select **Stop** or press Ctrl+. (Ctrl and the >. key).

You can see the score in action. The ***playback head*** is a black box that appears in the row marked "Frame," just above the frame numbers. It indicates the movie's current position.

Rewind the movie to the beginning with **Edit**, **Rewind** or Ctrl+R.

With the introductory screen showing, use the **Window** menu's **Score** command or Ctrl+4 to display the score.

The score should be its standard, initial size, as shown back in Figure 1.4, so that you can observe the movie and the score at the same time.

If it is not, resize the score to that size.

Use the scroll bar at the bottom of the score to scroll to the right so that frame 55, labeled "Lobby," is displayed in the Score window, approximately centered from left to right in the window.

Watching the Frame row, start the movie by opening the **Edit** menu and selecting **Play** or by pressing Ctrl+P.

The playback head crosses frame 55 just as the lobby appears. Then it goes out the window just as the woman says, "Oh, good. We were just about to start."

Stop the movie by opening the **Edit** menu and selecting **Stop** (or press Ctrl+.).

Tip: You can alternately play and stop a movie by pressing the Enter key on the keypad.

CREATING A MOVIE

Now it's time to try your hand at creating your own movie. We'll start with a very simple one and begin by creating a graphic of a balloon and string. Then we'll place the balloon on the stage and animate it to float from the bottom of the stage to the top.

Clear the movie by opening the **File** menu and selecting **New**.

Important: If Director asks you, "Save changes to the movie 'TOUR.DIR' before creating a new file?" be sure to click the Don't Save button so that you don't make any changes in the sample.

The stage's background is now black. It was changed to black when the TOUR.DIR movie was loaded and it remains black. We need to change it back to white. You use the Control Panel to do that.

If the Control Panel isn't showing, use the **Window** menu's **Control Panel** command or Ctrl+2 to display it.

Point to the Control Panel's **Stage Background** color chip (see Figure 1.6 if necessary), then **press** and **hold**.

A palette of colors appears. This is how you often change colors, as well as some other items in pop-up menus in Director: by pointing, pressing, holding, and selecting.

On the palette, point to the **white** swatch at its top-left corner and click.

The background changes back to white.

Display the Paint window by opening the **Window** menu and selecting **Paint** or press Ctrl+5.

The Paint window, shown in Figure 1.14, appears but without the balloon you see in the figure. We'll use this window to create the balloon. To do so, we'll use the two tools shown in color in the figure.

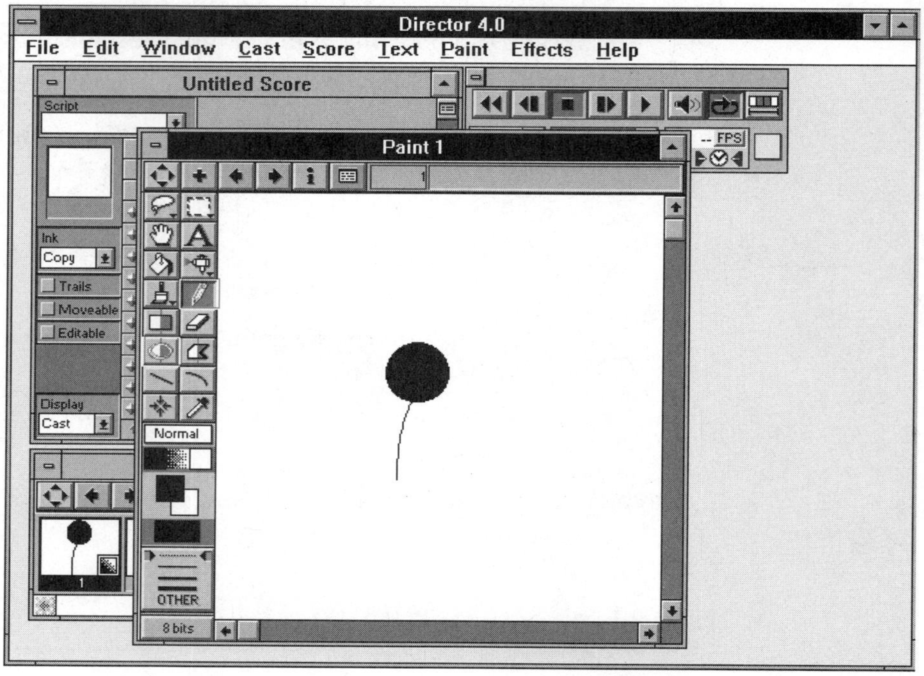

1.14

Art drawn in the Paint window to create a cast member

Begin by selecting the solid half of the **Ellipse** tool (lower-left color button in the figure) to create the balloon itself.

To restrict the ellipse to a perfect circle, hold down the **Shift** key.

With the Shift key held down, **point** to a spot for the top-left corner of the balloon and **drag** to the bottom-right.

The balloon appears. Now let's add the string.

Select the **Pencil** tool (upper-right color button in the figure).

To create the string, **drag** up from a point where the bottom end of the string will start, and continue into the balloon.

Creating a graphic like this in the Paint window creates a cast member in the Cast window. But we have finished with the Paint window for now.

Close the Paint window by selecting **Window, Paint** or by pressing Ctrl+5.

PLACING GRAPHICS ON THE STAGE

The balloon is showing in the Cast window, as Cast Member 1. Now to create the animation on the stage. We'll begin by creating a sprite of the balloon toward the bottom of the screen, which will appear in the first frame. Next we'll create another sprite, toward the top of the stage, in frame 20. Then we'll have Director automatically create the sprite positions in between these two. Finally, we'll run the animation.

Point to the balloon cast member in the Cast window and **drag** from that position to the bottom-right corner of the stage and **release**.

The sprite appears on the stage (Figure 1.15). Remember, the sprite is a copy of the cast member; if necessary, you can delete the sprite without affecting the cast member.

1.15

Copy of cast member dragged to the stage to create a sprite

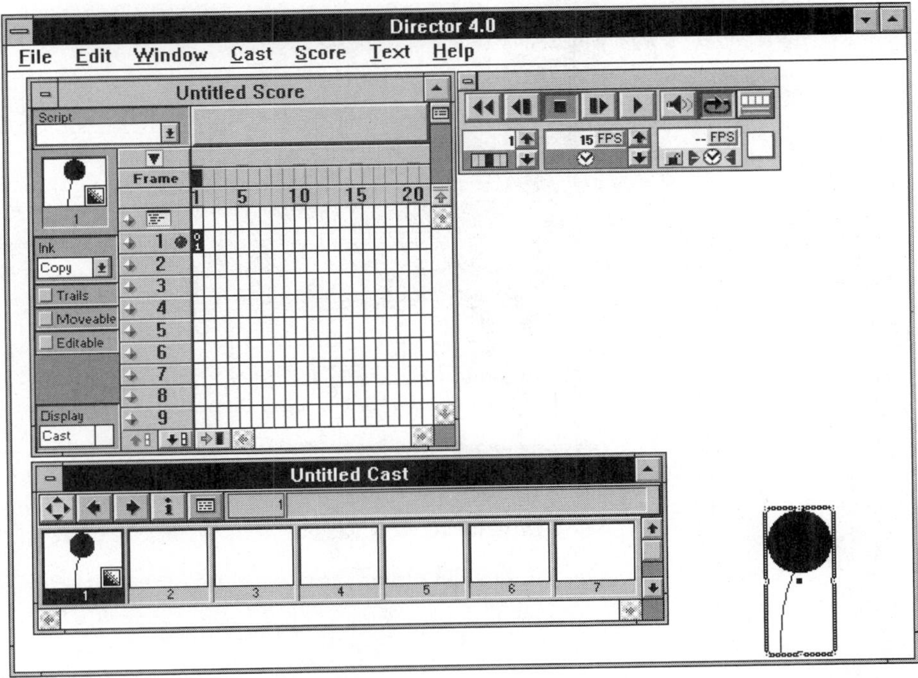

Of course, sprites can be placed anywhere on the stage, only a portion of which is now visible because of the three other windows. For now, though, we'll just use this visible portion of the stage.

At the same time that you create the sprite, the cast member's number (01) appears in the score, to the right of the Channel 1 label and beneath the Frame 1 label. Additionally, because the sprite's cell is selected (as indicated by the 01 showing as white-on-black), the cast member also appears in the cast indicator, in the top-left area of the score.

SAVING YOUR WORK

Since you've done some work, let's assign your movie a name and save it on disk. It's always a good idea to save frequently because your work is vulnerable to loss until you do.

Open the File menu and select either Save or Save As or press Ctrl+S.

The Save Movie As dialog box appears (Figure 1.16). Because you are saving this movie for the first time, you can use either command on the File menu (Save or Save As). Had you saved already, you would use Save to save the movie under the same name or Save As to make a copy of the movie under a new name.

1.16
Save Movie As dialog box

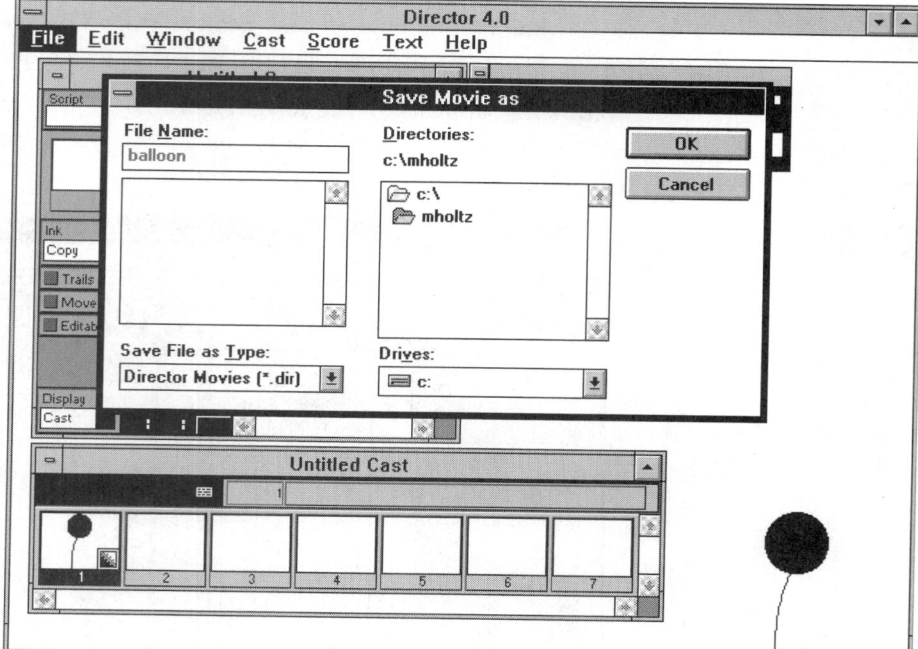

As your instructor indicates, change the dialog box's Drives box and its Directories box to set the appropriate drive/directory.

In the File Name box, enter balloon as shown in color in Figure 1.16.

Click the OK button or press the Enter key.

The file is saved and the full name of the file (BALLOON.DIR) appears at the top of the Director window. Director adds the .DIR extension automatically, indicating that the file is a Director movie. (Director *does not* assume the DIR extension when you open a file, as we'll do in the next chapter.)

CREATING ANIMATION AUTOMATICALLY

Now let's animate the balloon. We'll make it float from the bottom of the screen to the top. To do that, we'll first create the ending position of the balloon in the ending frame of the movie. Then we'll have Director automatically create the intervening or ***in-between*** positions in the intervening frames.

Dragging from the Cast window to the stage is one way to place a sprite on the stage and in the score. This automatically puts the sprite in the current frame, as indicated by the position of the playback head (in this case, Frame 1). Alternatively, you can drag to the score itself. This approach allows you to drag to a frame that is not currently displayed, an action that not only creates the sprite in that frame but automatically displays the frame for you. You can then position the sprite in the frame as desired. Let's do that now.

Point to the balloon in the Cast window, and **drag** from it to the cell in frame 20, channel 1, then release.

The cast member's number (01) appears in frame 20 as well. The sprite appears in the center of the stage. Additionally, the sprite in the bottom-right corner disappears. This is because frame 20 is now active. (The sprite is still in the bottom-right corner of Frame 1 but that frame is no longer being shown.)

Drag the sprite from the center of the stage to the top-right corner (Figure 1.17).

1.17

Sprite created for final animation position

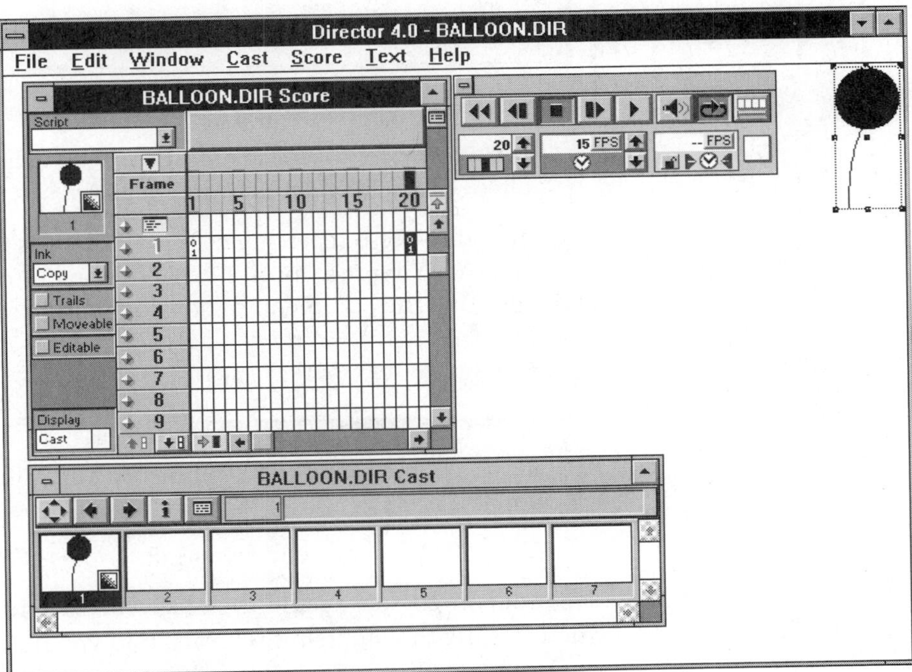

Now we'll create the animation.

Double-click Channel 1's channel number (shown in color in Figure 1.17).

This selects the first and last cell, with cast members assigned, and all cells in between.

Open the **Score** menu and select **In-Between Linear** (or press Ctrl+B).

In a direct line (hence the name *linear*) from the sprite you created in Frame 1 to the one you created in Frame 20, Director fills in the intervening cells with sprites. Dots appear just above the cast member number (01) in these Director-generated "in-between" cells (Figure 1.18).

Click away from the balloon sprite; that is, with the cursor off the balloon sprite and on the background, click so that the balloon sprite is no longer selected.

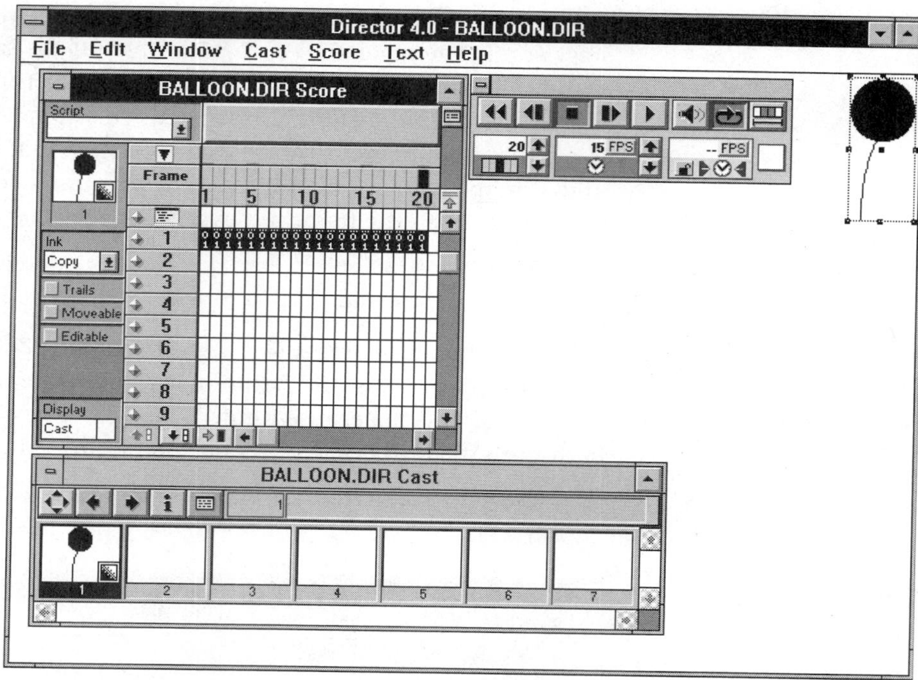

1.18

In-between sprites created with Score, In-Between Linear

> **Start the movie by opening the Edit menu and selecting Play (or press Ctrl+P or use the Control Panel's Play button).**

The animation keeps repeating because looping is turned on. You can turn off looping by clicking the Control Panel's Loop button (look back at Figure 1.6) or by selecting the Edit menu's Loop command or by pressing Ctrl+L.

QUITTING DIRECTOR

Now let us assume that you have finished with Director for the day. Exit the program as follows.

> **Open the File menu and select Exit (or press Ctrl+Q).**

The program goes away and the Macromedia program group that you used when starting the program reappears. Had you not saved your movie already, Director would have asked, "Save changes to the movie (with the name of the movie) before exiting?" (If you hadn't yet assigned a name to the movie, Director would simply call the movie "Untitled.")

ITEMS IN THE MACROMEDIA PROGRAM GROUP

We'll close out this chapter by examining the various icons in the Macromedia program group. Except for the first one, these icons start Windows' Write program and display text files. You can use Write to read, print, and search the files. It is important that you do not edit these files, though it is possible to do so. When exiting Write, should you see the message, "This document has changed. Save current changes?" be sure to respond No.

(The actual files that these icons open are given in parentheses. All are located in the \DIRECTOR directory or one of its subdirectories.)

- **Director 4.0** This is the icon you used to start the Director program and the one you will use almost always (DIRECTOR.EXE).
- **Director ReadMe** This Write file gives "late-breaking news about Director 4.0 for Windows"—that is, information that was too late for inclusion in the Director documentation or on-line Help system. Some of the information included in this file has been incorporated into this text. However, there may be additional information in your copy that has been added since the book went to press. You may wish to check this file from time to time as you become familiar with various aspects of the program (README.WRI).
- **XObject Developer's Kit** This document gives information for creating Windows XObjects for Director. XObjects are a type of dynamic link library (DLL) and are an advanced use of Director that won't be covered in this text (XOBJDEV.WRI).
- **Sample Movies** This gives information on the movie \director\samplmov\lingoexp\navigatr.dir, which is also known as the Director Lingo Expo. It tells how you can view this movie by using Director to load and play it (with Ctrl+P, for example). Playing this movie gives you access to other movies (Figure 1.19), which you can run by clicking a button. (Buttons on the right correspond from top to bottom to the listed movies.) The Lingo Index button gives information on how Lingo is used to create these samples. When you quit running one of these movies, you exit Director as well. Of course, when you quit, click the Don't Save button when asked, "Save changes to the movie 'NAVIGATR.DIR' before exiting?" (SAMPLMOV.WRI).

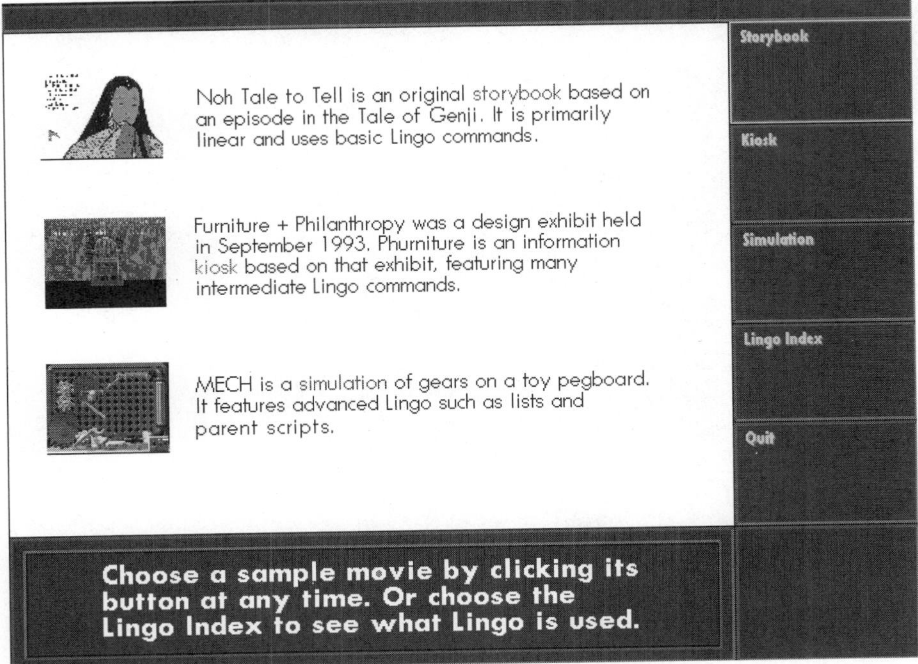

1.19
Director Lingo Expo (NAVIGATR.DIR) movie

CHAPTER REVIEW

KEY TERMS

author
movies
users
Control Panel
stage
cast members
score
sprites
channel
cell
playback head
in-between

REVIEW QUESTIONS

1. How do you restore the Director window when the Menu bar and Control-menu box are not visible?
2. Which menu can you use to display and take away Director's various windows?
3. **T F** Deleting a sprite deletes its cast member.
4. List four distinct ways to get help in Director.
5. Name one way to play a movie.

PROJECTS

1. Create an animation of a ball rolling.
2. Use Help to learn more about one of the windows.

2

Controlling, Printing, and Customizing

THIS CHAPTER WILL TEACH YOU HOW TO

- Open movies
- Rewind, advance, and otherwise control movies
- Turn movie sounds off and on
- Set the speed of a movie
- Change a movie's background color
- Print
- Customize aspects of Director's operations

The movie you created in Chapter 1 is a very simple one. It is, nonetheless, a full-fledged movie. We'll use it in this chapter to demonstrate how you can control movie playback and other operations with the Control Panel. That way, as you create increasingly complex movies, you'll be able to manipulate them easily for testing and other purposes. Your instructor may want you to print your assignments, and this chapter will show you how to print frames, cast members, and other aspects of movies. Finally, we'll show how you can customize Director with the File menu's Preferences dialog box.

OPENING A MOVIE

Before doing any of this, though, you must start Director again and retrieve the movie you created.

Start up Director as explained in Chapter 1 (Windows, Macromedia program group, Director 4.0 icon).

The Score window, the Cast window, and the Control Panel should appear, unless someone changed your Director in the interim.

If necessary, display these three windows by using the Window menu or an alternative method as described in Chapter 1.

Now to retrieve the movie we created in Chapter 1.

Open the File menu and select Open (or press Ctrl+O).

The File menu's Open dialog box appears (Figure 2.1).

2.1

File menu's Open dialog box

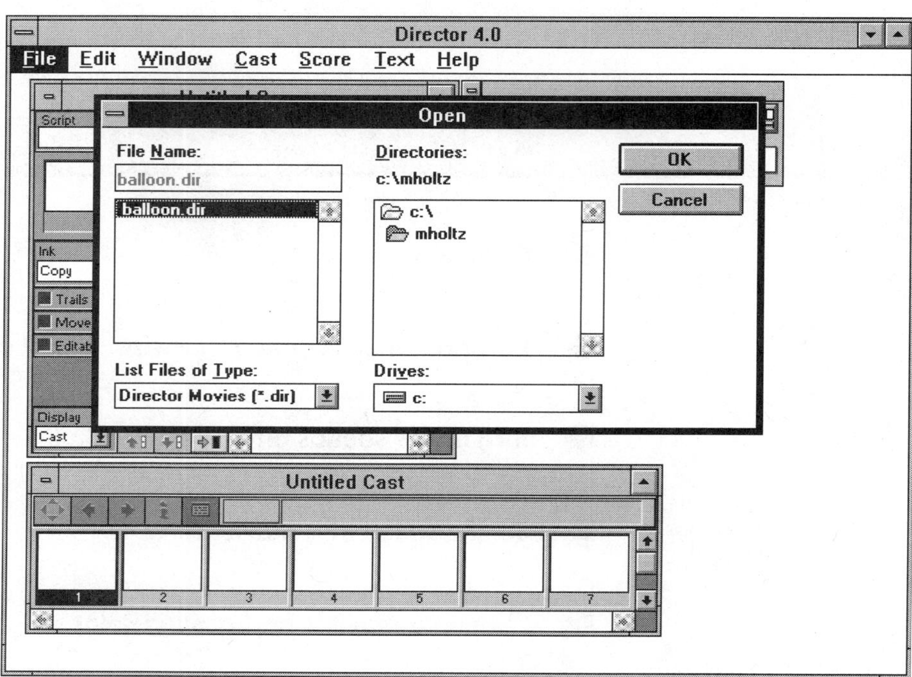

Check that the Drives and Directories boxes are set correctly.

Select or enter the file name balloon.dir (as shown in color in the figure).

Click the OK button or press the Enter key.

Director displays your movie as it was when you last saved it.

➡ *Troubleshooting:* When you provide a file name to open, Director does not automatically assume the DIR extension. So if you typed the name and got the message "Cannot find this file" it may be because you need to provide the full name, balloon.dir.

REWINDING MOVIES TO THE BEGINNING

Now let's examine use of the Control Panel, which was introduced in Chapter 1. As you saw back in Figure 1.6, which is reprinted as Figure 2.2, most of the operations managed with the Control Panel can also be controlled with the Edit menu. As we examine the Control Panel, use this figure to determine the button names if necessary.

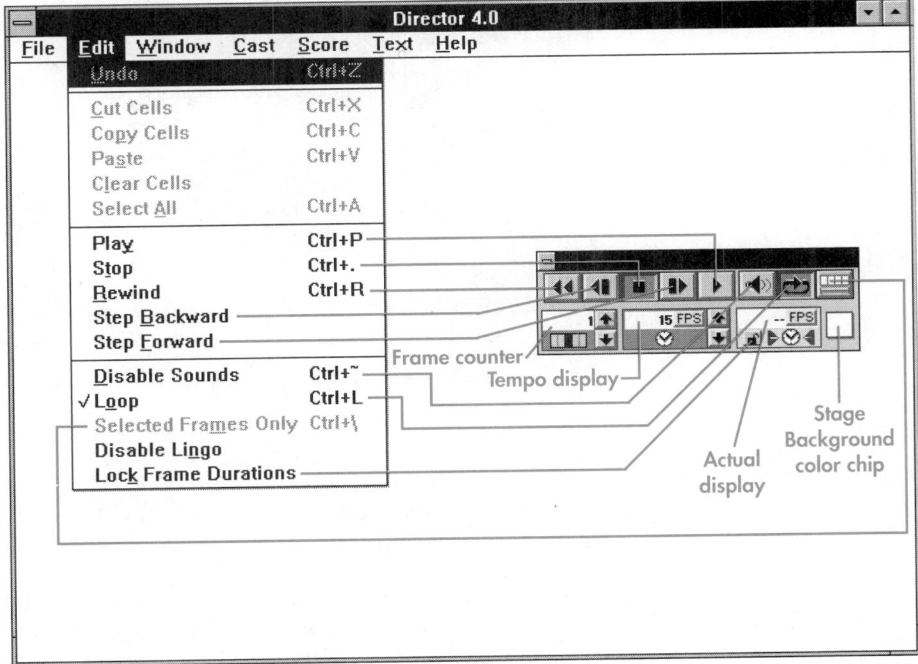

2.2
Edit menu and Control Panel

Let's start with the VCR-type buttons. The first one on the left (◄◄) is the Rewind button. It brings the movie back to the beginning. Be sure that your movie is at the beginning.

> Use the **Edit** menu's **Rewind** command or Ctrl+R or the Rewind button to bring the BALLOON.DIR movie back to the beginning.

When you click the Rewind button it remains depressed for only an instant as the movie jumps back to the beginning. Then the Stop button (■) immediately becomes depressed, as it was when you first opened the file.

INCREMENTALLY ADVANCING AND REWINDING MOVIES

Now consider the two buttons on either side of the Stop button. The Step Backward (◄I) and Step Forward (I►) buttons, respectively, rewind and advance the movie frame by frame. Try the Step Forward button first as follows:

> Move the movie ahead one frame by using the **Edit** menu's **Step Forward** command or the Step Forward button (shown in color in Figure 2.3) or Ctrl+→ (Ctrl with the → key) or Keypad 3 or 6 (with NumLock turned on, press the keypad's 3 or 6 key).

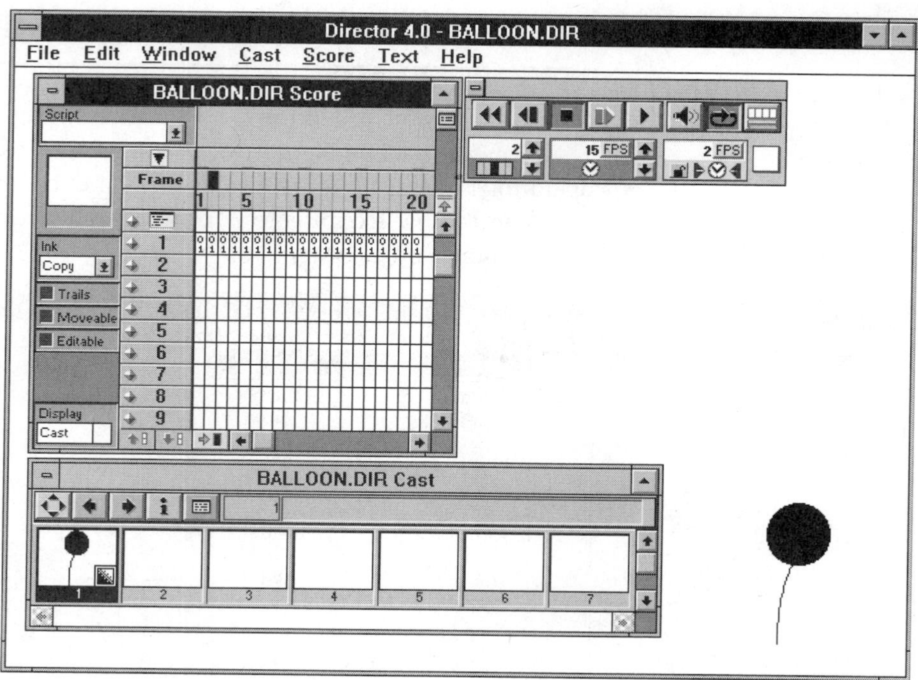

2.3
Step Forward button

The movie advances by one frame. This causes the balloon to rise slightly.

Notice, too, the position of the playback head (the black box in the score's Frame row, introduced in Chapter 1). It is now above the 2 position, indicating that Frame 2 is being displayed. Now try stepping backward as follows:

> **Move the movie backward one frame by using the Edit menu's Step Backward command or the Step Backward button (shown in color in Figure 2.4) or Ctrl+← (Ctrl with the ← key) or Keypad 1 or 4 (with NumLock turned on, press the keypad's 1 or 4 key).**

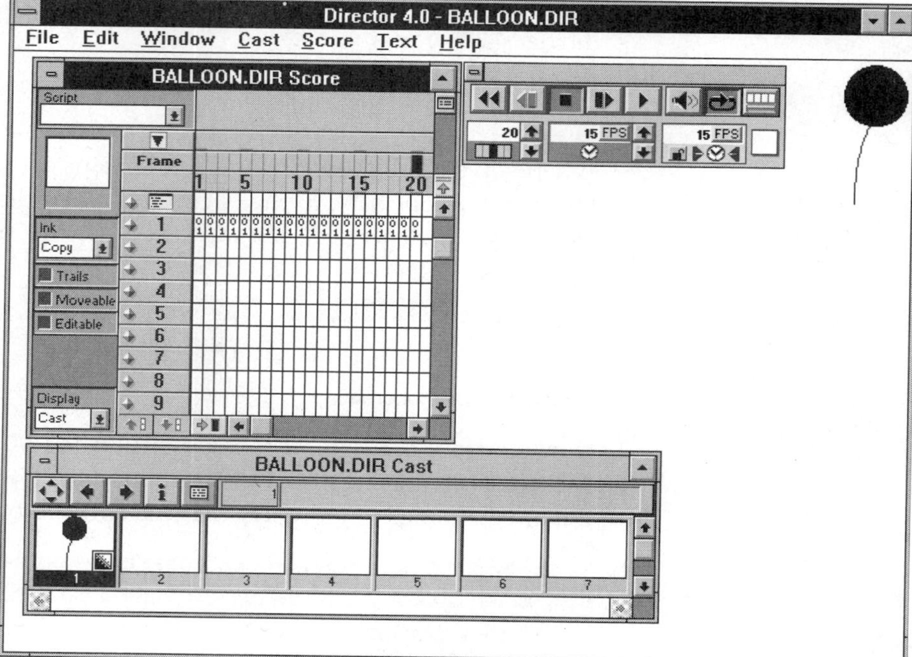

2.4
Step Backward button

The balloon drops, the playback head moves back to Frame 1, and the movie is back at its beginning. Now watch what happens:

> **With the playback head positioned in Frame 1, use Edit, Step Backward or equivalent once again.**

This causes the movie to "wrap around" to the final frame. The playback head is now in frame 20 and the balloon is at the top of the screen, as shown in Figure 2.4.

Next is the Play button (▶), with which you are familiar.

TURNING OFF SOUNDS

To the right of the Play button is the Disable Sounds button. When turned on (depressed) as shown in color in Figure 2.5, it suppresses the sound coming from the movie. Turned off, as it normally is, the movie's sounds are played.

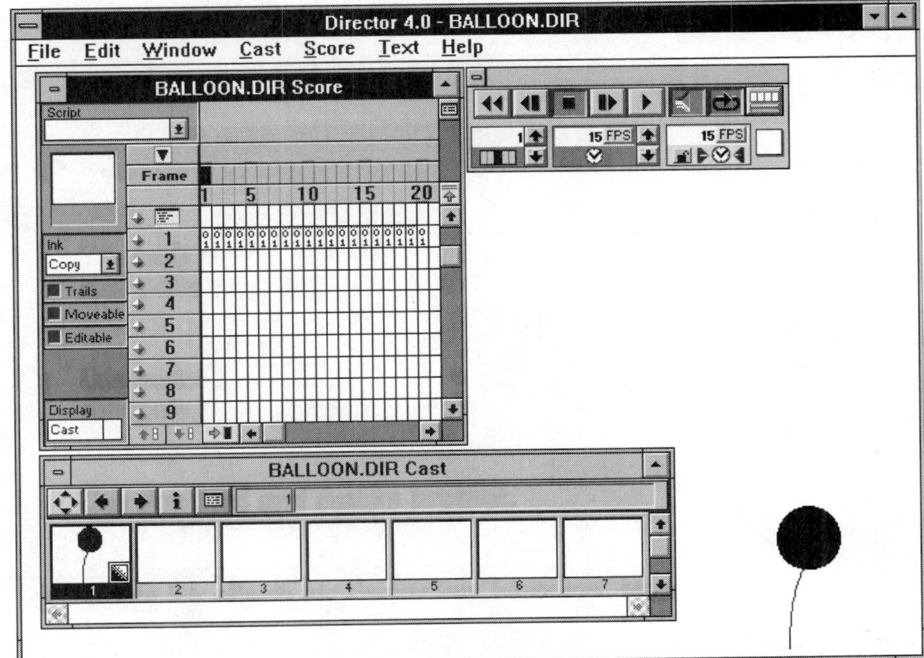

2.5
Disable Sounds button

Notice that the image on the icon changes when you change the Disable Sounds status.

> **Examine the Disable Sounds button when it is in the normal, turned-off position.**

Sound waves are shown being emitted from the icon's loudspeaker, as shown in Figure 2.4.

> **Use the Edit menu's Disable Sounds command or the Disable Sounds button or Ctrl+~ (Ctrl with the ~` key) or Keypad 7 (with NumLock turned on, press the keypad's 7 key) to turn on Disable Sounds.**

The Disable Sounds button becomes depressed and sound waves are no longer coming from the icon's loudspeaker (Figure 2.5). We'll be working with sounds in Chapter 6.

Turn off Disable Sounds.

Note: Be aware of the reverse way in which this button relates to the feature it controls. When the button is turned off, as normal, sounds are on. When the button is turned on, sounds are off. Thus, with this step, sounds are back on.

REPEATED PLAYBACK

The next button, to the right of the Disable Sounds button, relates to its feature in a more standard fashion. It's the Loop button and it is initially turned on. ***Looping*** refers to the repeated playing of a movie (or portion of a movie, as we'll see shortly) immediately and endlessly until stopped. It's as if the movie were a strip of film and its beginning and end were spliced to one another, creating a loop of film.

This button's icon also changes when you switch it off, as shown in Figure 2.6. Note the straightforward design in this figure as compared with the looping shape shown in Figure 2.5. Try it yourself:

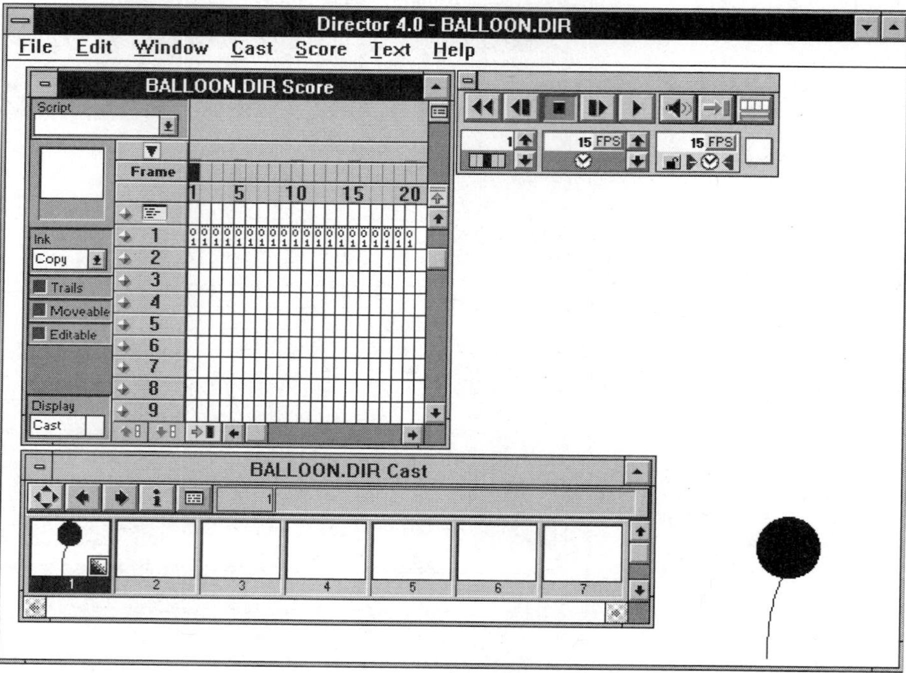

2.6
Loop Button turned off

Turn off looping with the **Edit** menu's **Loop** command or with Ctrl+L or Keypad 8 (with NumLock turned on, the keypad's 8 key) or the Loop button.

The button changes.

Rewind the movie, if necessary, and then play it.

The balloon rises once.

Turn on looping and play the movie.

The movie keeps playing repeatedly.

Stop the movie.

PLAYING PART OF A MOVIE

Next is the Selected Frames Only button, shown in color in Figure 2.7. Neither this button nor its equivalent Edit menu's command is available until you've indicated which frames you want to select. So let's discuss how to do that.

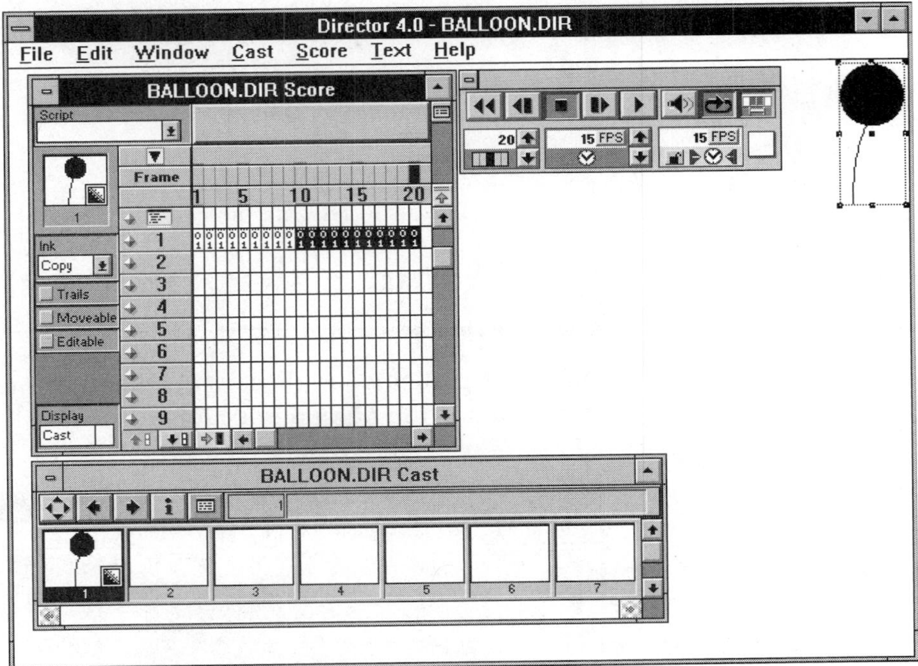

2.7 Cells selected and Selected Frames Only button

Suppose, for example, you wanted to play only the second half of this movie, from frame 10 to frame 20. You could do that by selecting the cells in any channel in frames 10 to 20. The Control Panel's Select Frames Only button would then be available and you could play only those frames. We'll use channel 1 as follows to do just that, but be aware that any channel would do.

> In frame **10**, select the cell in channel **1**.

The cell darkens to reverse highlighting, indicating that it is selected. The balloon appears at the midway point, with a ***bounding box*** (sometimes called a *selection box*) and handles around it (unless you are using a channel other than 1, in which case the bounding box and handles won't appear). The bounding box and handles also appear in Figure 2.7, which shows the results of the next step.

> Point at the frame 20 cell in the same channel and **Shift-click**.

The range of cells from 10 to 20 switches to reverse highlighting and the balloon moves to the top of the screen, its frame 20 position. Notice too that the playback head is now located at the frame 20 position. Also at this point, the Selected Frames Only button darkens, showing that it is now available.

> Open the **Edit** menu and turn on **Selected Frames Only** or click the Control Panel's Selected Frames Only button or press Ctrl+\ (the Ctrl key with the |\ key).

A green bar appears at the top of the selected frames (shown in color in Figure 2.7), indicating that only those frames will be shown when the movie is played.

With looping turned on, **play** the movie.

The balloon repeatedly rises from the middle of the screen to the top.

With the movie still playing, turn off **Selected Frames Only**.

Once again the entire movie plays, with the balloon rising from bottom to top.

Stop the movie and **rewind**.

Click the stage.

The balloon and the cells are no longer selected.

DISPLAYING A SPECIFIC MOVIE FRAME

Turning our attention to the lower half of the Control Panel, we see that the first section in this portion is the ***Frame counter***. It's shown in color in Figure 2.8.

2.8

Frame Counter (set to Frame 10)

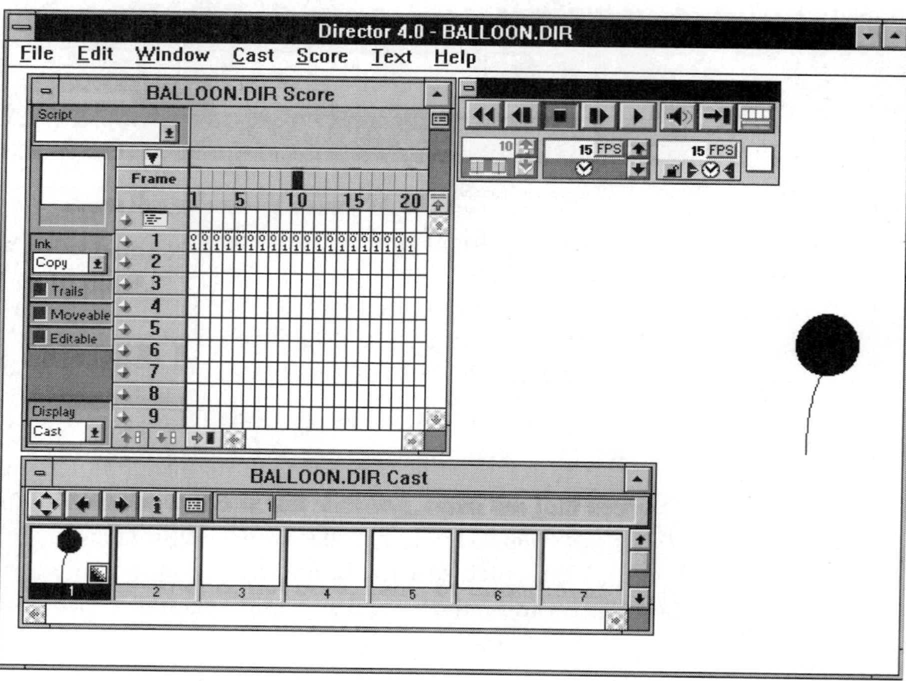

It shows the number of the frame that's currently displayed. Thus, it always corresponds to the frame indicated by the playback head. You can also use the Frame counter to make Director display a particular frame. Try that as follows:

In the Frame counter, point to the **frame number** and drag over it.

The Frame Number section darkens to reverse highlighting.

Type **10** as the frame to go to and press **Enter**.

The playback head moves to frame 10 and frame 10 is displayed (with the balloon at midpoint).

Also appearing in the Frame counter are two arrow buttons, one pointing up and one pointing down. Respectively, these buttons are quite similar in operation to Step Forward and Step Backward. The main way they differ is that they do not cause the movie to wrap around. In the first frame, clicking this down arrow has no effect. In the last frame with contents (for example, frame 20 in our movie), clicking the up arrow causes the movie to advance to the next frame, even though it is empty (frame 21 in this case).

These arrow-button operations accelerate when you use them. That is, initially these buttons move the playback head one frame at a time. As you hold down the mouse button, though, the speed with which the playback head advances increases.

SETTING THE TEMPO (SPEED) OF THE MOVIE

The next section of the Control Panel is the ***Tempo display*** (shown in color in Figure 2.9). This section allows you to see and control the speed with which the movie plays. Initially the display is set for 15 frames per second (***FPS***). You can see the same speed in seconds per frame (***SPF***).

2.9
Tempo display (showing seconds per frame)

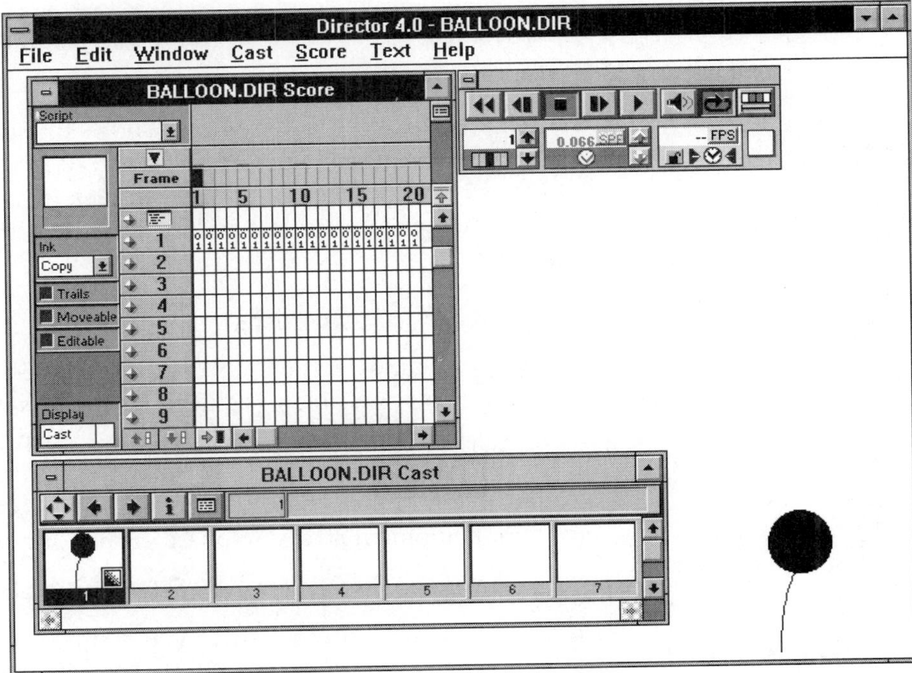

In the Tempo display, click the **Tempo Mode** button: the button labeled FPS.

The displayed value changes from 15 to 0.066. (0.066 seconds per frame is equivalent to 15 frames per second.) The button changes from FPS to SPF. The result is shown in Figure 2.9.

You can change the tempo either by entering a value, much as you did with the Frame counter, or by using the Tempo display's arrow buttons to increase (up arrow) or decrease (down arrow) the displayed value. FPS values may be entered in integers (whole numbers) only. Each click on an arrow changes the tempo by 1 FPS, whether the display is set for FPS or SPF.

Use one of the methods mentioned to increase the speed to **30** FPS.

Check the SPF display

It now reads 0.033 SPF.

With looping turned on, **play** the movie.

The movie should play at about twice the speed (though your equipment may present some limitations—more on this in the next section).

Change the Tempo display to **4** FPS.

The display slows to a crawl.

➡ *Question*: At 4 frames per second, what value represents the same speed expressed in seconds per frame?

Decide on an answer to this question, then click the **Tempo Mode** (FPS) button to change the display to SPF and check.

➡ *Preview:* You can change a movie's tempo on a frame-by-frame basis. We'll see how to do that when we examine the Tempo channel in Channel 4.

CHECKING AND LOCKING PLAY SPEEDS

The Tempo display we just examined shows the speed at which frames are set to appear. You can set values up to 60 or 120 FPS. However, all equipment is not created equal. Even though you can set a tempo for a particular rate, your equipment may not be fast enough to show the movie at the rate you assigned.

Checking Play Speeds

Once you run a movie, then, it's important to be able to determine just what speed the movie was able to achieve. The next section of the Control Panel (Figure 2.10) displays the *actual* duration of each frame when it was played. It's called the ***Actual display***. Its display too is initially set for frames per second (FPS). Until frames have been played, the display shows "--." Determine how your equipment stacks up by experimenting as follows:

In the Tempo display, enter **30 FPS** and press **Enter**.

Note that you must enter the speed you desire into the *Tempo* display, not into the Actual display. Values that appear in the Actual display may be viewed only, not edited; remember, they represent measurements of what actually occurred.

With looping turned on, play the movie.

Observe the Actual counter to determine whether your equipment is able to play this movie at 30 FPS. If it is, increase the tempo in steps to determine the approximate upper threshold of speed for this movie on your equipment.

2.10

Actual display (showing Sum)

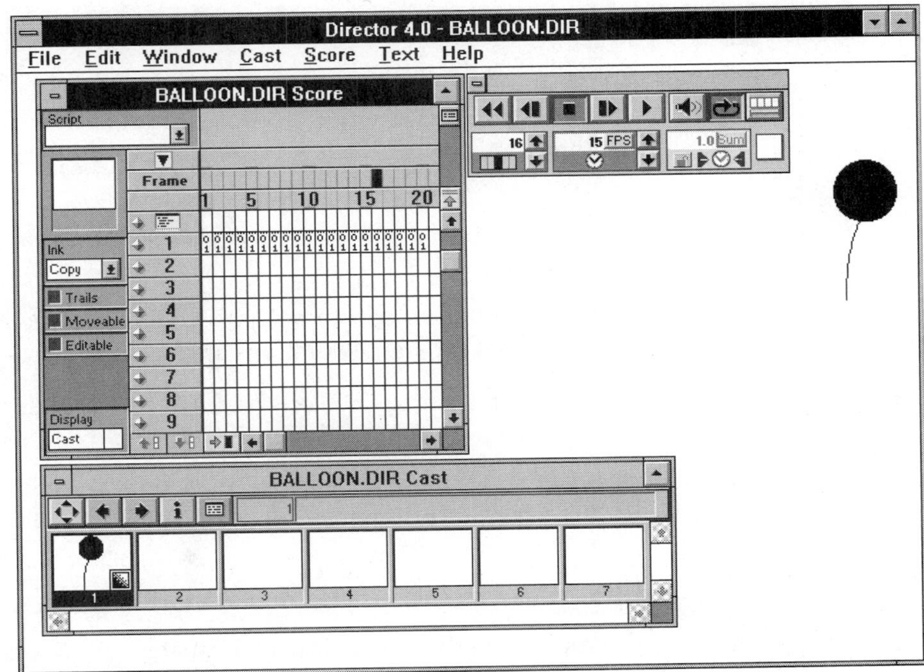

Like the Tempo display, the Actual display can also be shown in seconds per frame. In addition, the Actual display can show the amount of time accumulated from the beginning of the movie. Try these as follows:

Click the **Actual Mode** button (labeled FPS) two times.

On the first click, the button changes to SPF (with the displayed value adjusting accordingly). On the second click, the button changes to Sum, as shown in Figure 2.10.

Set the Tempo display to **15** FPS and play the movie at least once.

Move the playback head to frame **16** by clicking somewhere within that frame.

The Actual display shows 1.0 Sum. This shows that when the playback head entered this frame as the movie was playing, 1 second had elapsed.

Rewind the movie and use **Step Forward** to advance the movie frame by frame, observing the Actual display as you do.

As you step forward, the Actual display starts at none (--), for no elapsed time, in frame 1 and increases to 1.2 in frame 20.

The Actual Mode button has a fourth setting, Est. The Est setting is essentially like the Sum, except that it provides a more precise calculation. It takes into account changes made in transitions and color palettes, which are ignored by the Sum operation. However, these additional calculations can slow down the speed. Thus, Est mode should not be turned on while the movie is playing.

Locking Play Speeds

Finally, in the Actual display, consider the Lock button. This is the button with the icon shaped like a padlock on it. Turned on, it locks the speed of the movie. Try out this button as follows:

Set the **Tempo** display to **10 FPS**.

Play the movie through at least once.

Locking freezes the duration of all frames at their speed when last played. Therefore, you must allow the entire movie to play at the speed at which you wish to lock it.

Turn on the **Edit** menu's **Lock Frame Durations** command or click the Lock button.

The Lock button becomes depressed and the padlock icon on it closes, indicating that the frame durations are locked in place.

With Looping and Lock Frame Durations both turned on, increase and decrease the speed of the **Tempo display**, observing the Actual display as you do.

The Actual display remains at 10 FPS, the locked speed, regardless of changes in the Tempo display.

Turn off **Lock Frame Durations** and make changes in the Tempo display.

Once again, the Actual display fluctuates with changes you make in the Tempo display, within the parameters permitted by your system.

The Lock button serves another purpose. If you want to reset the Actual display so that all frames of the movie are back to none (--), hold down Alt and click the Lock button.

CHANGING THE COLOR OF THE STAGE BACKGROUND

The last item in the Control Panel could easily go unnoticed. It's the Stage Background color chip. You used it to change the color of the stage's background in Chapter 1.

Point to the **Stage Background color chip**, shown in color in Figure 2.11.

Press the mouse button and **hold** it down.

The color palette appears immediately to the left of the color chip, as shown in Figure 2.11.

Point to a color for the stage's background, perhaps a sky blue, and **click**.

The color palette disappears and the chip and the background change to match the color you selected.

There is a problem, however. A white box, whose edges match that of the balloon, surrounds it. This is the bounding box as mentioned earlier. It indicates the perimeter of the sprite. To make this box invisible so the background color appears instead, we must change the ink effect applied to all the sprites that generate the ascending balloon. Changing the ink effect is similar to the method used to change the color of the background, but different as well, so follow the instructions carefully. Begin by selecting the sprites as follows:

In the Score window, point to any cell with a balloon sprite (indicated with the cast member's number, **01**) and **double-click**.

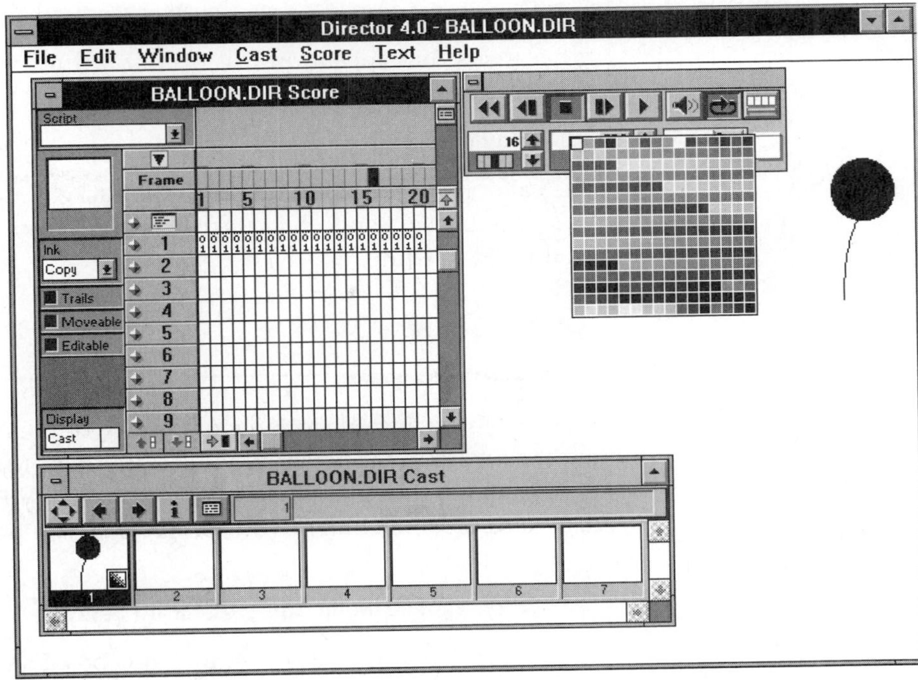

2.11
Stage Background color chip, showing palette

This selects the entire string of 01 sprites, as indicated by reverse highlighting. Double-clicking any sprite in a string of sprites created from the same cast member selects the entire string of similar sprites, from beginning to end. Now change the ink effect:

In the Score window, point to the **ink effect's pop-up arrow** (next to the ink effect's current setting, Copy).

Press the mouse button, **hold**, and with the pop-up list set to **Matte** (Figure 2.12), **release**.

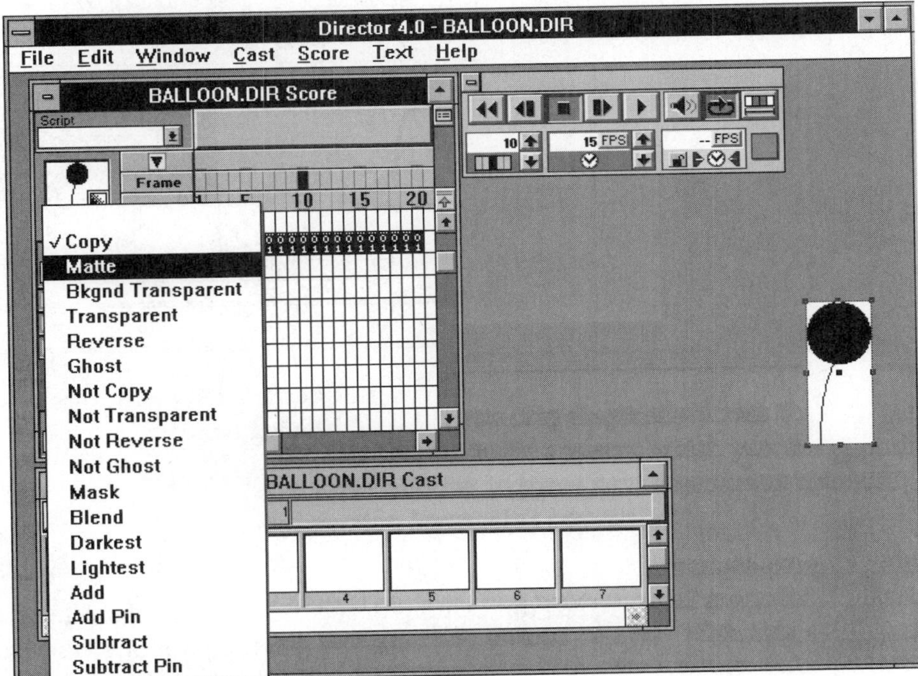

2.12
Score's Ink Effects pop-up list

The Matte ink is applied and the bounding box disappears. We'll examine other items that appear on this drop-down list when we study the score in Chapter 4.

Play the movie.

The balloon appears directly against the background in all the frames. You can leave the background you selected in place. For now we'll leave the background set to white.

PRINTING

Now you have a good working knowledge of the Control Panel and you can use it to work with movies as you create them throughout this book. Next, we'll examine printing with Director. That way you'll be able to create hard-copy output to document your progress as you proceed. Begin by checking your print setup.

Open the **File** menu and select **Print Setup**.

The standard Windows Print Setup dialog box appears (Figure 2.13).

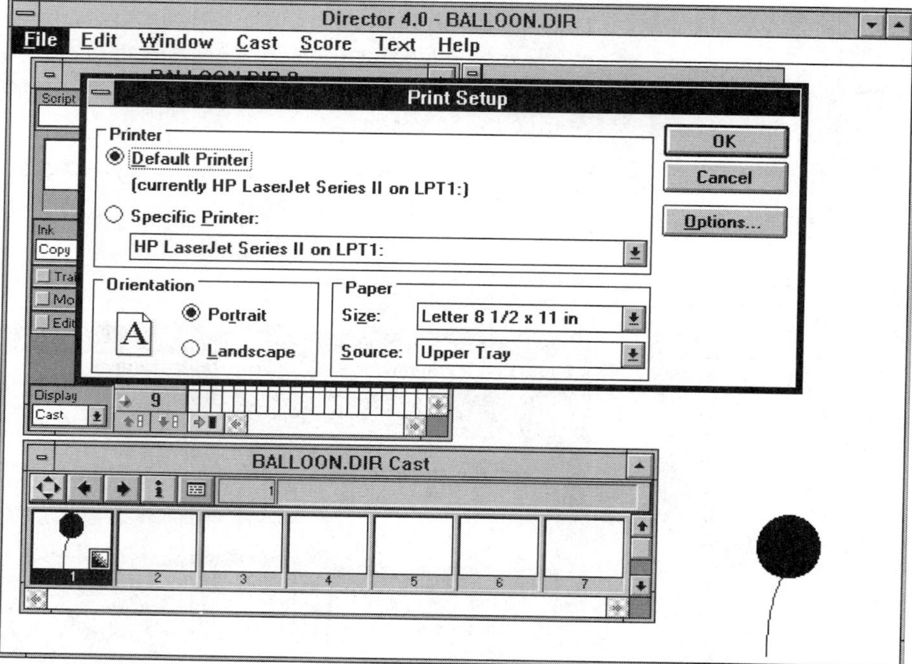

2.13
File menu's Print Setup dialog box

Following your instructor's directions, check that the print setup is correct and then close the dialog box.

Also check that your printer and other hardware, such as switch boxes, are set as instructed.

Open the **File** menu and select **Print** or press Ctrl+Alt+P.

The Print Options dialog box appears (Figure 2.14). Notice that its Print group, initially set to Stage, can be set to print one of several items as indicated by the list of radio buttons. The item selected for printing affects items in the Print Range group.

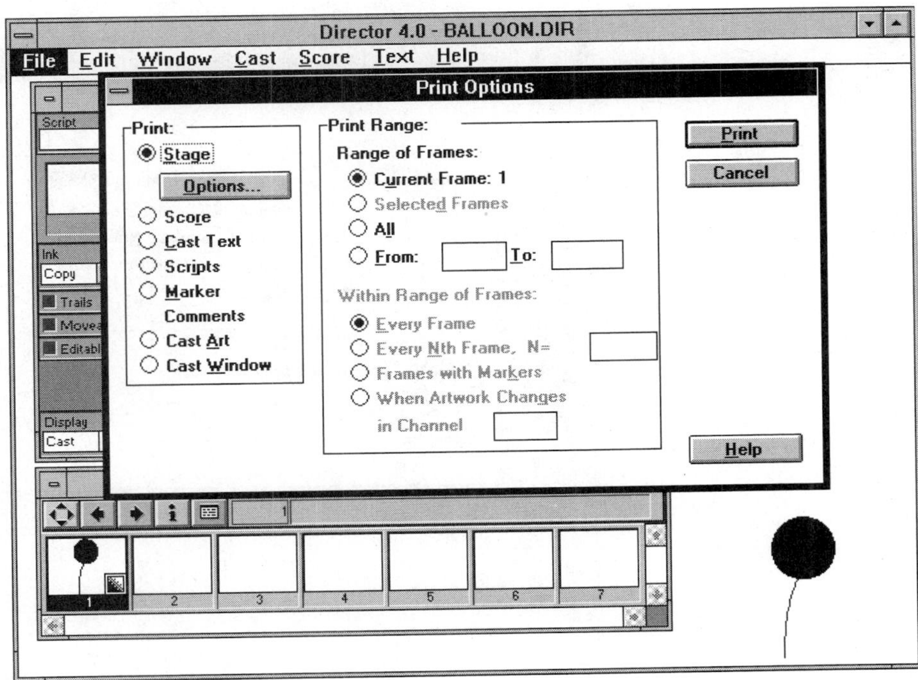

2.14
Print Options dialog box (displayed with File, Print)

In the **Print** group, click other radio buttons (not the Options button), observing how the Print Range group changes as you do.

Finish by selecting **Stage** once again.

Below the Stage button is an Options button. You may have noticed that this button is available only when the Stage button is selected. It allows you to set Stage Options and we'll use it now like this:

With the Stage button selected, click the **Options** button.

The Stage Options dialog box appears (Figure 2.15). In it you see a sample page only; it doesn't show your actual stage. For some items that are turned on, this sample shows where those items appear on the page. The figure shows the correspondence between the items and the sample.

Experiment with turning the check boxes on and off and observing the effect on the sample.

Most of the items in this dialog box are self-explanatory, but a word of explanation is in order about a few of them.

- **Registration Marks** These indicate the ***registration point***, which is a position you can set in the Paint window to line up sequential cast members accurately for smooth animation. You can turn on Registration Marks only when this dialog box's Image Size group is set to Full. We'll discuss registration points when we look at animation in Chapter 5.
- **Storyboard Format** This places the stage along the left edge of the page, providing blank space on the right for notes. It is available only if Image Size is set to 1/2 or 1/4.
- **Marker Comment** You can insert markers into the score, each of which is associated with a specific frame. In turn, comments can be assigned to the markers. If (and only if) the Storyboard Format button is

2.15

Stage Options dialog box

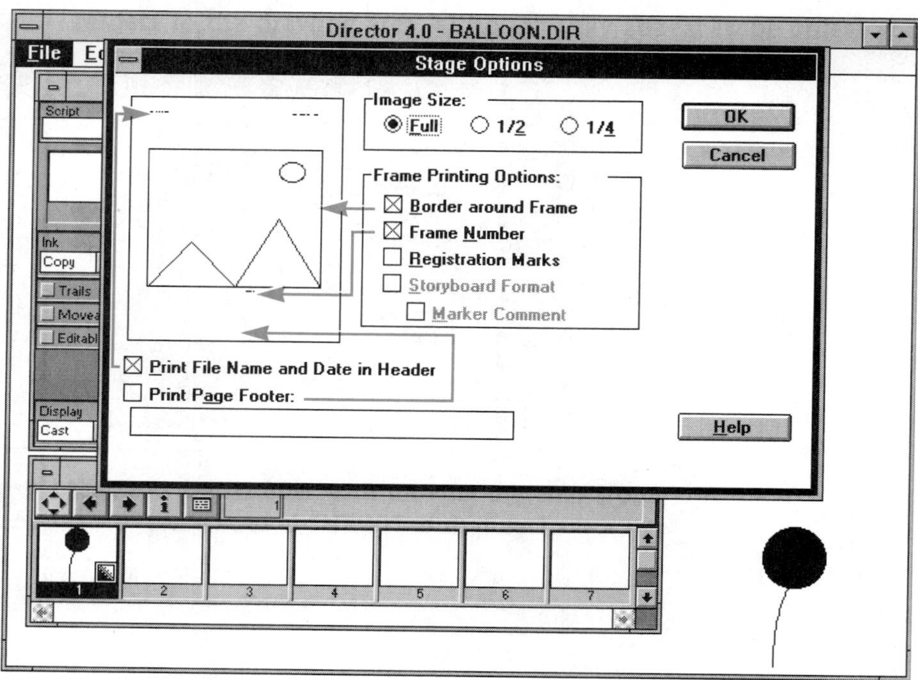

turned on, you can turn on the Marker Comment check box to have the comments printed on the right, alongside the appropriate frames. In Chapter 1, Figure 1.10 shows several markers (▼) in the score's top row, along with their comments ("Lobby" and "Crowd" for example).

- **Print Page Footer** When this check box is turned on, the page footer you provide in the text box just below appears at the bottom of each page.

Set **Image Size** to **1/4**.

Turn on the **Print Page Footer** check box and add your name in the box below it.

Click the **OK** button or press the Enter key.

The Print Options dialog box (Figure 2.14) reappears.

Now a few words about the Print Range group in this dialog box.

- **Range of Frames** *Current Frame* shows the current frame number as indicated by the Playback Head and the Frame counter. *Selected Frames* is available only when one or more cells are selected in the score; it reflects the frame numbers associated with those selected cells. The *From/To* button and boxes are provided so you can indicate a string of frames you want printed.
- **Within Range of Frames** This section is not available if the Current Frame button is turned on. *Every Nth Frame* causes the first frame to print, then adds the value you provide for *N*= and prints the frame corresponding to that. Thus, in our example, if you wanted to print only the first (1) and last (20) frames of the movie you could turn on this button and set N to 19.

Set **Range of Frames** to **All**.

Click the **Print** button.

The Print dialog box appears (Figure 2.16). At first, this dialog box may seem redundant, as ranges can be set with the previous dialog box. However, this dialog box allows you to select printed *page* ranges, whereas the previous dialog box could be used to select *frame* ranges. For example, setting images in 1/4 size allows you to print 15 frames to the page, which means that it will require 2 pages to print all 20 frames in the BALLOON.DIR movie. Your instructor may want you to print the first page only. You can do this by turning on the Pages button and setting both the From and To boxes to 1.

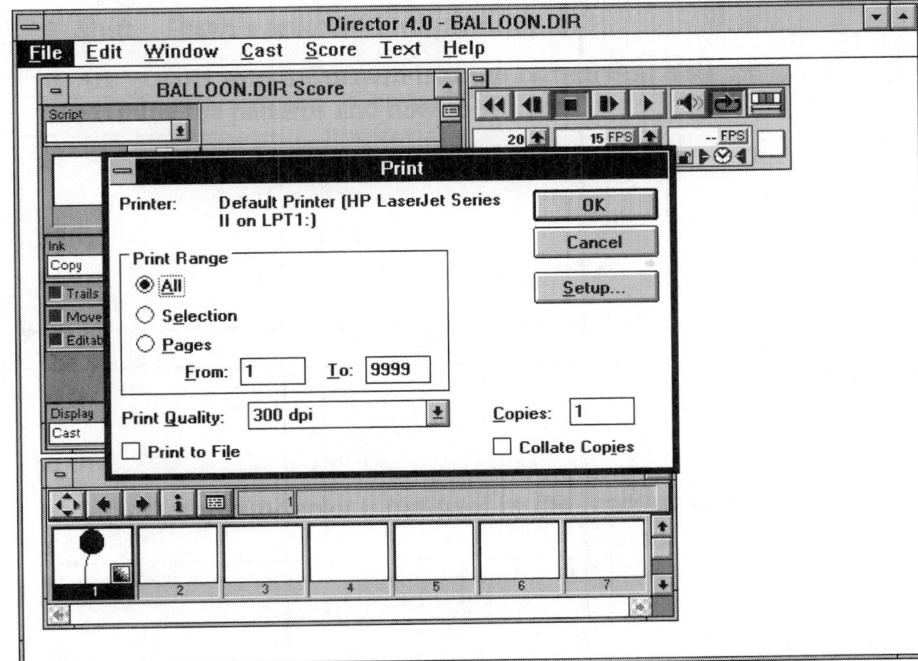

2.16
Print dialog box

Set the Print dialog box as instructed.

Click the **OK** button or press the Enter key.

Figure 2.17 shows the result when you print the first page of stage frames. Figure 2.18 shows some other items you can use File, Print (or Ctrl+Alt+P) to print.

CUSTOMIZING DIRECTOR

Finally, consider customizing Director by setting Preferences (Figure 2.19).

Open the **File** menu and select **Preferences** or press Ctrl+Alt+U.

- **Stage Size** Used for setting the size of the stage. Normally, it's the same size as the screen, but that's not required. With Custom, values can be entered into Width and Height; selecting one of the other settings provides these values automatically.
- **Stage Location** When the stage is smaller than the screen, you can use this group to position the stage.

2.17
Printed stage

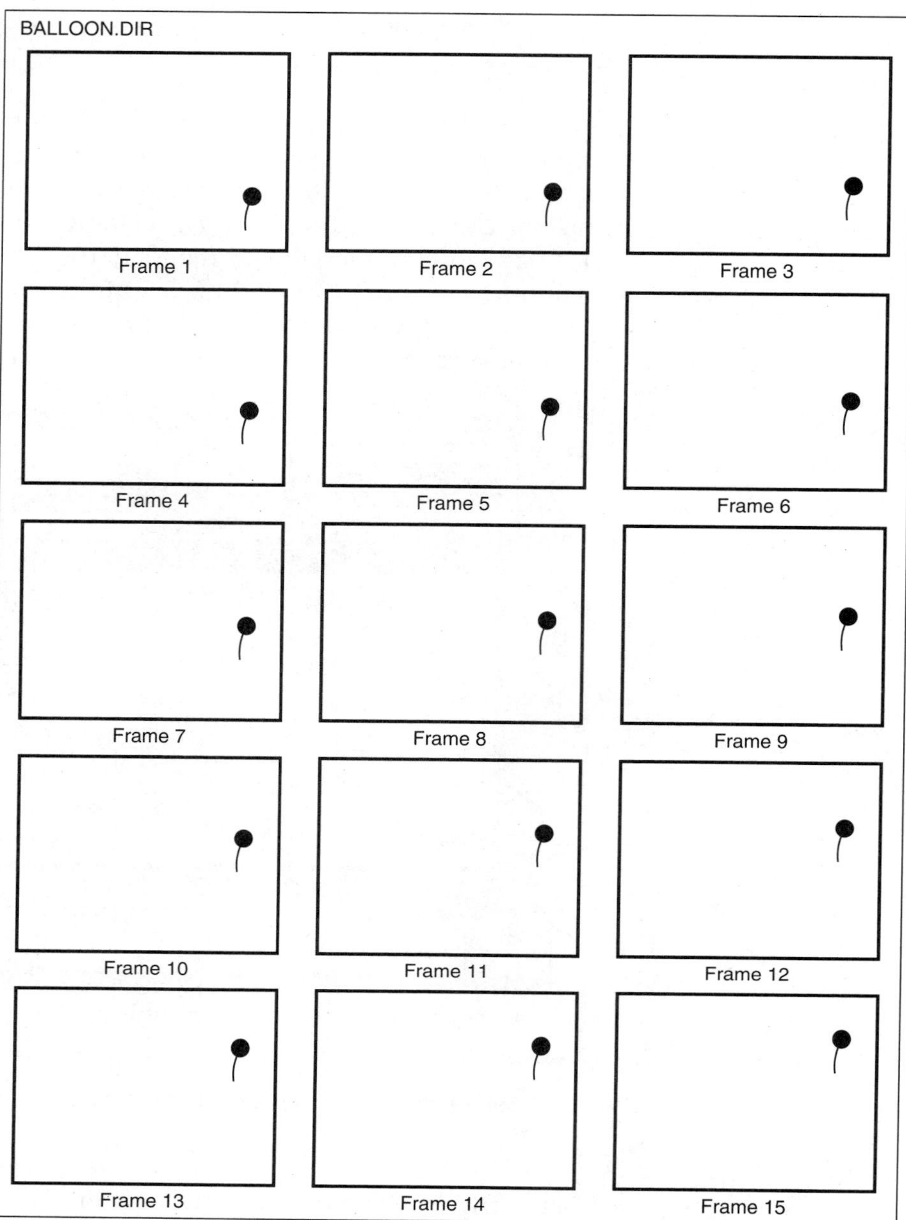

- **When Opening a Movie** With this group you indicate where you want the movie placed when you open it.
- **Save Settings** Use this to indicate whether you want your settings saved when you exit this dialog box (*Now*) or when you exit Director (*When Quitting*).
- **Black and White User Interface** This check box is helpful when you are using some color palettes, as their color combinations can make it difficult to see Director's ***interface:*** dialog boxes, menus, and other aspects of the display. We'll be examining color palettes in Chapter 4.
- **Dialogs Appear at Mouse Position** Causes the dialog boxes to appear where the mouse is pointing, rather than centered as normal.
- **Animate in Background** Allows animation to continue running when you use other applications.

2.18.

Additional printed items

Cast Window

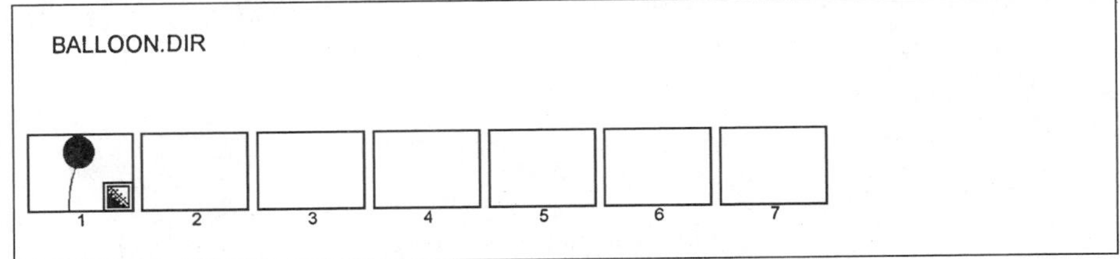

Score

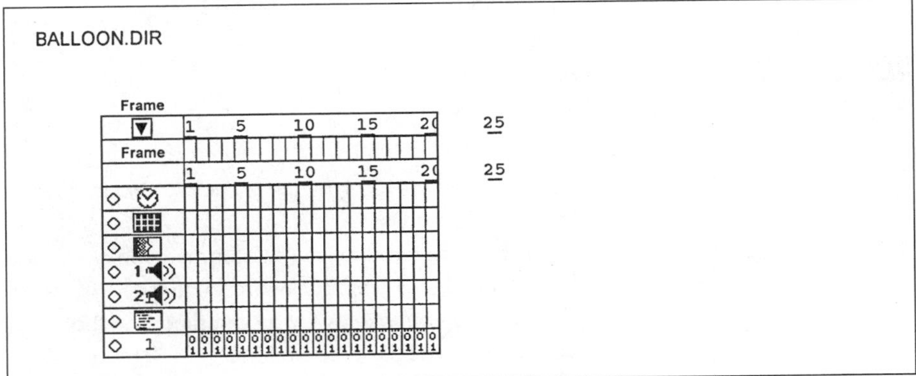

2.19

File menu's Preferences dialog box

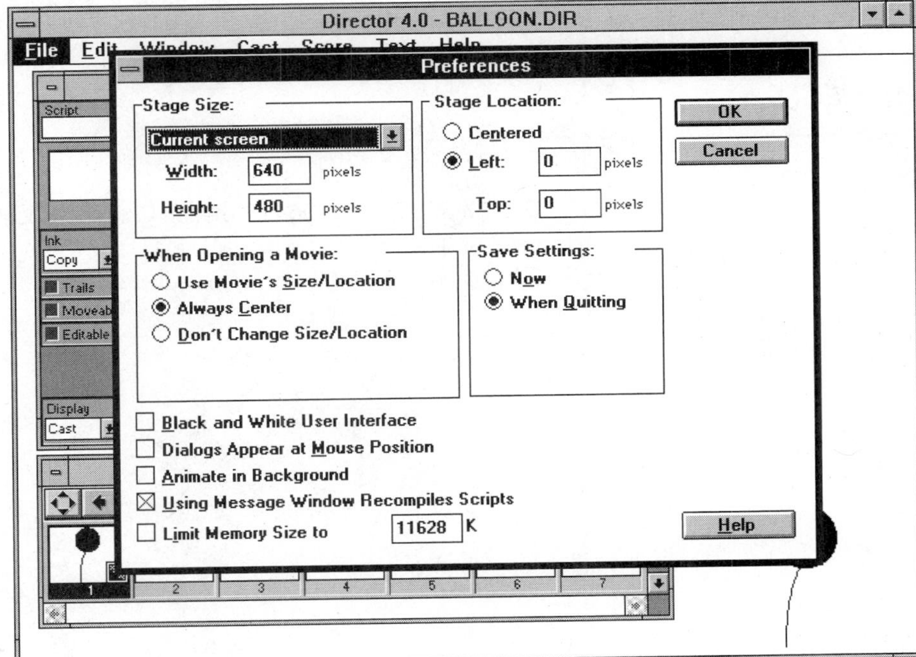

- **Using Message Window Recompiles Scripts** For use when Lingo scripts are created (Chapter 6).
- **Limit Memory Size to** Allows you to insert a value that limits the amount of memory Director can use, permitting you to test how movies will behave when they are played on computers with less memory than yours.

KEY TERMS

looping
bounding box
Frame counter
Tempo display
FPS
SPF
Actual display
locking
registration point
interface

REVIEW QUESTIONS

1. **T F** When you type the name of a file to open in Director, it is not necessary to provide the DIR extension.
2. **T F** Arrow buttons in the Frame counter are identical in operation to the Step Forward and Step Backward buttons.
3. How do you take away a bounding box that appears around a sprite?
4. How do you set print options?
5. Name two kinds of ranges you can choose to print.
6. When a color palette makes it difficult to see Director's interface, what can you do?

PROJECTS

1. Using the rolling ball you created in Chapter 1, lock the second half of its movement at slow speed.
2. Print out your rolling ball movie as instructed.

3

Using Paint and Working with the Cast

THIS CHAPTER WILL TEACH YOU HOW TO

- **Use tools in the Paint window to add text, select, move, add color and patterns, erase, and create shapes.**
- **Use buttons in both the Paint window and the Cast window to navigate through movies when editing.**
- **Use standard and custom brushes.**
- **Apply ink effects for darkening, blending, smudging, and so on.**
- **Customize the Cast window and Paint window.**

In this chapter we'll look more closely at the Paint window, which you used in Chapter 1 to create the balloon. You'll see how you can use the Paint window to enhance cast members you create from scratch. We'll also examine the Cast window. These two windows closely interact with each other.

EXAMINING EXISTING ART

Figure 3.1 shows the Paint window in its default size and position, with its major areas labeled. Examine this figure as necessary throughout the chapter. Cast member 1, the balloon you created, appears in the Paint window. Its cast

3.1
Paint window

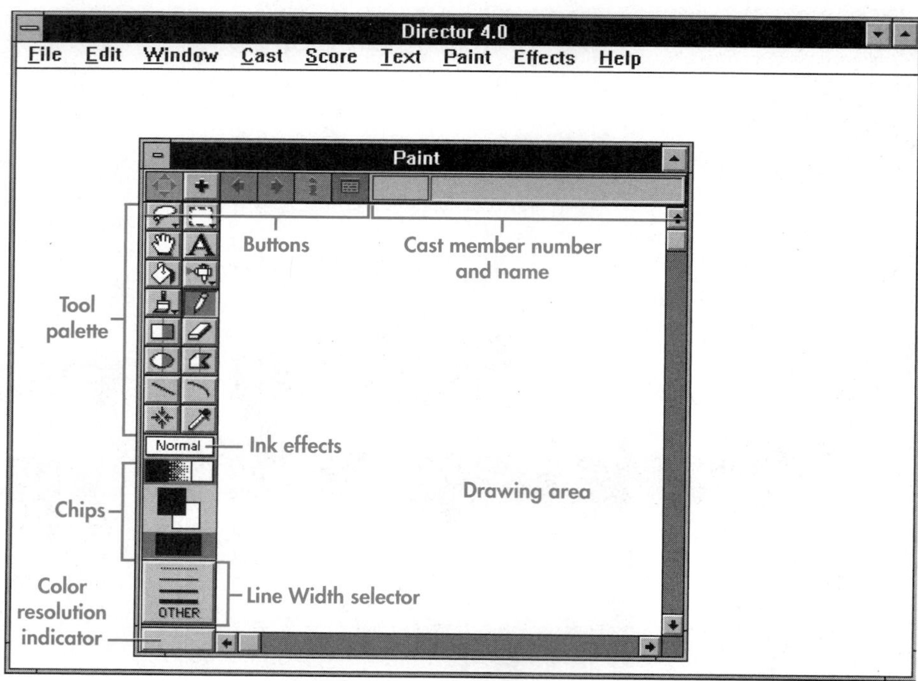

Begin by opening the BALLOON.DIR movie.

Assuming the Paint window is not yet open, use Window, Paint or Ctrl+5 to open it.

number (1) is indicated in the Paint window in two places: the Title bar at the top of the window, where "Paint 1" appears, and the small box just below that.

ADDING TEXT TO ART

We'll begin by adding some text to our art. Assume the BALLOON.DIR movie is to be used in conjunction with a grand opening, perhaps in a kiosk. Let's add a sign that says "NEW!" to the end of the balloon's string. By adding it in this Paint 1 window, we will make it a part of the balloon graphic. As such, the sign will rise with the balloon when you play the movie, just as the string does. If you want to look ahead, Figure 3.11 shows the sign we'll be creating. (Figures have a background added.)

You'll begin by entering "NEW!" below the string, approximately where it's shown in Figure 3.2. As you do this, it is not important that you get this text in the exact position; soon you'll see how to select and move art in the Paint window. However, it is better to position the text lower than higher. Do not allow the text to come in contact with the string or balloon. In the Paint window, items that touch, in a way, meld together and lose their identity as independent items. Keep white space or some other solid color between areas of art until you are sure you will not need to control them separately.

Click the Text tool, shown in color in Figure 3.2.

Position the mouse cursor well below the balloon's string.

As you cross into the working area, the mouse cursor assumes the I-beam shape.

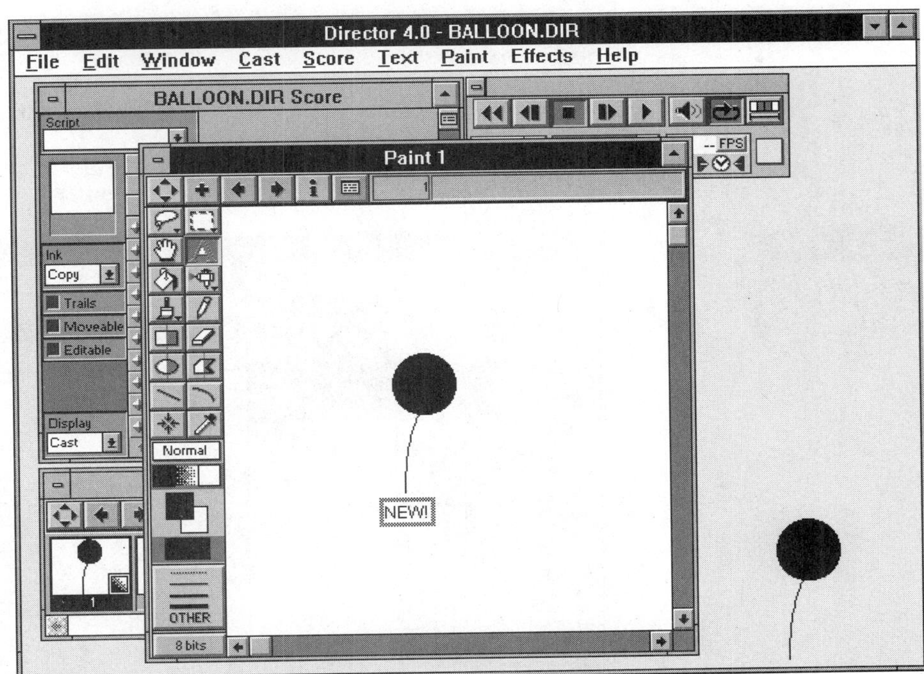

3.2
Using the Text tool to add text

Click below the string.

A ***text box***, a temporary container you can use to type in text, appears.

Troubleshooting: If you clicked in the wrong location, just go back to the Text tool and click again.

Use the text box to enter the text **NEW!** as shown in Figure 3.2.

Important: For now, don't do anything to the text box to make it disappear, like clicking away from it. Don't switch to another program or quit, as these actions also take the text box away. We need to keep things as they are for the moment.

CHANGING FONT SIZE

Director has some text formatting that can be applied as you initially enter text in the Paint window. Such formatting *cannot* be added to existing text; you would have to erase or immediately undo such text and reenter it to apply the formatting.

Text formatting you apply in the Paint window is applied to the entire text box that is active at the time, regardless of where the cursor is positioned. You do *not* drag the mouse cursor over text before changing formatting, as you might in a word processing program. Thus, you can change formats before even typing a letter, or at the very end, or somewhere along the way, as long as you keep the text box active. The results are the same: The formatting is applied to the entire contents of the text box.

Although this is convenient, the flip side is the disadvantage that you can't combine different formatting styles in text as you enter it. For example, you couldn't enter an entire sentence and have just one word appear in italics. Instead, you would have to enter italicized and plain text separately, or type the sentence and later place an italicized version of the word on top of the plain version.

With the text box still showing, open the Text menu and select Size.

The submenu shown in Figure 3.3 appears. The check mark indicates the current font size.

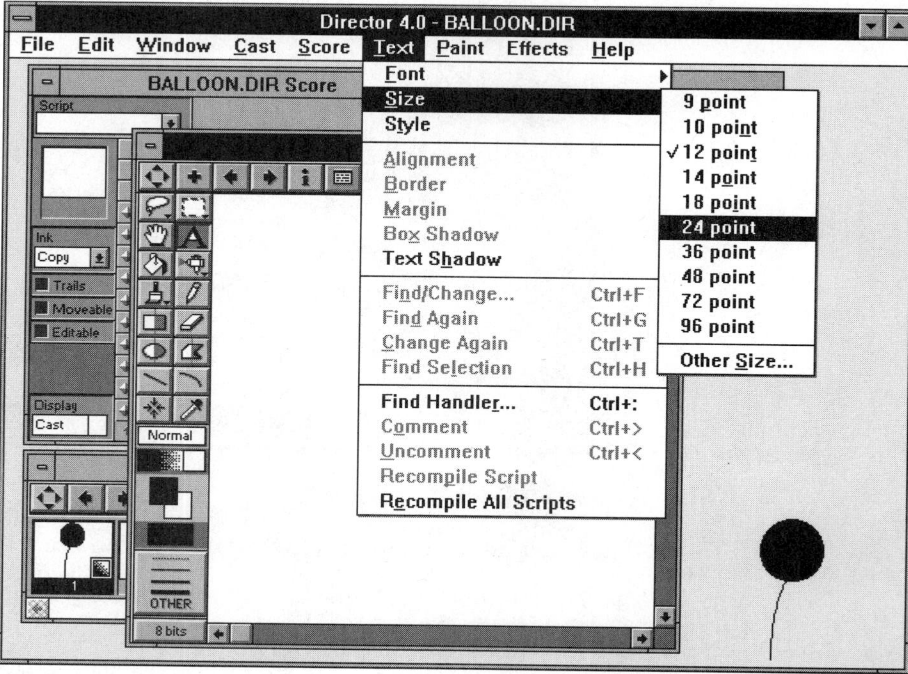

3.3
Text, Size submenu

From the submenu, select 24 points.

A ***point*** being 1/72 inch, the text increases to about 1/3 inch in size. Keep the text box in place.

ADDING BOLD, ITALIC, AND UNDERLINE

Now to apply boldface to the text.

With the text box still showing, open the Text menu and select Style.

The submenu shown in Figure 3.4 appears. The check mark indicates that the text is plain—that is, not bold, italic, or underlined.

From the submenu, select Bold.

The bold style is applied and the result of that and the increase in size is shown in Figure 3.5.

Now that the typing and formatting are complete you can take away the text box. One way to do so is this:

Click on the Text tool (A).

The text in the Paint window is set into place. Note the change in the ***thumbnail*** as well (that is, the depiction of cast member 1—balloon, string, and sign—as it appears in the Cast window).

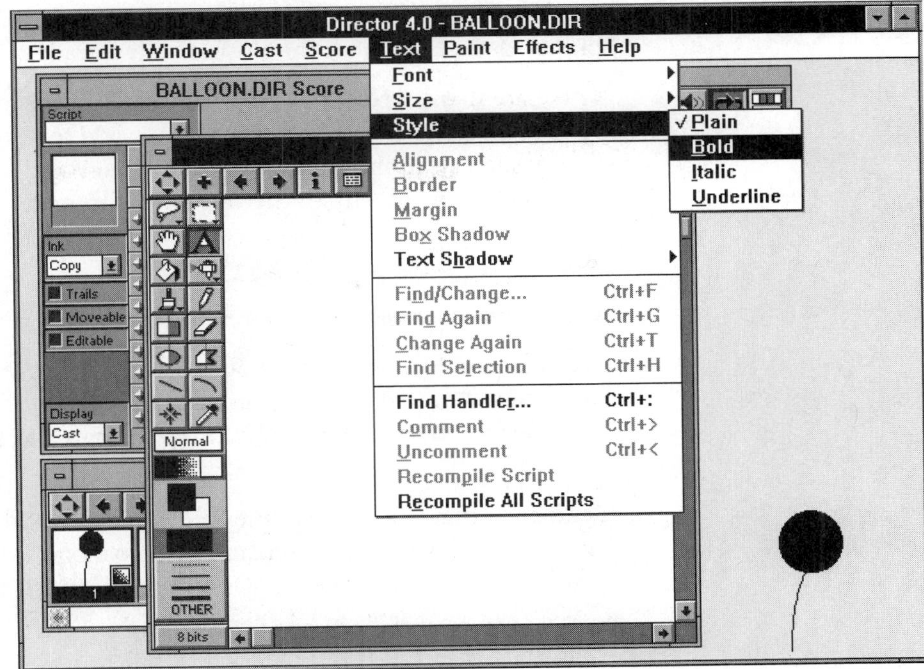

3.4
Text, Style submenu

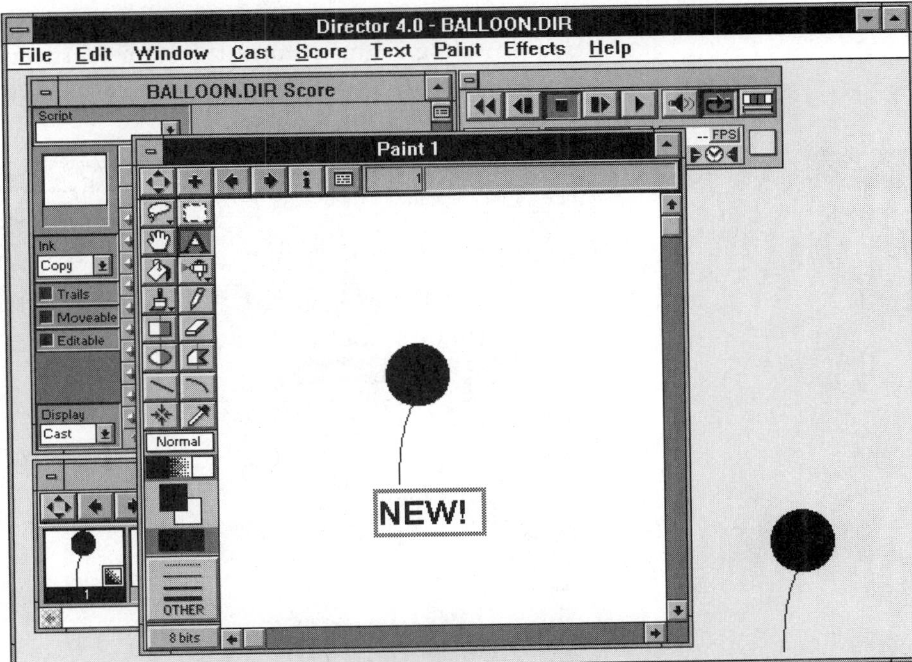

3.5
Bigger, bold text in place

OTHER TEXT FORMATTING

Besides size and styles such as bold, you can also use the Text menu to change the font of newly entered text. The Font submenu is a list of the available typefaces.

The Text Shadow submenu is for providing a letter-by-letter duplicate of the text offset from the original by the ***pixel*** value (picture element or screen dot, the smallest size available) you select. It appears only after you take away the text box. This effect works best on larger sizes; should you decide to use it, be prepared to experiment for most effective results.

There are many items that are "ghosting" on this menu, indicating that they are not available. There are other ways to add text to a movie; formatting paint text has less flexibility than other methods. You'll see how you can add text as an object more directly to the stage in Chapter 4.

SELECTING AND MOVING

We need to add a box around our text and then connect the box to the string like a sign. But first, in case you need to adjust the position of your text, let's look at how to select a portion of the bitmap and then at how to move that portion.

Remember that all you see in the Paint window at this point is one cast member. However, with white space separating the balloon's string and the word "NEW!" you can easily select the word. Once it has been selected, you can then move it.

The Lasso

Director provides two tools at the top of the Tool palette that you can use for selecting. The first is the ***Lasso tool*** (shown in color in Figure 3.6). With this tool, you drag a line around the item you want to select and, when you release, the line connects, selecting what is within it, the edges of an item selected with the Lasso tool blinks.

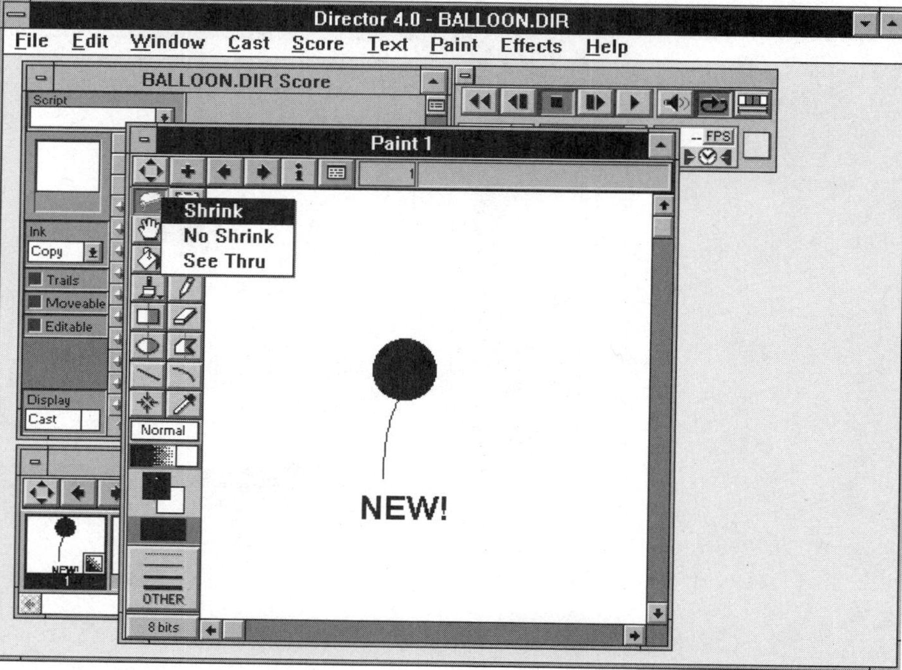

3.6
Lasso tool and its menu

At the bottom-right corner of the Lasso tool in the Tool palette you can see a small, downward pointing arrow (▼). This marking indicates that the tool has a pop-up menu available, which you see in Figure 3.6 just to the right of the Lasso tool. (The telltale arrow is hidden by the menu in this figure; however, it is visible in the previous figure.) To display this menu, you point to the tool and press and hold the mouse button. While holding the mouse button, you select by dragging to one of the items on the menu and releasing there.

Items on the Lasso menu consist of the following:

- **Shrink** When selecting with a shrink lasso, the lasso ignores white area around the object it encloses and, like a vacuum-packed envelope, wraps itself tightly around the object. When you move the object, only the object itself moves, not the white area that existed around the object when it was encircled with the lasso.
- **No Shrink** With No Shrink selected, enclosed white space between the lasso and the object is selected as well as the object. Should you move the object on top of another object, say a red splotch, that white space would be evident and reflect the shape of the lassoed area.
- **See Thru** This is similar to Shrink but with an important difference. Not only is white space around the object not selected, but white space *within* the object is not selected either. For example, should you use See Thru to lasso and drag the word "SOON" over a red splotch, the red would show through the center of the O's. With Shrink, that white space would drag along, obscuring the red paint.

The points made with regard to white space also apply to solid color backgrounds. Thus, if you had "NEW!" against a solid color rectangle, you could use a shrink lasso to select only "NEW!" as long as you dragged the lasso only in the color area.

Practice selecting with the lasso:

Select the **Lasso** tool and position it in the drawing area.

The mouse cursor changes into the shape of a lasso.

Position the mouse above and to the left of the "N" in "NEW!"

Drag around, below, to the right, and up, as shown in Figure 3.7.

When you release, the word begins to flash, indicating it is selected.

Note that you need not connect both ends of the lasso. Director does that for you, completing the lasso by connecting its two ends in a straight line across the space between them.

Careful: Be careful where you position the beginning and end points of the lasso, so there's a clear path between them. In the figure, for example, if you ended too high, you could inadvertently snag a bottom part of the string. That part would also move when you move the "NEW!"

Troubleshooting: If you inadvertently selected incorrectly, just click the Tool palette's Lasso tool and try again.

Now that the word is selected, you can move it.

With the word flashing and the Lasso tool still selected, position the cursor over the flashing material.

The mouse cursor turns into an arrow shape, indicating that you can drag with it.

3.7

Lassoing a portion of the bitmap

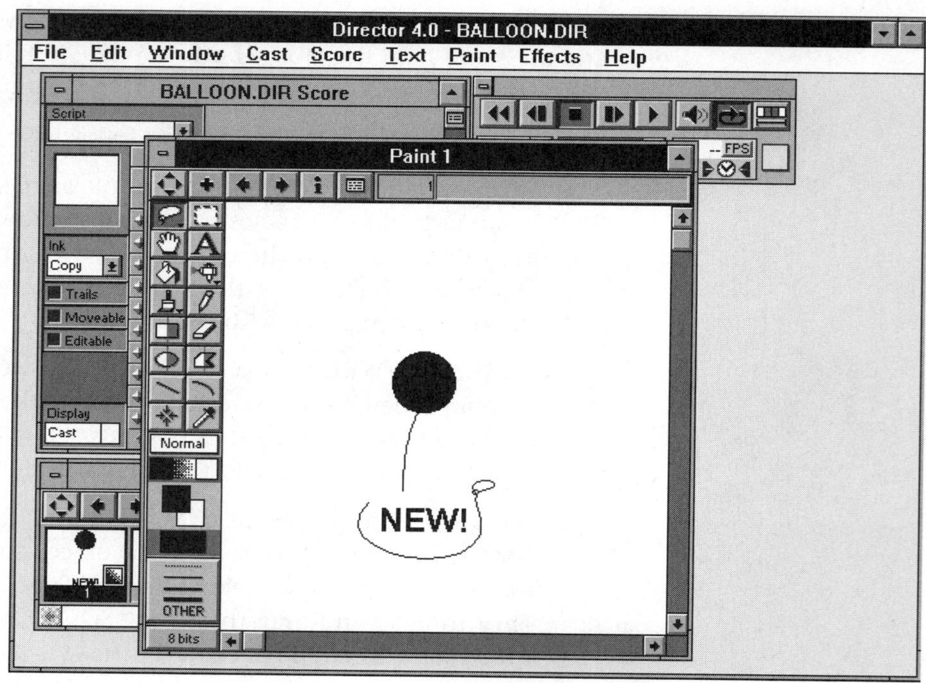

Drag the selected material around white space and temporarily over the balloon to observe its effects.

Keep the "NEW!" selected while it is over the balloon. Otherwise it could become a permanent part of the balloon. Should you make a mistake you can use Edit, Undo Bitmap (or Ctrl+Z) if you catch it right away.

You can also move art in fine increments. To do that, you press the arrow keys.

With the "NEW!" still selected, try the **arrow** keys and watch closely to see the material move in small increments.

With the "NEW!" in the white area, change the **Lasso** menu and experiment again.

Holding down the following keys causes them to affect the lasso.

- **Alt** When you are selecting, it makes the Lasso tool select in straight lines and operate with clicking, like the Polygon tool. (We'll see how this works when we study the Polygon tool shortly.) When you are dragging a selected item, it makes a copy of the item, leaving the original in place.
- **Shift** When you are dragging the item, it allows you to drag only horizontally or vertically (depending on which way you move first).

You can combine these effects when dragging. Holding down Alt+Shift allows you to drag a copy in a constrained direction.

The Selection Rectangle

Another tool you can use for selecting is the ***Selection Rectangle tool***. It is shown in color in Figure 3.8. The figure also shows this tool's pop-up list. You display this list in the same way as the list for the Lasso tool—that is, by pressing and holding the mouse button. Still holding, you make a selection by dragging to it and releasing.

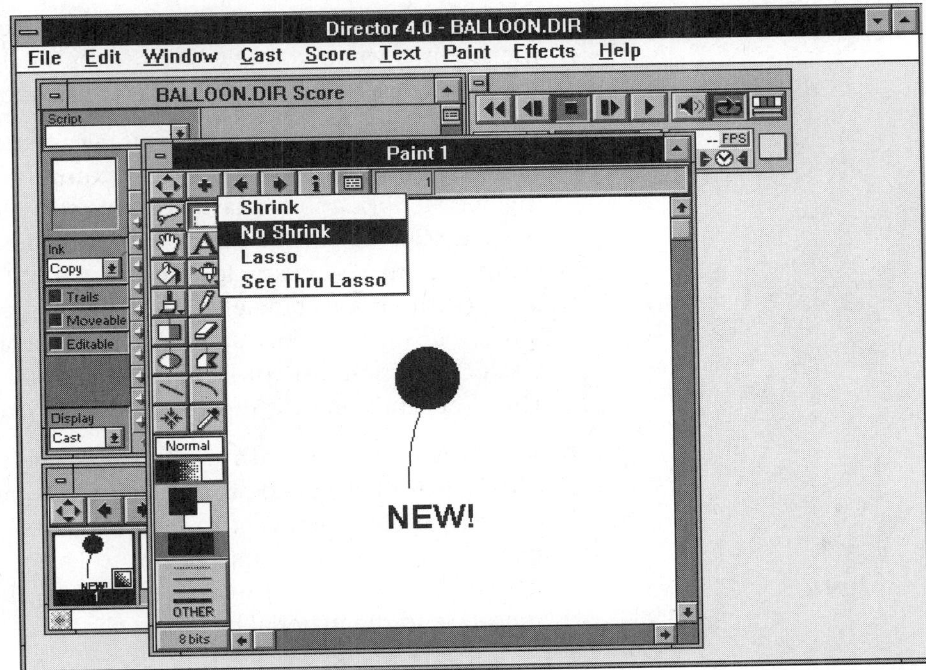

3.8
Selection Rectangle tool and its menu

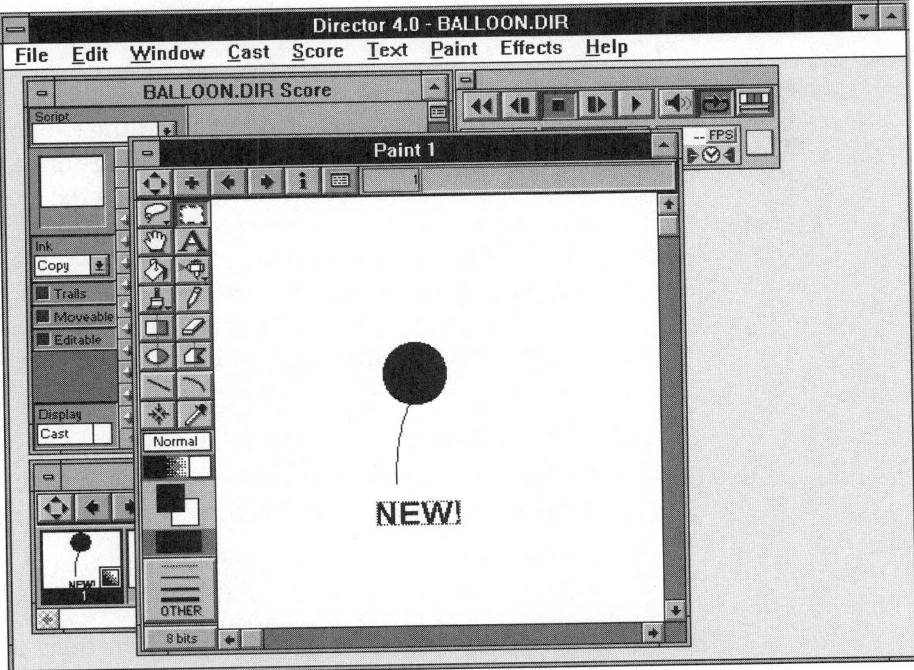

3.9
Part of bitmap selected with Selection Rectangle tool set to Shrink

To select with the Selection Rectangle, you drag diagonally across the area you want to select. As you do, a dotted rectangle appears, which you use to indicate the area you want to include. What happens next depends on the setting you've chosen from the Selection Rectangle's pop-up list.

- **Shrink** As with the shrink lasso, the Selection Rectangle ignores white area around the object it encloses and tightens itself around the object. The result is shown in Figure 3.9, around "NEW!" With this setting, as the figure shows, a fair amount of white space can remain selected because a rectangular area is used.

- **No Shrink** With No Shrink selected, the Selection Rectangle remains the size it is when you release to select. Enclosed white space between the rectangle and the object is selected and moves with it when you drag.
- **Lasso** With this setting, once you release the mouse button, the Selection Rectangle disappears, the cursor turn into a lasso shape, and selecting operates like a shrink lasso, causing the selection to shrink. No white space is selected outside the graphic, and the edges of selected material begin to blink. For example, selecting "NEW!" would cause that text to blink (without a rectangle), and no white space would be selected. The mouse cursor then looks and behaves like a lasso (should you decide to reselect). Which type of lasso it becomes—Shrink, No Shrink, or See Thru—depends on how the Lasso's pop-up list is set.
- **See Thru Lasso** As with the lasso, this setting excludes white space within as well as outside the object. Selecting "SOON" with the Selection Rectangle's menu set to See Thru Lasso will not select the white space in the center of the O's. Set to Lasso, it will. As with the Lasso setting, the cursor turns into a lasso shape, the Selection Rectangle disappears, and the material begins to blink.

Use the **Selection Rectangle** to practice selecting and moving "NEW!"

As with the Lasso tool, you can use the arrow keys to move in small increments.

Careful: The caveat noted with the Lasso tool in regard to positioning over the balloon applies here: "NEW!" and the balloon should not touch or they meld. However, be aware that, when using Shrink or No Shrink Selection Rectangles, Undo is not available *while* material is selected. If you are moving material and decide you want to undo, turn off selection of the material (by clicking the Selection Rectangle tool or one of the other tools, for example) to complete the erroneous positioning, *then* use Undo. Do *not*, however, complete the selecting by clicking inside the work area, as this will start a new selecting process, making Undo unavailable. You will have lost your chance to undo.

As a last comparison to the Lasso tool, the ability to shrink against a color background applies only to the Lasso and See Thru Lasso settings. It does not apply to the Shrink (and of course, No Shrink) setting.

Holding down the following keys causes them to affect the dragging of material selected with the Selection Rectangle.

- **Alt** Creates and drags a copy of the item, leaving the original in place.
- **Shift** Allows you to drag only horizontally or vertically (depending on which way you move first).
- **Ctrl** When you are dragging a selected area, allows you to stretch or compress the area.
- **Ctrl+Shift** If you first drag horizontally or vertically, these cause the combined effect of the two keys—that is, constrained stretching in the direction in which you are moving. Dragging diagonally keeps the material proportional as you stretch or compress it.

Other combinations operate as well. For example, use Alt+Shift when you want to drag a copy in a constrained direction.

Finally, you can also place a shrink Selection Rectangle around the entire graphic assigned to the cast member. You do this by double-clicking the Selection Rectangle tool in the Tool palette. Once the entire graphic has been selected, you can move it by dragging, and dragging combined with the various keys listed above will affect all the graphics in the window.

Moving with the Hand

There is another way you can move the entire graphic. You can use the ***Hand tool*** (shown in color in Figure 3.10). Try using it.

3.10

Hand tool and cursor

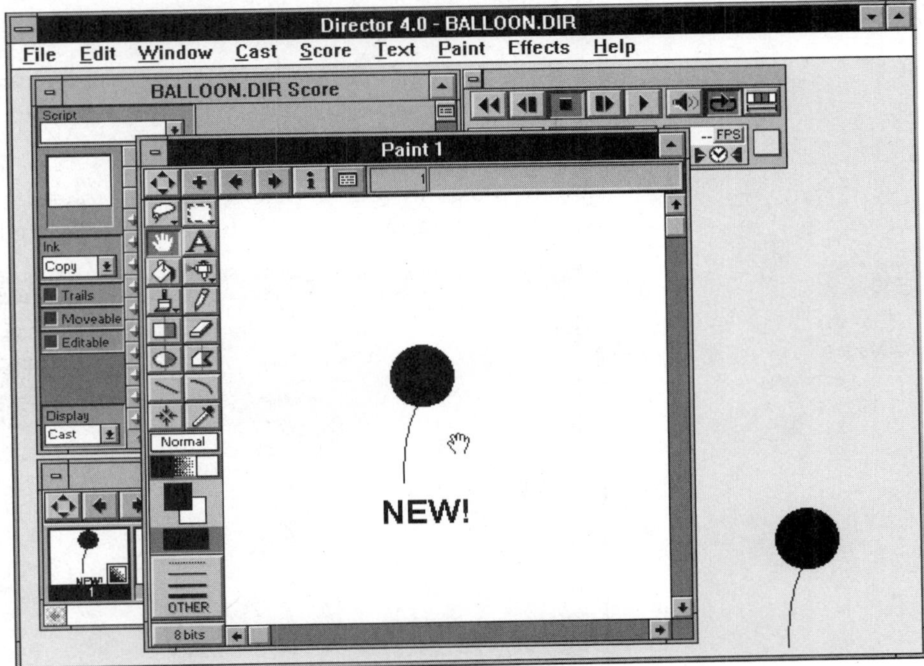

Select the **Hand** tool.

Over the drawing area, the cursor turns into a hand shape as shown in the figure.

Drag to move the art.

As you do, observe the Cast window. The position of the balloon and "NEW!" do not change. This is because the background is not considered in creating the cast member, so where you drag the art does not matter. This may seem to limit the tool's usefulness. However, it is helpful when graphics are too close to one edge of the window, say the top edge, and you have to move everything down to make room for something else you need to draw.

The following keys affect the Hand.

- **Shift** Shift-dragging allows you to drag only horizontally or vertically (depending on which way you move first).
- **Alt** Alt-dragging makes the Hand scroll the Paint window, just as the Paint window's scroll bars do. The objects aren't repositioned with

respect to the drawing area, although they appear to be unless you observe the scroll bars.

- **Spacebar** When you are using any Paint tool *except* the Text tool, pressing the Spacebar activates the Hand tool. It remains activated, and you can use it to move, as long as the Spacebar is pressed. Releasing the Spacebar reactivates whatever tool you were using when you pressed the Spacebar.

These keys do *not* combine. For example, pressing Alt+Shift activates the Help cursor ($+_?$), as it normally does.

DRAWING RECTANGLES AND SQUARES

Now that you are familiar with moving material around on the screen, let's create a rectangle around "NEW!" so that we have a sign. Then we'll connect the sign to the balloon's string.

Several tools in the Tool palette are used to create shapes. To create our box we'll use the Rectangle tool, shown in color in Figure 3.11.

3.11 Hollow portion of the Rectangle tool used to draw a rectangle

With tools such as this, you can create two basic versions of the shape. You use the left side of the tool to create a hollow version of the shape and the right side to create a filled version. We'll use the left side to create a hollow rectangle around "NEW!"

Begin by selecting **NEW!** and moving it far enough away from the string that you don't risk collision with the string while drawing.

Click the hollow (left) side of the **Rectangle** tool.

Position the mouse past the upper-left corner of the "N" in "NEW!"

Have it in place for the upper-left corner of the rectangle.

Drag to the bottom-right of "NEW!" to create a rectangle around the text, and release.

Now that the sign has been created, it can be attached to the balloon.

Use a **shrink-style selection rectangle** to drag the sign below and close to, but not touching, the string.

With the sign still selected, use the ↑ key to nudge the rectangle so that it just touches the string.

The result is shown in Figure 3.11.

The following keys affect drawing with the Rectangle tool.

- **Shift** Draws a square.
- **Alt** Draws with the pattern that the Pattern chip is set for. (Shortly we'll examine the patterns and how to set them.)

These two keys can be combined to create squares with a pattern.

CHANGING COLORS

Now, let's add a little color to the sign. Say you want the white area of the sign to be yellow so that the resulting yellow sign with black lettering attracts greater attention. To do this, we'll use the Paint Bucket tool. However, the Paint Bucket tool uses the current foreground color to pour paint into an area, and the foreground color now is black. We need to change it to yellow.

The current foreground color is indicated by the Foreground Color chip, which is shown in color in Figure 3.12. Change it to yellow as follows:

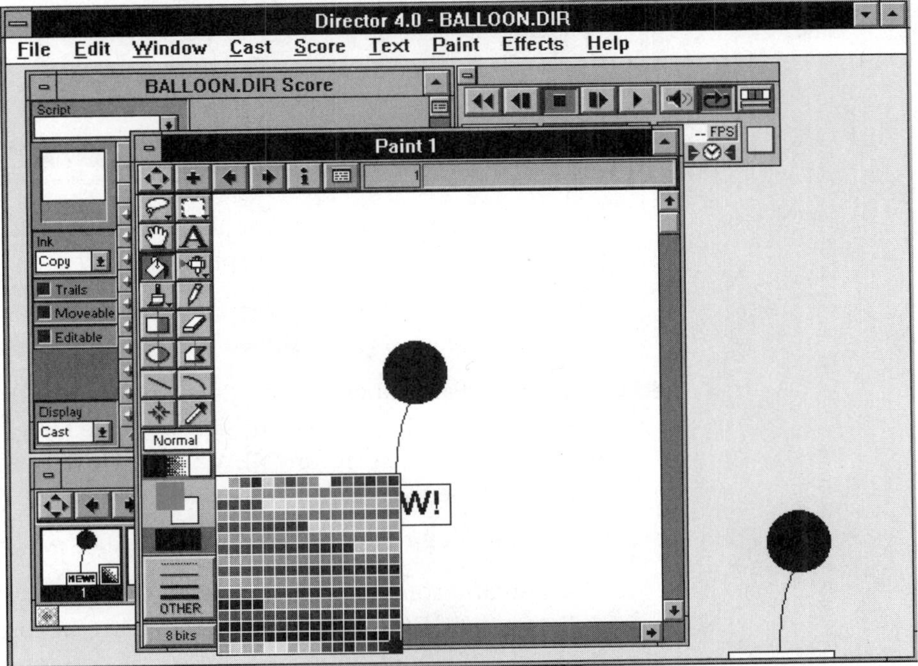

3.12
Foreground Color chip and its palette

Point to the **Foreground Color** chip, **press**, and **hold**.

The palette appears just to the right of the chip, as shown in the figure.

> **Release** the mouse.
>
> In the palette, point to a **yellow** chip and **click**.

The Foreground Color chip changes to yellow. Two other chips change color as well. We'll discuss them later in this chapter.

POURING PAINT

Now that we've changed the foreground color to yellow, we're ready to pour that yellow with the ***Paint Bucket tool***.

> Click the **Paint Bucket** tool (shown in color in Figure 3.13).

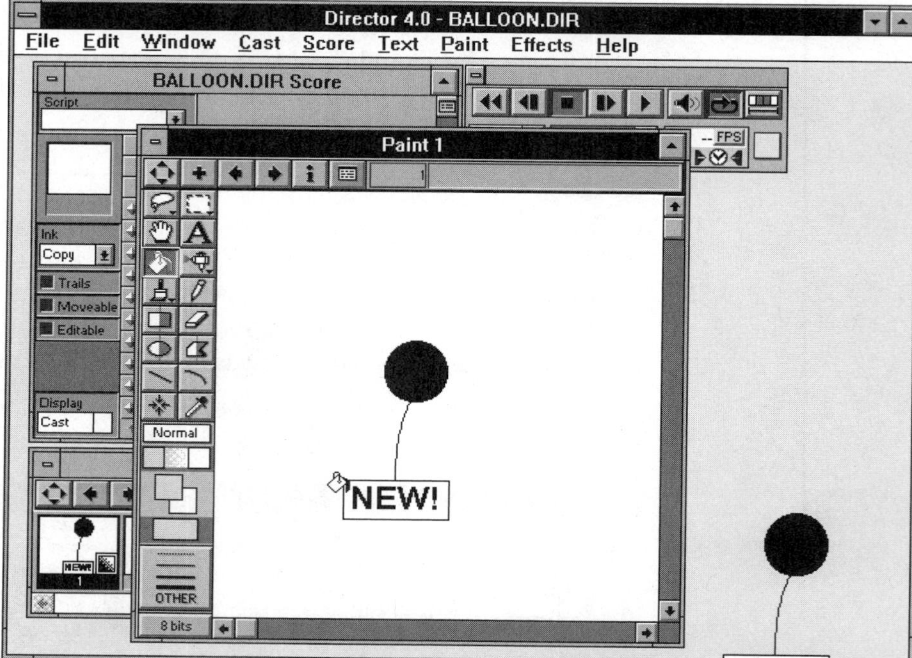

3.13
Using the Paint Bucket tool to fill color

With the mouse cursor in the drawing area of the Paint window, the cursor changes into the shape of the paint bucket.

> Position the cursor so that the tip of the pouring paint is within the **white** area of the sign, as shown in Figure 3.13, and **click**.

Note: The Paint Bucket tool fills in areas of continuous color only, replacing whatever color is at the cursor's tip with the foreground color. Thus if the sign said "SOON!" instead of "NEW!" the white space in the center of the O's would not be filled in.

> Change the **Foreground Color** chip back to black.

A command somewhat similar to the Paint Bucket tool is the Effects menu's Fill command. It fills the area selected with the foreground (for black) or background (for white) colors.

DUPLICATING CAST MEMBERS AND RELATED EDIT COMMANDS

Now let's say that we want to create another balloon, with a sign that says "SOON!" We want the balloon to be the same size, so we'll create a duplicate of our first cast member, the balloon, string, and sign. Then we'll remove the "NEW!" sign and replace it with the "SOON!" sign. Begin by activating the Cast window as follows:

> Bring the Cast window forward by selecting **Window, Cast**, or pressing Ctrl+3, or clicking the Cast window's Title bar.

The thumbnail of cast member 1 should be selected.

> With that cast member selected, select **Cast, Duplicate Cast Member** or Ctrl+D.

The cast member duplicates itself in position 2, the next available position. In the next section, we'll edit the new cast member 2.

Rather than using the Cast menu to duplicate like this, you can also use the Edit menu to copy and paste the cast member. First, with cast member 1 selected, you would copy the cast member to the clipboard. Then you would have to select the (empty) position 2 in the cast window and paste the cast member there from the clipboard.

Cut, copy, paste, clear, select-all, and undo operations (items in the second section of the Edit menu) work in various windows in various ways. In the Cast window they operate on selected cast members. In the Paint window, they work on bitmap material. In the Score, they work on selected cells. The exact wording of these commands varies, depending on the window that is activated (or on the Clipboard in the case of Paste). For example, Cut Bitmap appears when the Paint window is activated, compared with Cut Cast Members when the Cast window is activated.

Here are those items in the Edit menu, along with their shortcuts and description.

- **Cut** (or Ctrl+X or Shift+Delete) Removes the selected material and places it on the clipboard. You can't cut more than one cast member at a time.
- **Copy** (or Ctrl+C) Leaves the selected material in place but makes a copy of it on the clipboard. (The Accelerator or "Hot" key, indicated with underline, varies.)
- **Paste** (or Ctrl+V or Shift+Insert) Inserts a copy of the material that is on the clipboard into the window. (The original remains on the clipboard.)
- **Clear** (or, sometimes, the Backspace or Delete key) Removes the selected material permanently (does *not* place it on the clipboard).
- **Select All** (Ctrl+A) Selects all the items in the window. (It has no effect in the Paint window. Instead, double-click the Selection Rectangle tool to place a shrink-style selection rectangle around all material.)
- **Undo** Reverses the effect of your most recent edit. Using it a second time in succession restores the edit (Ctrl+Z).

ERASING

Now that we have a copy of cast member 1 in the Cast 2 position, we can edit cast member 2. After duplicating, the new cast member (2) is selected, as indicated by highlighting in the Cast window. Additionally, the cast member displayed in the Paint window is also cast member 2, as you can see by the Paint window's Title bar ("Paint 2" in Figure 3.14, as opposed to "Paint 1" in Figure 3.13). So activate the Paint window as follows:

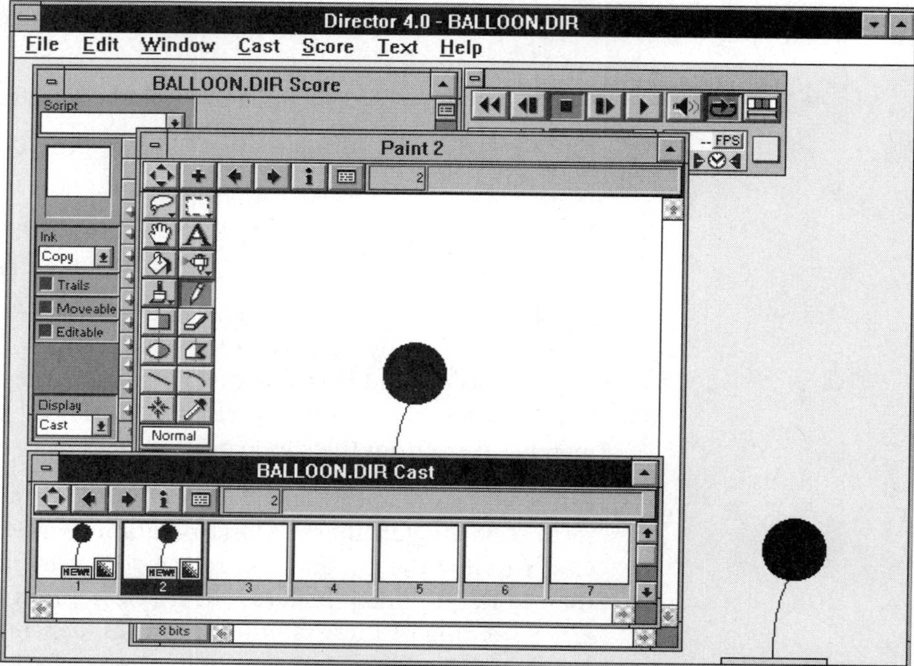

3.14 Cast member copied

Bring the Paint window forward by selecting Window, Paint, or pressing Ctrl+5, or clicking the Paint window's Title bar.

Now let's wipe away the sign and replace it with a new sign. Remember, this will only eradicate the duplicate sign in cast member 2. The original sign remains intact as part of cast member 1. Eventually we'll use both of these cast members in our movie.

In the Paint 2 window, click the Tool palette's Eraser tool (shown in color in Figure 3.15).

In the drawing area, the mouse cursor appears in the shape of an opaque square. First, we'll use this tool to make big sweeps. But don't get too close to the point where the sign connects to the string. Next, we'll magnify the art so you can erase carefully without accidentally removing any of the string.

Being careful not to get too close to the sign/string junction, drag the Eraser across the sign to wipe (Figure 3.15). Except for a small spot near the string, remove all the sign.

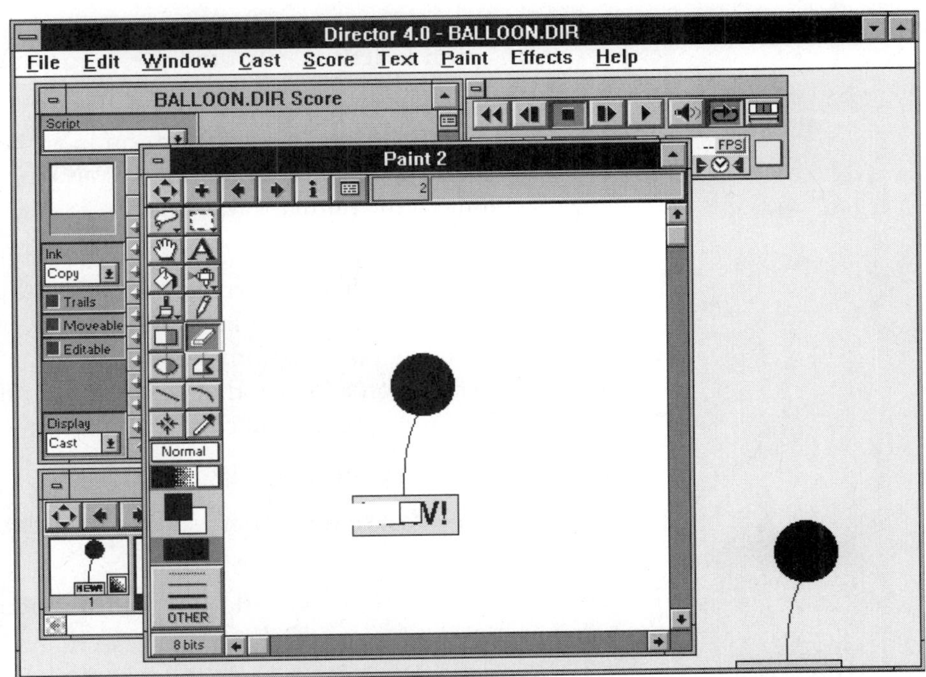

3.15
Eraser tool used to remove part of bitmap

MAGNIFYING

Now let's zero in on the area where the sign and string connect so we can erase with precision. To do this, we'll use ***zooming***, the process of magnifying in the Paint window.

The Paint window has three levels of magnification (2, 4, and 8 times normal). When you magnify, an inset window appears in the top-right corner of the Paint window. The size of this smaller window is determined by the amount of magnification. It shows the *actual* size of the area appearing in the main Paint window. Thus, the greater the amount of the magnification, the smaller this special window appears. (You may want to look ahead at Figure 3.17 to see the result of maximum magnification.)

Following are implements you can use with magnifying in the Paint window.

- **Paint, Zoom In** or **Ctrl++** (the Ctrl key with the += key) Magnifies the Paint window up to the next level.
- **Paint, Zoom Out** or **Ctrl+-** (the Ctrl key with the _- key) Reverses magnification of the Paint window down to the next level.
- **Double-clicking the Pencil tool in the Tool palette** Switches between normal and the most recent level of magnification.
- **Ctrl-clicking** Regardless of the selected tool, pressing the Ctrl key causes the mouse cursor to change to the shape of a magnifying glass. Holding Ctrl down, you can then click a spot in the Paint window. In the normal (nonmagnified) Paint window, this switches the window to the most recent magnified view. In a magnified Paint window, Ctrl-clicking returns the window to normal.

- **Clicking within the upper-right window** (which appears when magnification is active) Returns the Paint window to normal (turns off magnification).
- **Hand tool** In a magnified Paint window you can drag the Hand tool to scroll the window. You do not need to also use the Alt key as you do with scrolling in the normal Paint window.
- **Pencil tool** In the normal Paint window, double-clicking the Pencil tool in the Tool palette switches the window to the most recent magnified view. In a magnified Paint window, double-clicking the Pencil tool returns the window to normal. Also, you can use the Pencil to turn individual pixels off and on—that is, in the magnified view, select the Pencil tool, point to a pixel, and click to change it.

Follow these steps to magnify.

> Starting with a normal Paint window, use **Paint, Zoom In** or Ctrl++ **four** times.

The result is maximum magnification, but not necessarily of the part of the window you need to see.

> **Click** in the small, upper-right window.

The Paint window returns to normal.

> Position the mouse cursor over what's left of the string/sign junction (Figure 3.16).

3.16
Magnifying tool

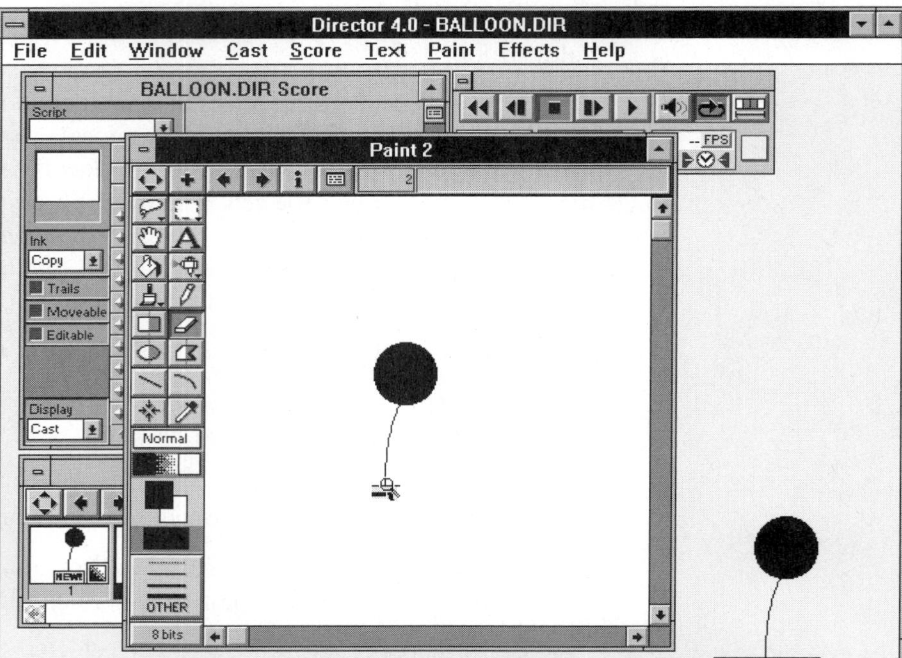

> Press the **Ctrl** key and **click**.

This makes the window switch to the most recent magnified view of the spot you clicked. The result is maximum magnification on just the area you need (Figure 3.17).

3.17
Bitmap enlarged with Magnifying tool

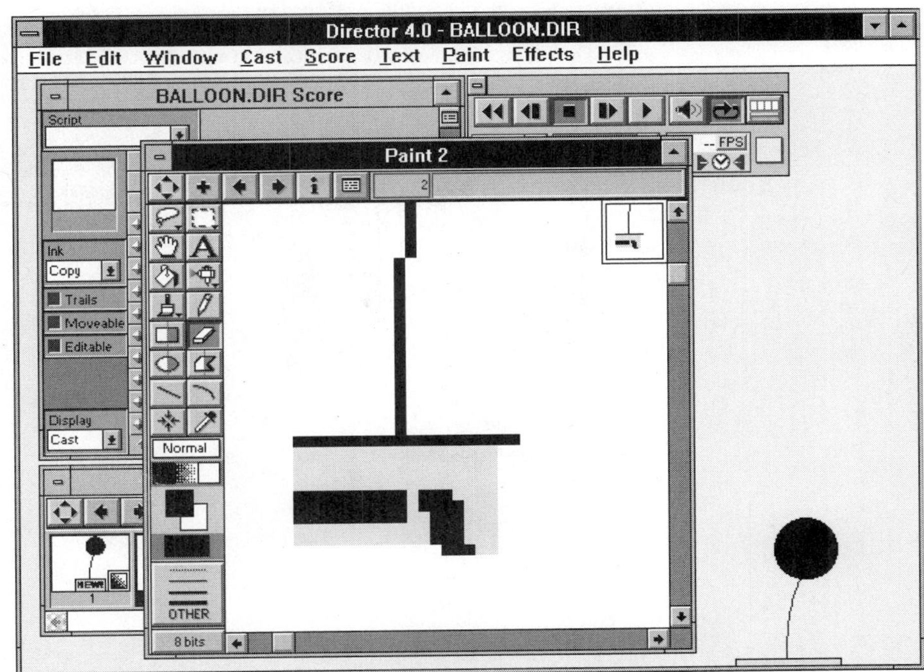

Use the Eraser tool to remove what's left of the sign without removing any string.

You can also use the Pencil tool to click individual pixels.

Return to the normal, nonmagnified view by double-clicking the Pencil tool in the Tool palette.

USING RULERS

Now to create the new sign to hang from the new balloon. We'll make this one different. We'll create a long banner that hangs down from the balloon. Then we'll fill it with sideways text.

The distinctive shape of the banner is shown in Figure 3.18. It should be about 1½ inches long and ½ inch wide, with a tip centered at the top. As shown in the figure, you can display rulers to assist in making measurements to create this shape.

Open the Paint menu and select Show Rulers or press Ctrl+Shift+K.

The rulers appear in the Paint window.

The ruler positions shown in Figure 3.18 are Director's initial positions. You can relocate the zero (0) position on either ruler by dragging the mouse along the ruler. When you release, the zero jumps to that position and the other values on that ruler adjust accordingly.

You can adjust the zero position in both rulers simultaneously by dragging from one of the rulers into the drawing area. A pair of cross hairs follows your mouse as you drag. The point in the working area at which you release determines the position of zero on both rulers.

Experiment with the zero position on one and then on both rulers.

3.18

Polygon tool and rulers

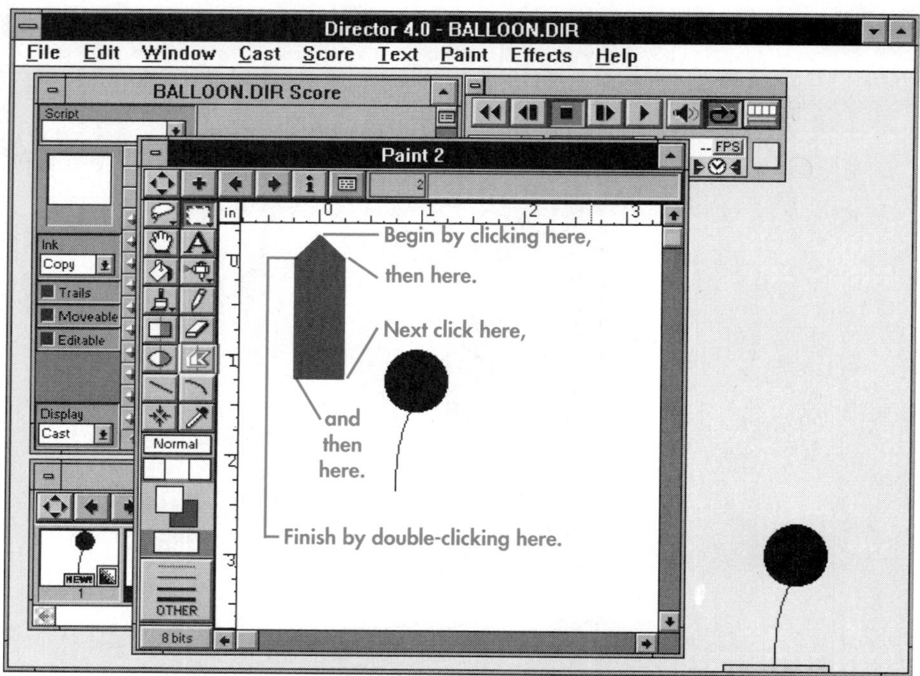

Rulers initially appear in inches, as evidenced by the indicator (in) that appears in the top-left corner of the Paint window, where the rulers converge. You can change the system of measurement used for the rulers by clicking this indicator. Each click changes both the indicator and the markings that appear on the ruler. Here is what's available:

- **in** Inches. This is the initial setting.
- **cm** Centimeters
- **Pixel** More accurately, this displays in hundreds of pixels. Each number (1, 2, 3, . . .) represents that many hundred pixels (100, 200, 300, . . .). Each marking between these numbers represents 10 pixels.
- **Pica** A pica (a typesetting measurement) is ⅙ inch. Each number on the rulers represents one inch, but each inch is divided into 6 parts. Markings, then, are in 1-pica increments.

Experiment with changing the system of measurement displayed on the rulers.

Note: To turn off the rulers, you use Paint, Hide Rulers (or Ctrl+Shift+K). If the Paint window's Tool palette is turned off, the underlined keys for turning rulers on and off will change. (Turning the Tool palette on and off is accomplished with Paint, Show/Hide Paint Tools or Ctrl+Shift+J.)

CREATING A FILLED POLYGON

Now that you are familiar with the rulers, you can use them to create the shape shown in Figure 3.18 with the dimensions given earlier. To create this shape, we'll use the Polygon tool (shown in color in the figure). We'll use the filled (right) half of the tool to create a filled polygon.

When you create a filled shape such as this, the shape appears in whatever color is set for the Foreground Color chip. Let's create a red shape.

Change the **Foreground Color chip** to **red**.

On the Tool palette, click the **Polygon** tool on the filled (right) side.

In the drawing area, the mouse cursor assumes the shape of a plus sign (+). As you proceed with this tool, you draw with lines that are initially black. As each line is completed, it changes to red. When you finish drawing, Director connects the final point with the first point and fills the shape with red.

Position and **click** the mouse as shown in the figure, being sure to **double-click** at the final point as indicated.

CREATING WHITE-ON-RED TEXT

Now to put some text on the banner. To do that we'll create white text against a red background. Then we'll rotate the text and place it on the banner. The color of the text is whatever the Foreground Color chip is set to.

Set the **Foreground Color** chip to **white**.

Just behind the Foreground Color chip is the Background Color chip (the lower item in color in Figure 3.19). Text, when entered, will appear against whatever color this chip is set for.

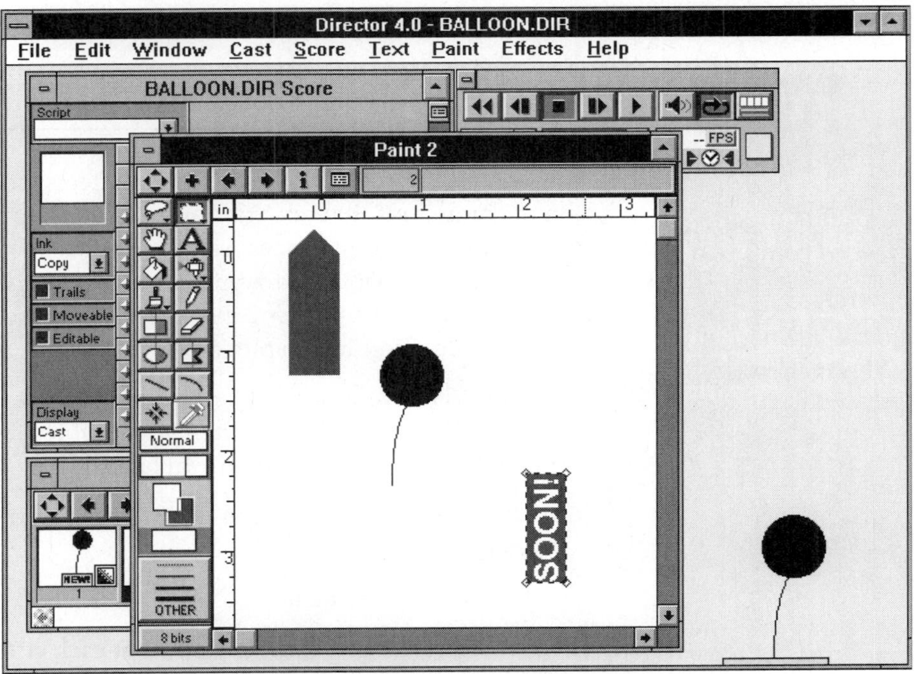

3.19
Using the Effects menu's Rotate Left command

Once the colors are correctly set and you enter the text, you will have a block with white text against a red background. You can then move that block in front of the banner, the red block will disappear, and you'll be left with white text against the red banner. For this to work, before typing you must set the Background Color chip to the same shade of red you used to create the banner.

Now you probably recall which red you used. But suppose you weren't sure. Fortunately Director has a method for drawing the color right from the page. That tool is the Eyedropper tool (the upper item in color in Figure 3.19).

Once you've activated the Eyedropper tool, you position the mouse on the color you want. How you click determines which color chip gets set to the color you're indicating:

- **Click** Foreground Color chip
- **Shift+click** Background Color chip
- **Alt+click** Destination Color chip (discussed later in this chapter)

Click the **Eyedropper** tool and use it to set the Background Color chip to the red of the banner.

Now you're ready to type the text.

Warning: Because you are using white for the text, when you type you won't see anything initially, since you will be placing white text against a white background. When you finish, though, white text on red will appear.

Using the **Text** tool (A), enter "SOON!" in the bottom-right area of the Paint window. (Nothing should show as you type.)

Format the text as **24-point**, **bold**.

Click the Tool palette's **Text** tool.

The white-on-red text appears.

SIDEWAYS TEXT

Now we need to rotate the text. On the Effects menu, Director provides a section of commands that you can use to change shapes in a variety of ways (the menu's Rotate commands, as well as Perspective, Slant, and Distort). In addition, you can use Director to animate these effects. Thus your Paint art can be made to change into one of the effects. We'll see how to do this when we examine animation in Chapter 5.

Important: These effects work only when you use the Selection Rectangle tool set to Shrink or No Shrink or when you double-click it to select the entire cast member. It does not work when you lasso.

Use a **shrink-style selection rectangle** to select the white-on-red "SOON!" you created.

Open the **Effects** menu and select **Rotate Left**.

The text rotates, Rotate handles appear at each corner of the text, and moving dotted lines appear along the text's perimeter (Figure 3.19).

Click the Tool palette's **Selection Rectangle** tool to complete the effect.

Figure 3.20 shows some examples of effects available by using the various items on the Effects menu. The examples show text but you can use the effects on any selected area of art. You can re-do an effect with Effects, Repeat Effect or Ctrl+Y. Now to combine the banner and the text and "attach" them to the balloon's string.

3.20

Effects available from the Paint window's Effects menu

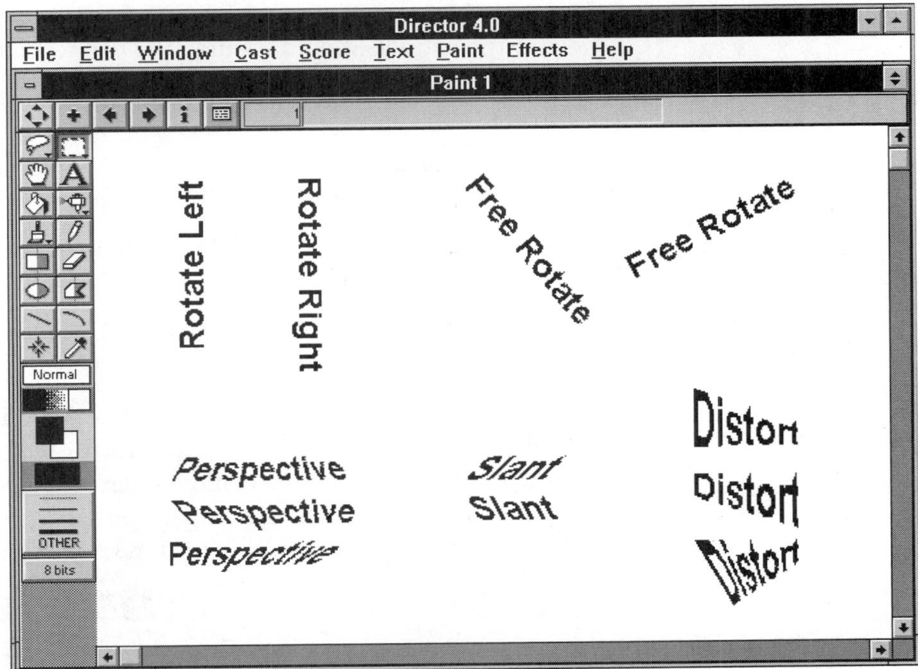

Select the banner and **drag** it to the string. Use nudging and/or magnification as necessary to position it correctly.

Select the text and **drag** it on top of the banner.

The result is shown in Figure 3.21. You may need to scroll down to see the entire cast member.

3.21

Portions of bitmap combined

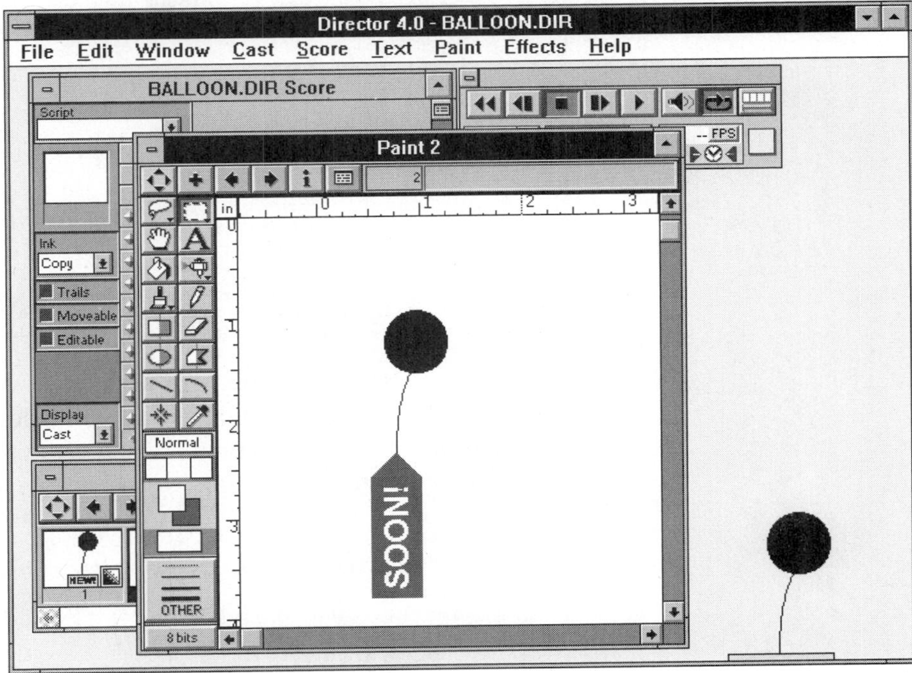

Warning: Be careful to position the text on the banner just as you want it before proceeding. Use Undo if necessary, following the rules discussed earlier (p. 50). Once the text is set in place it's difficult to readjust.

Note that because we wanted to place the text on the banner, we dragged the text to the banner. Should we drag the banner to the text, it would cover the text and obscure it.

PATTERNS

Now let's add a little pizzazz to the balloon. To do this, we'll apply a pattern to it.

Director provides a wide array of patterns. You can use these or you can custom design your own. Additionally there are tiles you can use or create.

The Pattern chip is shown in color in Figure 3.22. You use it to display the Pattern palette, also shown in this figure. (You display and select from this palette as you do with the Foreground and Background palettes.) Normally this palette is set for the solid pattern, the chip in the top-left corner of the palette. If you want to turn off all patterns you must reset this palette to that solid chip.

3.22
Pattern palette

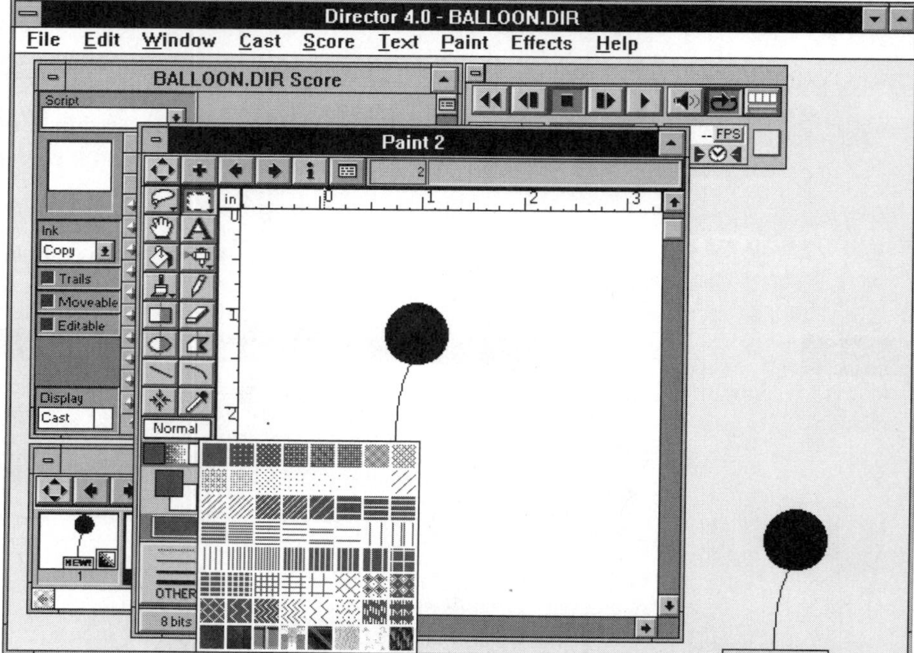

The Pattern palette displays patterns using the two colors that are set for the foreground and the background. Because our colors are set for red and white, the patterns appear in those colors. (The bottom row displays the tiles. If you want to use more than two colors, you must use a tile. Tiles are discussed in the next section.)

> Use the **Pattern** chip to display the Pattern palette.
>
> In the top row, select the fifth chip from the left.
>
> Use the **Paint Bucket** tool and fill the balloon with this pattern.

Because the Pattern chip is set to a pattern, the Paint Bucket uses that pattern.

Figure 3.23 shows the dialog box you can use to customize the patterns. Display it as follows.

3.23

Paint menu's Patterns dialog box

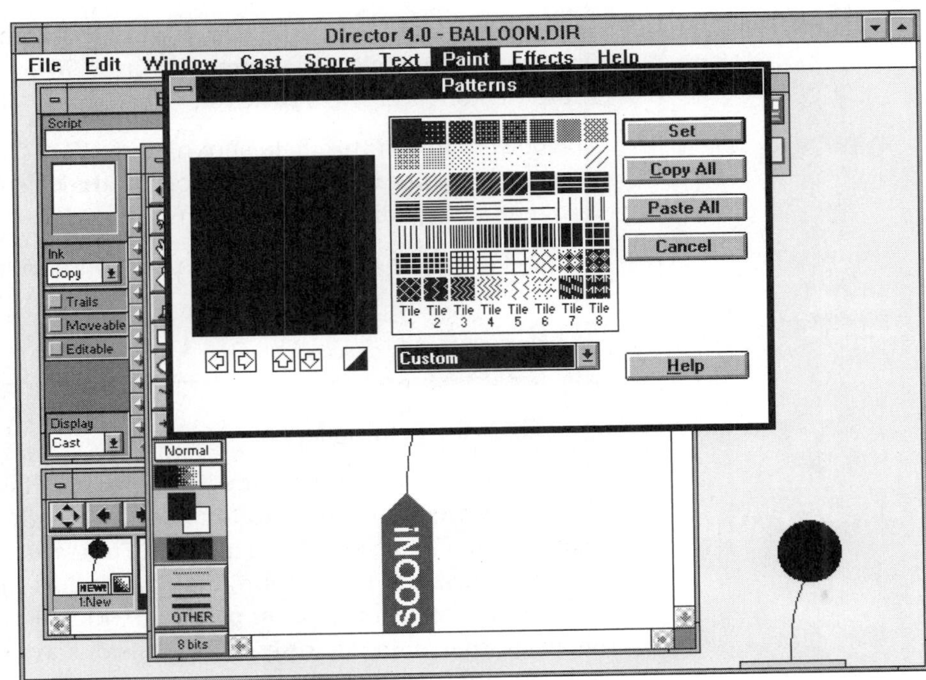

Open the Paint menu and select Patterns or double-click the Pattern chip.

In this dialog box, the drop-down list toward the bottom has four settings you can use: Custom, Grays, Standard, and QuickDraw. Each is a different pattern palette. You can edit the Custom palette (which originally is a copy of the Standard palette) but not the other three.

To edit a pattern, you first select it on the palette in the center of the dialog box. Then you can click an individual pixel in the blowup on the left, to switch it from black to white or vice versa. Below the blowup you can use the arrow buttons to move the pattern around in the blowup. You can also click the diagonally divided black/white box to swap all the black and white pixels in the blowup.

Should you create a custom palette, you can save it with the movie. To do that, first click this dialog box's Copy All button. This copies the displayed pattern palette to the clipboard. Then you close the dialog box and open the Paint window. Next you paste the palette from the clipboard into the Paint window. (The Paint window should probably be empty.) The palette appears in the Paint window just as it looks in the center of the Patterns dialog box. This makes it a cast member in the movie.

Later, you can apply the patterns saved as a cast member to the Custom palette. You open the Paint window on that cast member, then use a shrink-style selection rectangle to select the pattern palette. Then you copy the selected pattern palette to the clipboard and use Paint, Patterns (or equivalent) to display this dialog box again. With the drop-down list set to Custom, you finish by using the Paste All button to paste the pattern palette from the clipboard into the dialog box. Select the Set button and the patterns are once again available.

Similarly, you can copy the Grays, Standard, or QuickDraw palettes to the Custom palette should you want to use one of them as a starting point for your own version of that palette. You just set the drop-down list to the one you want to copy and click the Copy All button. Then you switch the drop-down list to Custom and select Paste All.

The bottom row of this dialog box shows "Tile 1" through "Tile 8" indicating that the tiles appear in these positions in the palette. Tiles are controlled by a different dialog box that we'll examine next.

In the Patterns dialog box, click the Cancel button.

TILES

Open the Paint menu and select Tiles.

The dialog box shown in Figure 3.24 appears. The eight tiles you see in this dialog box are built into Director. You can use them or you can create your own tile from a cast member. This ability to create from an existing cast member and the ability to use more than two colors (mentioned in the previous section) distinguish tiles from patterns, which do not have such capabilities. Be aware that there are only eight positions available for tiles; should you decide to insert one of your own, you must first use this dialog box to select a built-in tile to replace (by clicking one of the tiles displayed in the Select Tile To Edit line). Then you turn on the Created From Cast Member # button and click the arrows below this button to rotate among the cast members until the one you want appears in the large left display.

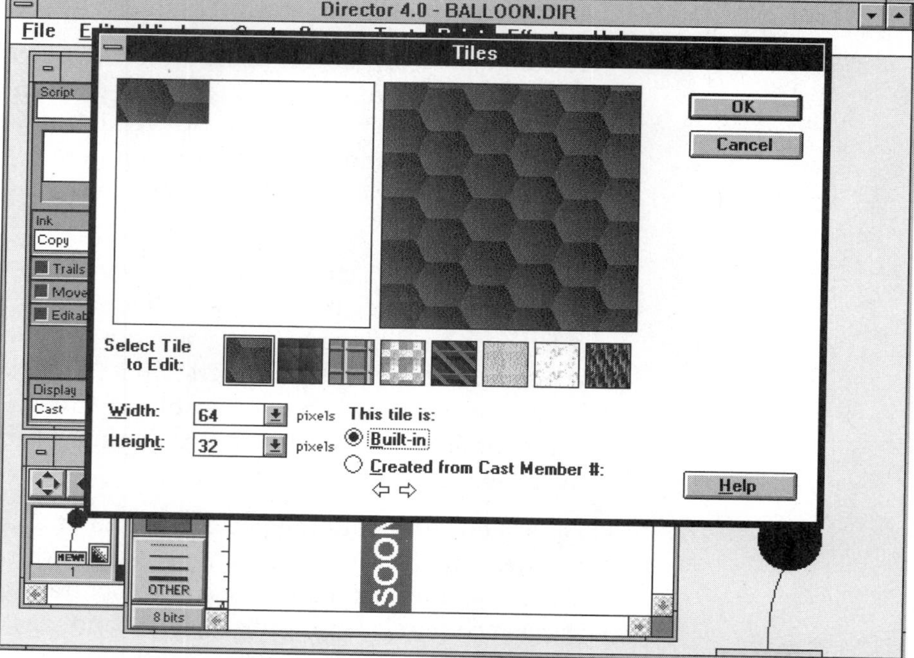

3.24
Paint menu's Tiles dialog box

Once you have the appropriate cast member displayed you can, within certain limitations, set the size of the tile. (Initially it has the same size as the built-in one that it replaces.) A dotted rectangle around the cast member shows the tile you are creating and it is replicated in the large right display to show its appearance in a large area. You use the Width and Height drop-down lists to select from among the four sizes available (16, 32, 64, 128 pixels). Should the size you select for the tile be smaller than the cast member, you can drag the dotted rectangle to pick out the area of the cast member you want to use.

Once the tile is created, you can use it to cover large areas like wallpaper. You need only set the Pattern chip to your custom tile and then use the Paint Bucket tool to pour the tile into the area you desire.

GRADIENTS

Another implement useful in covering large areas is the ***gradient***, the result of a process that creates transitions from one color to another. For example, we can create a more convincing sky by creating a gradient that goes from a darker blue at the top to a lighter blue at the bottom. To do that, use the Gradient Color selector, shown in color in Figure 3.25.

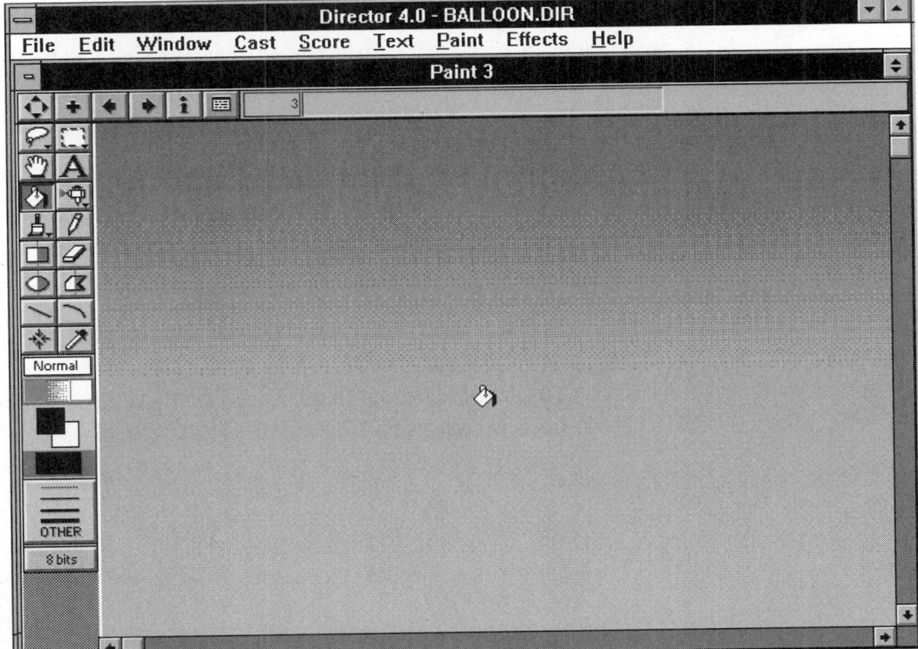

3.25
Gradient and Gradient Color selector

The Gradient Color selector has three parts. On the left is a copy of the Foreground Color chip. This chip and the Foreground Color chip are always the same and you can change the foreground color with either one. On the right of the Gradient Color selector is the Destination Color chip. With it, you set the color you want the foreground color to become when you apply the gradient. Between these two is a depiction of the gradient. This middle ground is for display only. You can't change it directly; it's always a result of how you set the other two chips.

Let's create the sky as the third cast member.

Activate the **Cast** window and select thumbnail number **3**.

Activate the **Paint** window.

Set the **Foreground Color** chip to a medium blue (for example, 5th row from the bottom, 2nd color from the right).

Set the **Destination Color** chip to a light blue (for example, 5th row from the top, 2nd color from the right).

Select the **Paint Bucket** tool.

Set the Paint window's **Ink Effects** pop-up menu to **Gradient**.

We want the gradient to cover a large area.

Maximize the Paint window.

Turn off the rulers by using **Paint, Hide Rulers** or Ctrl+Shift+K.

Turn off the Tool palette by using **Paint, Hide Paint Tools** or Ctrl+Shift+J.

With the mouse cursor in the shape of a paint bucket, click within the Paint window's **Drawing** area.

The gradient sky appears (Figure 3.25).

Troubleshooting: If your version doesn't look right (the gradient goes from left to right instead of top to bottom, for instance), your gradient settings may be different from the defaults (shown in upcoming Figure 3.26). Use Undo, change the settings discussed next, and try again.

Director provides a variety of ways that you can apply gradients. To see what's available, proceed as follows:

Open the **Paint** menu and select **Gradients** or double-click the Rectangle, Ellipse, or Polygon tool on the shaded side or the Paint Bucket tool.

The dialog box shown in Figure 3.26 appears. At the top-left is a large sample of how the gradient is set to appear. It's dynamic, changing as you adjust the settings below it. To its right are copies of the various chips that appear in the Paint window. You can change these chips right here in the dialog box if necessary, by pointing, pressing, and holding as usual. In the following, except for the item under discussion, examples assume the standard settings, including that of the foreground color (black) and destination color (white).

3.26
Paint menu's Gradients dialog box

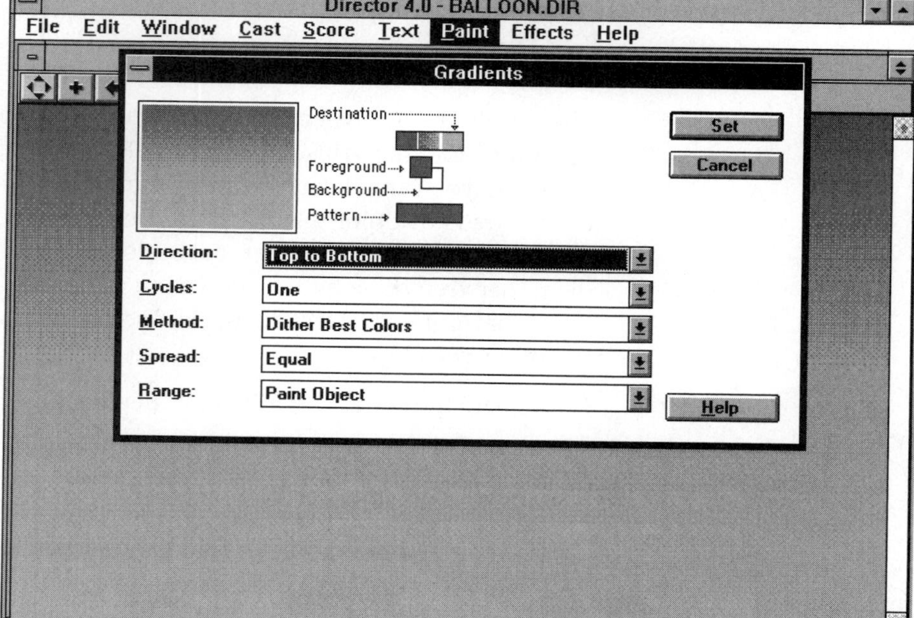

- **Direction** Sets the way the gradient proceeds, foreground to destination. In the normal setting, *Top to Bottom*, black would be at the top. It can be set to *Bottom to Top*, *Left to Right*, and other directions. (The *Directional* setting allows you to set the direction of the gradient when you paint the area. A line appears, which you can position to specify the gradient direction—perpendicular to the grain. When you have the desired direction, you click.)
- **Cycles** In the normal setting, *One*, the gradient goes from the foreground color to the destination color only once. Alternatively, you can have it cycle through 2, 3, or 4 times, in Sharp or Smooth fashion. *Sharp*, when the destination color is reached, causes the color to jump directly to the foreground color. *Smooth* causes the color gradient to reverse direction, gradually changing back to the foreground color for the next cycle.
- **Method** Director provides ten different methods for creating the gradient. Shortly we'll examine these methods and allow you to experiment.
- **Spread** This is normally set to *Equal*, so that the foreground, middle, and destination colors are treated equally. If you want to increase the amount of foreground color in the gradient, you select *More Foreground*. Similarly, you can choose *More Middle* or *More Destination*.
- **Range** This controls the area over which the gradient, from foreground color to destination color, is made. *Paint Object* is the usual setting; with other standard settings this would cause the foreground to start at the top of the paint object and finish at the bottom. When pouring into a circle, for example, the top of the circle would be black and the bottom would be white. With the setting *Cast Member*, the top of the cast member would be black, the bottom of the cast member white. An object filled with a gradient would not receive the complete gradient, from full foreground color to full destination color; instead, it would receive only a portion, depending on the object's position. With the setting *Window*, the top of the Paint window is black, the bottom white.

Now let's examine the gradient methods.

In the Gradients dialog box, verify that the settings are the standard ones, as shown in Figure 3.26.

Still in the Gradients dialog box, set the **Foreground Color** chip to the black chip that appears in the top row of the color palette (sixth chip from the right).

Also set the **Destination Color** chip to the white chip in the top-left corner of the color palette.

Open this dialog box's **Method** drop-down list.

The two main categories of this list are *Pattern* (the first 4) and *Dither* (the last 6). The Pattern methods use whatever pattern is set by the Pattern chip (which you can change from within this dialog box). Normally, of course, the pattern is solid. ***Dithering*** is the process of mixing pixels of different colors together to create a new color. In a gradient, dithering can give the impression of subtle changes in color. Without dithering, colors are limited to those on the palette, resulting in more sudden changes in color.

With Method set to Dither Best Colors, notice the gradual gradient from black to white as a result of dithering used to create a wide array of grays.

Select **Method: Pattern Best Colors**.

As pattern is solid, the gradient consists of solid bars that use only grays that are in the color palette.

In the Gradients dialog box, change the **Pattern** chip to some other pattern, but do not select a tile.

The gradient appears with the pattern you selected.

Now change the **Pattern** chip to a **tile**.

The tile takes over and the gradient and its colors disappear. Taking over like this is standard behavior with tiles.

Set the **Pattern** chip back to the solid pattern (in the Pattern palette's top-left corner).

Two other categories that several of the methods fall into are Best Colors and Adjacent Colors. *Best Colors* causes Director to use the colors that are logically best for making the transition from foreground color to Destination color. Thus, to go from black to white, it would make sense to use several shades of gray, as we have seen. *Adjacent Colors* makes Director use the colors that appear in the palette between the foreground color and the Destination color, regardless of what they are.

With Method set to Pattern Best Colors, the intervening colors are shades of gray.

Select **Method: Pattern Adjacent Colors**.

A variety of colors appear.

Open the **Foreground Color** chip's color palette.

It should still be set for the black chip in the top row. Notice that the colors between this chip and the white (top-left corner) chip correspond to those in the gradient sample.

Close this color palette. (You can simply click away from it somewhere.)

Two last terms are worth discussion. *See Thru* is available for pattern. When you select this, the pattern's white pixels become transparent. *Multi Dither* uses a variety of dithering patterns rather than just one, as others do.

Cancel the Gradients dialog box.

BUTTONS, NAVIGATING, AND OTHER PAINT/CAST OPERATIONS

Now that you have three cast members, let's see how to navigate the Paint and Cast windows. To accomplish this, you can use buttons in these windows as well as menus and keyboard shortcuts. Let's examine how to perform these and other Paint window and Cast window operations.

Placing cast members

Drag up the bottom of the **Paint window** so that you can see both the Cast window and the Paint window at the same time, as shown in Figure 3.27.

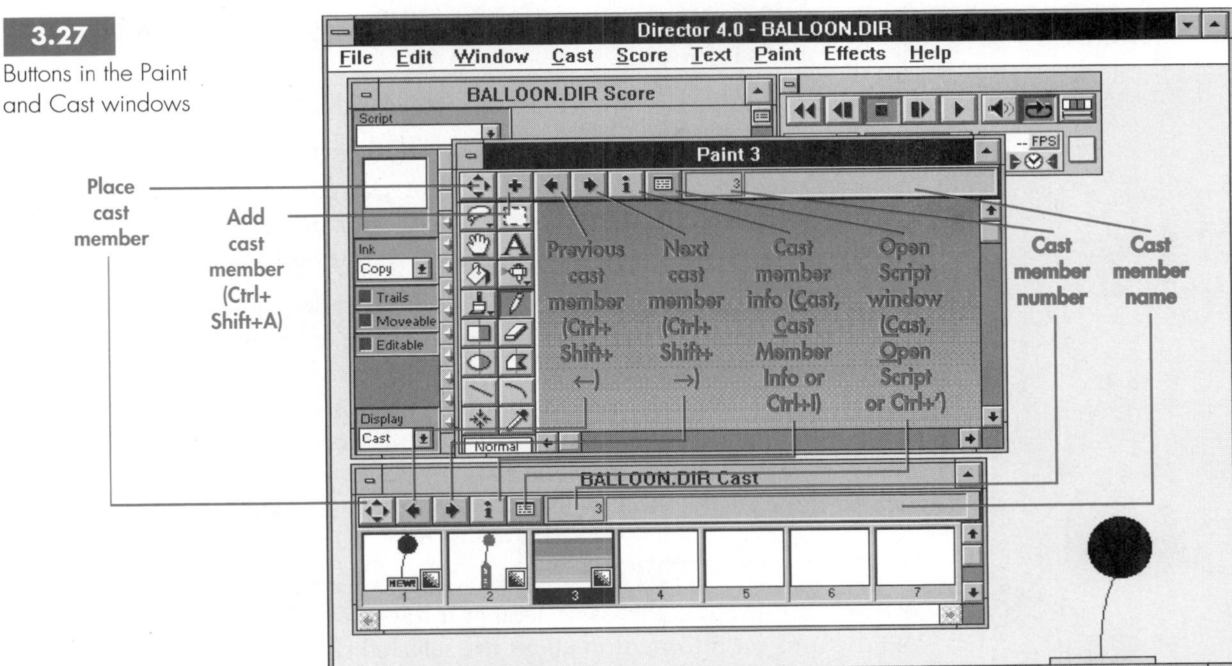

3.27
Buttons in the Paint and Cast windows

In the Cast window you should now see three cast members: the two balloons and the gradient sky. The sky cast member, still in the Paint window, should still be selected in the Cast window. Use Figure 3.27 as a guide as you proceed and observe both windows.

The Place Cast Member button (or *Place* button for short) represents another way that you can place cast members in the movie. Dragging from this button drags the current cast member. The mouse cursor changes into a clutching hand as you drag. As with the previous method we examined—dragging the cast member from its number position in the Cast window—you can drag from this button either to the stage or to the score.

Adding cast members

The Add Cast Member button (or Ctrl+Shift+A) is another way to add a cast member to the movie. As we saw, you can also simply click an empty position in the Cast window. (This is called the *Add* button for short.)

Click the **Add Cast Member** button (or press Ctrl+Shift+A).

A blank Paint window appears, entitled "Paint 4." You could use it to create a new cast member. Be aware that, regardless of the active cast member, Director displays the next empty cast position. Thus even if cast member 1 was selected, clicking this button would still display cast member 4.

Notice that this button is available only in the Paint window.

Navigating

Click the Paint window's **Previous Cast Member** button or press Ctrl+Shift+←.

The gradient sky appears in the Paint window and is now selected in the cast window. The Paint window's Title bar is now labeled "Paint 3" indicating that cast member 3 is showing.

Click the Paint window's **Next Cast Member** button or press Ctrl+Shift+→.

Director wraps around and cast member 1, the "NEW!" balloon, appears and becomes selected. Because you did not enter anything into cast member 4, you did not create that cast member, so Director now ignores that position. These buttons are also called the *Previous* and *Next* buttons.

Important: Remember that you can have a variety of types of cast members. For example, you can have sounds, film loops, color palettes, and scripts. The Paint window can only show paint objects. Therefore, when you are using the Paint window's Next or Previous button, Director will skip any cast member that is not paint art and display the next cast member that is paint art. This note applies to other windows as well. Thus the Text window shows only text cast members; the Digital Video window shows only digital video cast members.

Getting Information

The next button (i) is the Cast Member Info button (or *Info* button for short). You use it to get information about the selected cast member. It is equivalent to Cast, Cast Member Info or Ctrl+I.

With the "NEW!" balloon selected, use one of these methods to display the **Bitmap Cast Member Info** dialog box (Figure 3.28).

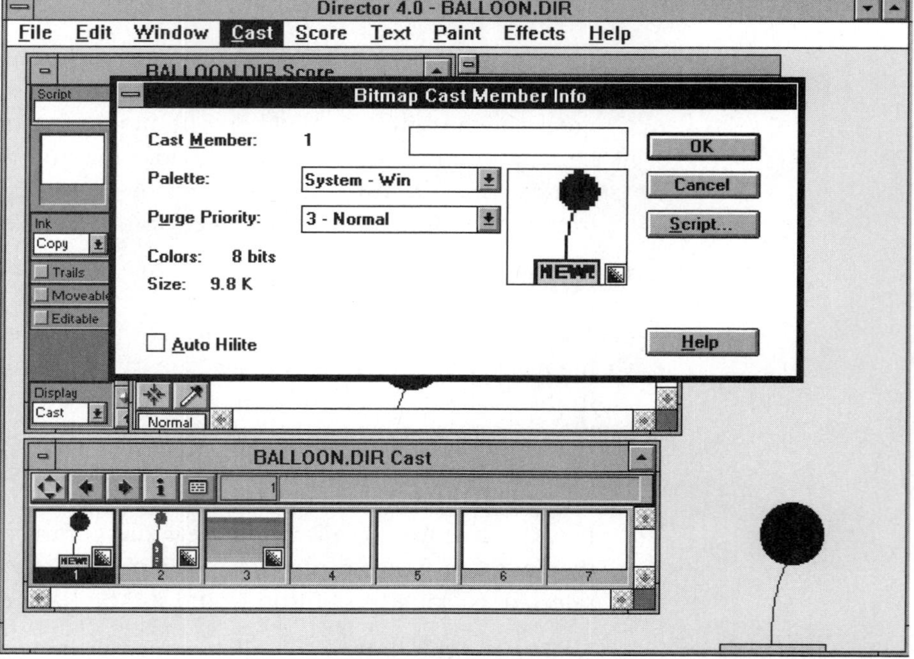

3.28
Bitmap Cast Member Info dialog box

Be aware the dialog box that appears is specific to bitmap cast members. Other types of cast members have Cast Member Info dialog boxes that are displayed in a similar fashion, but their contents vary depending on the type of cast member.

In this dialog box, **Cast Member** shows the position number of the cast member in the Cast window. To the right of that number is a box you can use to provide a name to the cast member.

Enter the name **New** into this box.

You can set the **Palette** list to a particular color palette for this cast member. More on this when we examine color palettes in Chapter 4.

With the **Purge Priority list** you can provide your movie with some guidelines for dealing with memory while the movie is running. Settings control how readily you allow the cast member to be removed from memory. Settings are from 3 (the default, which allows it to be removed as necessary) to 0 (never removed).

Colors and **Size** provide information about the cast member and cannot be adjusted here. (8 bits equals 256 colors.)

Auto Hilite causes the cast member to be highlighted when it's clicked by the user. It's chiefly for use with buttons. To make the cast member a button, you must assign a programming script to it. The *Script* button is for doing just that, as we'll see when we look at scripts in Chapter 6.

Click the **OK** button or press the Enter key.

The "NEW!" cast member name now appears in four positions: the two positions for "Cast member name" indicated in Figure 3.27 (where it can be edited), the Paint window's Title bar, and below the cast member's thumbnail in the score. When its sprite is selected, the name will also appear in the score.

Use the Bitmap Cast Member Info dialog box to add names to the other two cast members.

PAINTBRUSH AND AIR BRUSH TOOLS

Now let's examine two more important tools in the Paint window: the Paintbrush tool and the Air Brush tool. These two tools operate the same way in some aspects.

Paintbrush Tool

The ***Paintbrush tool*** is on the Paint window's Tool palette. Its position is shown in color in Figure 3.29.

As you can tell from the marker (▼) in its bottom-right corner, this tool has a related pop-up menu (not the dialog box you see in the figure). As with the Lasso and the Selection Rectangle, you can display this menu by pressing the mouse button and holding.

The menu has five items on it, Brush 1 through Brush 5. These five brushes have default shapes assigned to them. To change one, you can use the dialog box shown in the figure. But first you must use the Paintbrush tool's menu to set the Paintbrush tool to the shape you want to change.

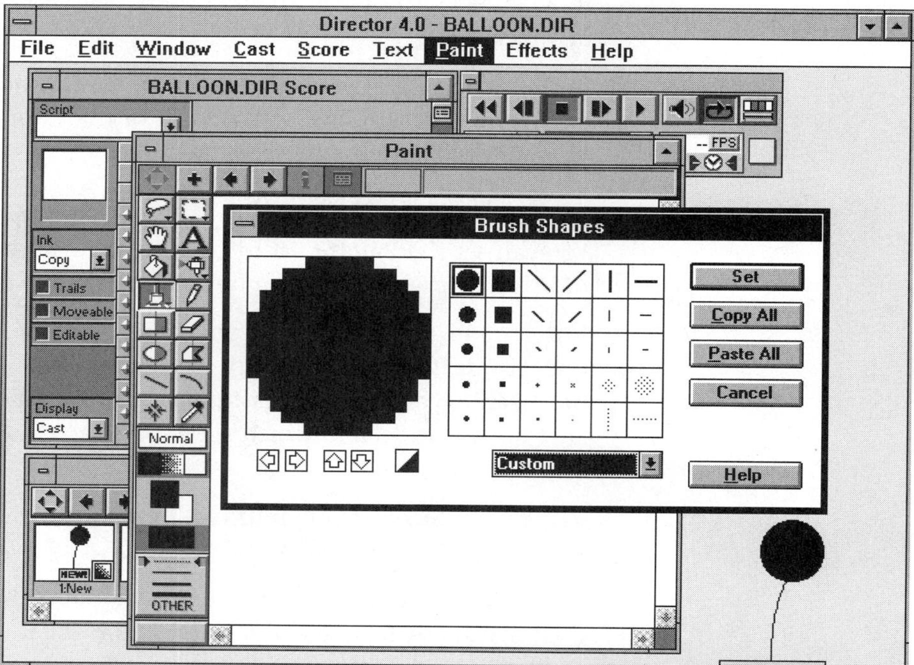

3.29
Paint menu's Brush Shapes dialog box

Check that the Paintbrush menu is set for Brush 1.

Open the Paint menu and select Brush Shapes or double-click the Paintbrush tool.

The dialog box in Figure 3.29 appears.

If your Brush 1 is set for the default, your dialog box should look like the one in the figure (although the figure's dialog box has been repositioned slightly to show the Paintbrush tool). The graphic in the display area on the left should appear. It corresponds to the shape in the top-left corner of the center portion and should be selected (as indicated by the black box around it).

The initial brush shapes, 1 through 5, correspond to the first five brush shapes in the top row of this dialog box. For the sake of consistency (and your own sanity in remembering the shapes assigned to brushes) you may want to follow this convention; that is, to use one of the shapes in the first column, assign it to Brush 1, and so on. (You can use brush 5 for both columns 5 and 6.) However, following this convention is not required.

The drop-down menu has two settings, Custom and Standard. These settings and other items in this dialog box operate as they do in the Paint menu's Patterns dialog box (shown back in Figure 3.23). You can click the display to change a pixel, the arrow buttons to position the display, the black/white button to swap black and white, and the Copy All and Paste All buttons to reassign the standard shapes and—in conjunction with the Paint window and a selection rectangle—to store and retrieve custom brush shapes.

We'll work with the Paintbrush tool shortly. In the meantime:

Practice changing the Paintbrush tool's menu to other brushes and using them in an empty Paint window.

Air Brush Tool

The ***Air Brush tool*** is shown in color in Figure 3.30. Like the Paintbrush tool, its menu has five settings, Air 1 through Air 5. As with the Paintbrush tool, you can customize the five brushes by selecting the one you want to change and using the dialog box in the figure.

3.30

Paint menu's Air Brushes dialog box

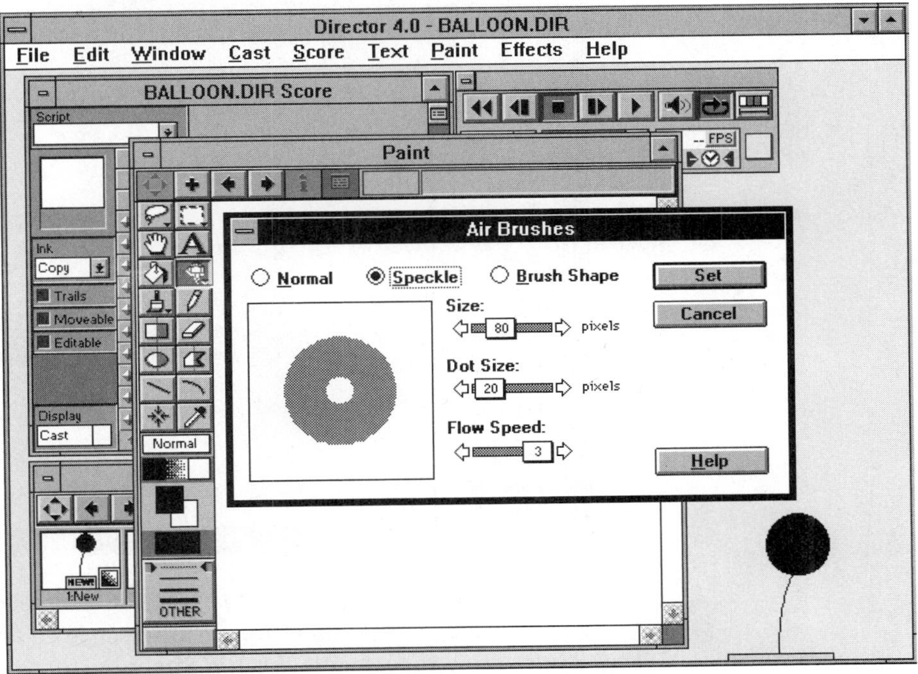

Open the Paint menu and select Air Brushes or double-click the Air Brush tool.

First in this dialog box is a set of three radio buttons that govern the shape of the spray. *Normal* causes a spray of dots, each in the dot size indicated later in the dialog box. *Speckle* also causes a spray of dots, but they vary in size, from the dot size indicated downward. *Brush Shape* causes a spray of paint in the shape of the current paintbrush. This is handy for reproducing lots of simple objects. For example, you could create a paintbrush in the shape of a tree and then spray it on a mountainside to create a forest.

You can change the next three items in this dialog box either by dragging the appropriate slider switch or by clicking or press/holding the appropriate arrow buttons. *Size* controls the area covered by the spray. *Dot Size* controls the size of the Normal or Speckle dots sprayed, as discussed. (It has no effect on Brush Shape sprays, which are set by the size of the brush shape.) *Flow Speed* controls the rate at which the ink is spewed and has a range of 0 (slowest) to 3 (fastest).

Experiment in creating air brush effects of various sizes.

INK EFFECTS

Director has a wide variety of ***ink effects*** you can assign to various tools. An ink effect changes the way an ink looks or the way two inks affect each other.

Be aware that not all ink effects are available for all tools. They're shown on the menu displayed in Figure 3.31.

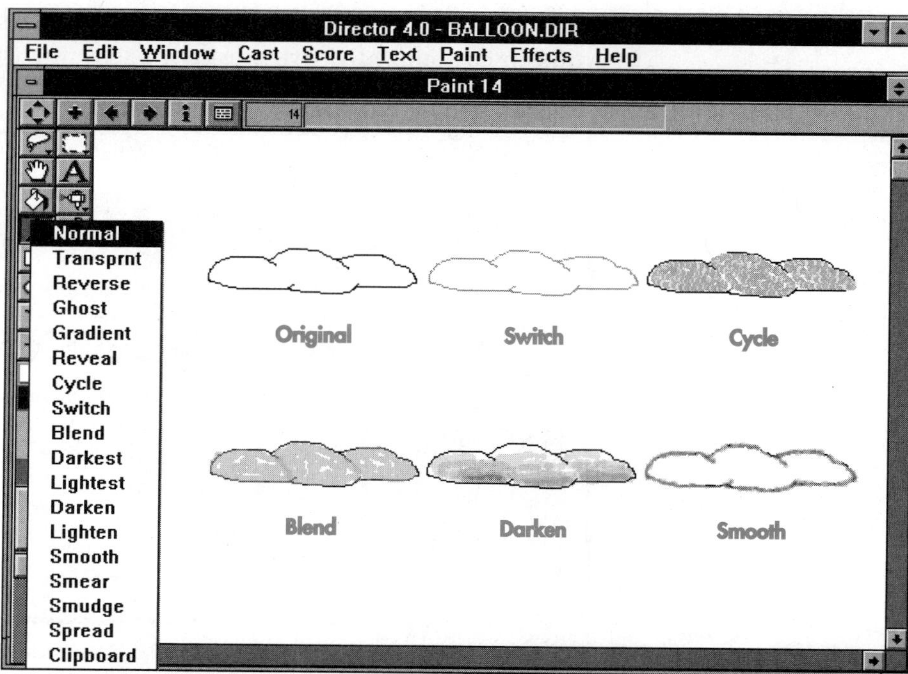

3.31
Paint window ink effects

To use an ink effect, you must first select the tool that you want to use. Then you can use the Ink Effect menu to select from among what's available. You activate this menu with the Ink Effect button, a part of which is shown in color in Figure 3.31. The button should currently display the word "Normal" on it; you can see it clearly labeled back in Figure 3.1.

Preparing for Ink Effects

You'll create the clouds with various ink effects shown in Figure 3.31. This figure shows all six clouds as part of the same cast member. But you should create separate cast members so they can be animated separately. Create them in one row of the Cast window.

In the **Cast** window, select cast position **8**.

Activate the Paint window and set the **foreground color** to **black**.

Use the **Pencil** tool to create a cloud, like that labeled "Original" in the figure.

Duplicate the cloud in cast positions 9 through 13.

You should now have a total of 6 identical cast members, drawn with black ink and numbered 8 through 13.

Name cast member 8 **Original**.

Color Switch

The first ink effect we'll examine is Switch. When you paint with a Paintbrush that has the Switch ink effect applied to it, the brush switches the ink of some art as it passes. Anywhere the color of the Foreground Color chip appears it is removed and the color of the Destination Color chip is put in its place. Use this effect to change the outline of the cloud from black to gray.

Select cast member **9**.

Set the **Destination Color** chip to a shade of gray.

Select the **Paintbrush** tool.

Set the **Ink Effect** menu to **Switch**.

Now to create the switch.

With the Foreground Color chip still set to the same black you used to create the original cloud, **drag** along the cloud's black outline.

The cloud's outline changes to gray, like the Switch cloud in Figure 3.31.

Label the cast member **Switch**.

You can also use the Effects menu's Switch Colors command to switch colors in selected art. Using it changes the foreground color to the destination color (Effects, Insert Colors reverses colors according to the color palette.)

Color Cycle

When you paint with the Cycle ink effect, the ink changes from the assigned foreground color to the destination color as you apply the color. Then the cycle starts again.

Look at the palette closely to determine foreground and destination colors. You'll want to carefully consider the intervening colors and use those that create an appropriate cycle. For example, should you use the air brush and a tree-shaped brush to create a forest as discussed earlier, you could select a light green at the beginning and a dark green at the end of a continuous set of greens to spray trees with a variety of appropriate colors.

The Cycle cloud in the figure was created with the standard Brush 1 and some of the colors in the bottom row of the palette. Brushing was performed with an inward spiral motion in each of the three sections of the cloud. The result is what might be described as a storybook cloud.

Create the Cycle cloud as cast member **10** and label it **Cycle**.

Color Blend

When you paint with the Blend ink effect, Director adds the color you're applying to whatever color you're painting on top of. The result is a new color that's a combination of the two.

The Blend cloud in the figure was created with standard Brush 1, which was allowed to overlap the outline of the cloud in some spots. Where the blue and the black outline overlap, the two colors are added together and a darker shade of the blue appears. The result is a color cloud with a softer edge.

Create the Blend cloud as cast member **11**, named **Blend**.

Darkening

Darken is an effect that operates in the same way, no matter what colors the chips are set for. Each time you apply this effect, any ink that you pass over is simply made darker.

The Darken cloud was created by painting the three sections several times in a zigzag fashion from top to bottom. On the first pass, painting was started near the top, on the second pass closer to the center, and so on.

Create the Darken cloud as cast member **12**, named **Darken**.

The Lighten ink effect produces the opposite results. On each pass the colors become lighter.

You can use the Effects menu's Darken command to darken a selected object by one increment. The Effects menu's Lighten command does the same with respect to lightening.

The Darkest ink effect causes Director to favor display of the darker of two colors: the one you're painting with or the one you're painting over. The Lightest ink effect does the same with regard to the lighter color of the two.

Smoothing

The Smooth ink effect is another effect that operates in the same way, regardless of the color chips. Dragging with it smooths out hard edges between colors by combining the two to create related colors at their boundary.

Create the Smooth cloud as cast member **13**, named **Smooth**.

You can use the Effects menu's Smooth command to apply Smooth to all art in the selected area.

Similar to the Smooth ink effect is the Smear ink effect, which drags one color into another in the direction you are dragging, combining to create related colors as well. Smudge is also similar but the effect is more pronounced. Spread moves one color into another full strength while dragging (does not combine the colors).

CUSTOMIZING THE WINDOWS

Let's finish out our examination of the Cast and Paint windows by examining how you can customize some aspects of these windows.

Customizing the Cast Window

To customize the Cast window, proceed as follows:

Open the **Cast** menu and select **Cast Window Options**.

The dialog box shown in Figure 3.32 appears.

- **Maximum Visible** Limits the number of cast members that the Cast window can accommodate. For efficient scrolling you can set this to the lowest number necessary. (Values are various numbers from 512 to 32,000.)

- **Row Width** For indicating the number of cast members that are placed across the Cast window. Choices range in value from 8 to 20 thumbnails. *Fit To Window,* the usual setting, causes the number to vary depending on the size of the window. If you restrict the number, you won't be able to widen the window beyond what you set.

3.32

Cast menu's Cast Window Options dialog box

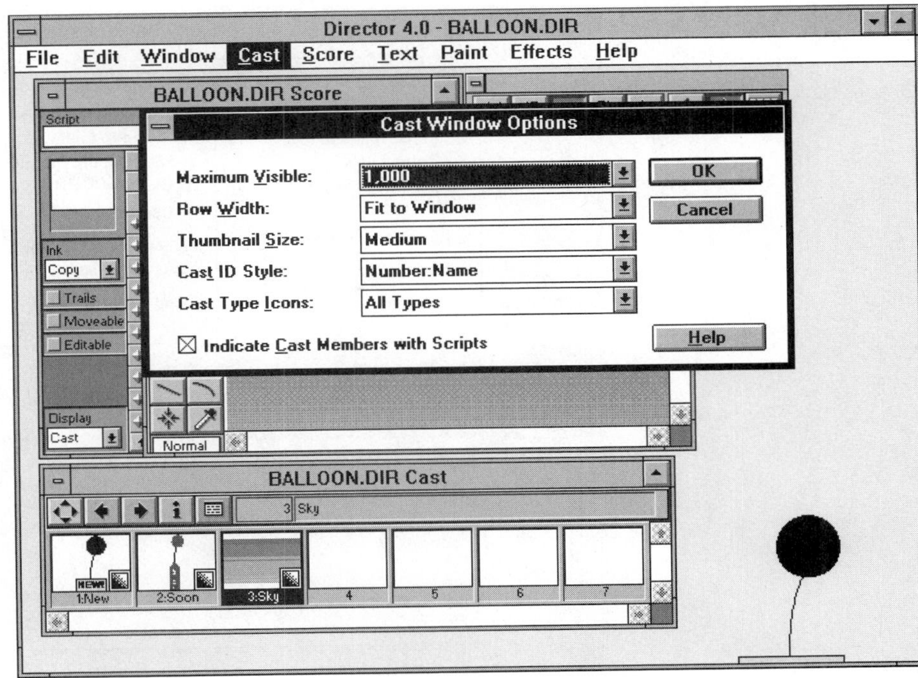

- **Thumbnail Size** Can be set to *Small*, *Medium*, or *Large*. You may wish to use smaller thumbnails for movies with many cast members, or with which you are quite familiar.
- **Cast ID Style** How the cast member is identified below the thumbnail and elsewhere in Director. The standard is the number and name separated with a colon (*Number:Name*). You can also choose *Number* alone or *Name* alone. (A fourth type, *A11*, is now obsolete.)
- **Cast Type Icons** Controls whether Director displays a small icon in the bottom-right corner of the thumbnails. (You can see some displayed in Figure 3.28). *All Types* shows type-indicating icons in all thumbnails. *All but Text and Bitmap* displays such icons for all thumbnails except for those cast members that are text or bitmaps (apparently assuming that those types would be more easily apparent and the space would be better used to display the thumbnail). *None* takes away icons from all thumbnails.
- **Indicate Cast Members with Scripts** If you turn on this check box, those cast members to which you have assigned script will have that indicated in their thumbnails by showing a small L-shaped bracket in the bottom-left corner (see Chapter 6).

  Experiment with changing values in this dialog box and checking the results in your Cast window.

Customizing the Paint Window

Finally, let's look at customizing the Paint window. The menu you need is available only from the Paint window.

Activate the **Paint** window.

Open the **Paint** menu's **Paint Window Options** dialog box (Figure 3.33).

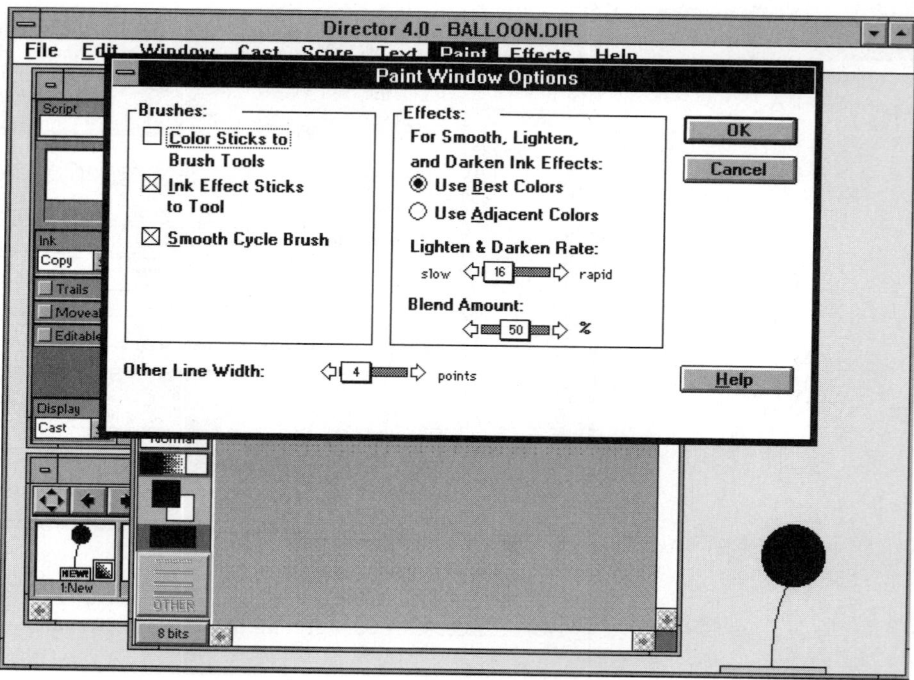

3.33

Paint menu's Paint Window Options dialog box

As you examine these items, you may find it particularly helpful to refer to Figure 3.31, which shows ink effects.

- **Color Sticks to Brush Tools** Turned on, this check box causes whatever color was last applied to the particular brush you are using (Brush 1 to Brush 5 and Air 1 to Air 5) to remain on the brush, even if you've changed Foreground Color chip in the meantime. When this box is turned off, brush tools take their color from the color chips.
- **Ink Effect Sticks to Tool** Turned on, this check box ensures that, when you use an ink effect on a tool (other than the Paintbrush or Air Brush tools), then switch to the Paintbrush or Air Brush tools, and then switch back to the original tool, that tool has the effect you assigned to the Paintbrush or Air Brush tool. With this box turned off, the ink effect originally assigned to the first tool is with the tool when you switch back.
- **Smooth Cycle Brush** When this check box is turned on and you use the Cycle ink effect, the colors progress from the foreground color to the destination color and then reverse and progress from destination to foreground. With the box turned off, the colors progress from the foreground color to the destination color but then jump back to the foreground color to start the next cycle.
- **For Smooth, Lighten, and Darken Ink Effects** The buttons allow you to choose between *Use Best Colors* and *Use Adjacent Colors*. The distinction between these two categories is the same as earlier discussed with respect to gradients.
- **Lighten & Darken Rate** Controls how much the ink is lightened or darkened when you use these ink effects, thereby controlling how many times you have to swipe a color to make it completely white (in the case

of lightening) or completely black (in the case of darkening). It ranges in value from 1 (slowest, most number of passes) to 255 (most rapid, fewest number of passes).

- **Blend Amount** Controls the percentage of color that is to be the new color when you are using Blend ink effect (page 77). At the 100% setting, the ink is entirely the new color (same as the Normal setting).
- **Other Line Width** This check box is for use in conjunction with the Line Width selector near the bottom-left corner of the Paint window (shown in color in Figure 3.33, which you can double-click to open this dialog box). With this selector, you set the thickness of lines used when you draw with the hollow versions of the various shapes (or with solid versions when the outline shows, such as with gradients and patterns), as well as when you use the Line and Arc tools. You can select from one of the lines shown or you can select OTHER. Use this slider switch to set the thickness of the line that is to be used when OTHER is selected. Another way to outline selected art is with Effects, Trace Edges.

CHAPTER REVIEW

KEY TERMS

text box
point
thumbnail
pixel
Lasso tool
Selection Rectangle tool
Hand tool
Paint Bucket tool
Eraser tool
zooming
gradient
dithering
Paintbrush tool
Air Brush tool
ink effects

REVIEW QUESTIONS

1. **T F** You can easily make formatting changes to text after it is permanently entered into the Paint window.
2. **T F** For easily selecting art in the Paint window, it's important to keep a solid color all around it.
3. **T F** To move only selected art, you use the Hand tool.
4. What key do you press to switch between no magnification and the most recent magnified view?
5. **T F** Using the arrow buttons in the Paint window displays the previous and next cast member, regardless of the type of cast member.
6. **T F** To create an ink effect, you set the Ink Effect menu and then select the tool you want to use for the effect.
7. **T F** To change the OTHER line width, you use the Paint menu's Paint Window Options dialog box.

PROJECTS

1. Create a sign with your name on it and use the Selection Rectangle with appropriate keys to stretch the font.
2. Use a tree-shaped air brush to create a mountainside forest as discussed in the text.
3. Save the Pattern palette with this shape as a cast member. Then copy the Standard palette back to the Custom palette. See if you can retrieve your cast member/palette and copy it back as a Custom palette.
4. Create and use a tile of the balloon. (You needn't include all the string.)

Positioning Graphics in Time and Space

THIS CHAPTER WILL TEACH YOU HOW TO

- Get around in the score
- Select, move, copy, and display cells, channels, and frames
- Change the size of sprites on the stage
- Place markers and comments in the score
- Add text, lines, and shapes directly on the stage
- Allow users to edit and move sprites on the stage as a movie plays
- Assign a variety of effects to sprites, such as transparent, ghost, mask, and blend effects, and create animation trails
- Change a movie's tempo and colors and add transitions
- Customize the score's display and operation

In the previous chapter you learned how to create graphics in the Paint window. In this chapter you'll see how to use the score to place and manipulate the bitmap (paint) cast members you created and to control their behavior over time as the movie is played. You'll also work with the stage, where you directly manipulate cast members and add new ones.

NAVIGATING THE SCORE AND OTHER SCORE BASICS

Two implements we'll examine in this chapter are shown in Figure 4.1. One is the score (maximized in the figure); the other is the Score menu. As we make our way around the score, there will be references to the Score menu, and our examination of this menu will continue into the next chapter.

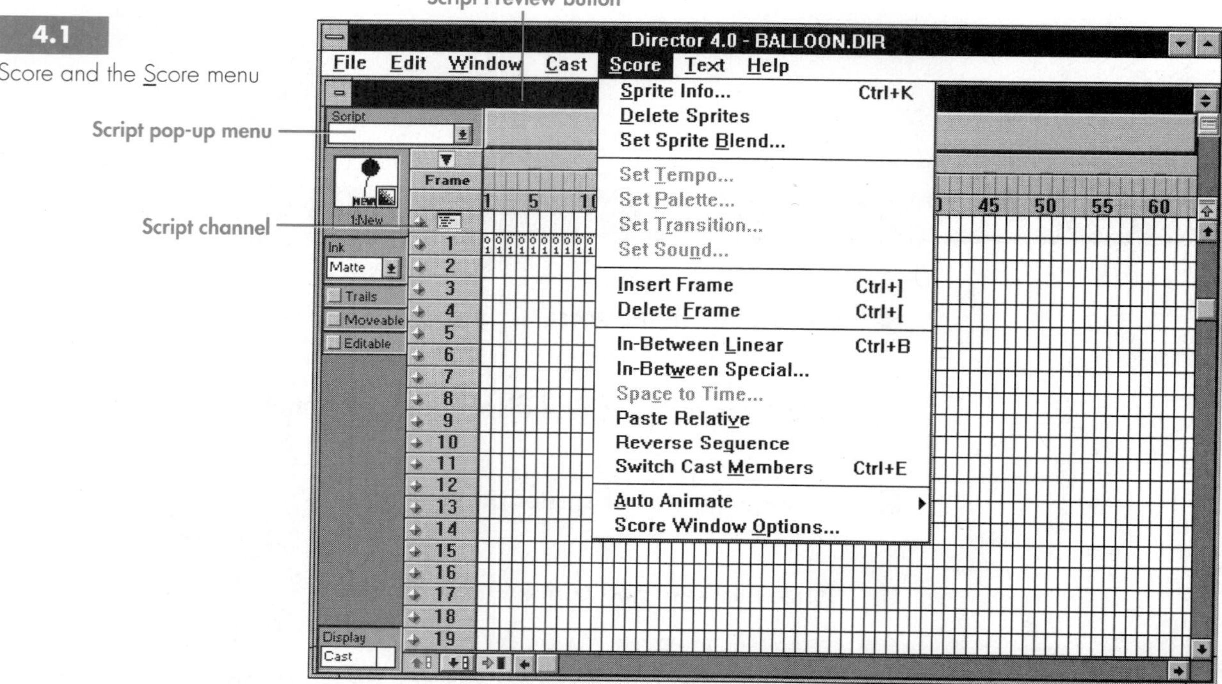

4.1
Score and the Score menu

Open your **BALLOON.DIR** movie.

Maximize the **Score** window.

Making up the bulk of the score are the numbered channels. (Remember, each row of cells is called a *channel*.) These are the ***sprite channels***, so called because their cells can hold sprites.

Toward the top-left of the score is the Script button (shown in color in Figure 4.1). We'll examine scripts later (Chapter 6). Clicking this button takes away the area at the top of the score occupied by the Script pop-up menu and the blank Script Preview button (as labeled in Figure 4.1). This provides more room for other elements in the score, which is fine when you're not working with scripts. Experiment with this button as follows.

Click the **Script** button.

The script area at the top of the score goes away.

Click the **Script** button again.

The script area comes back. We'll leave the script area turned on as that is the default setup. You may wish to leave the script area off as we won't be working with scripts now; if you do, there will be that minor discrepancy between your screen and the figures in this text.

Another script element that appears in the score is the Script channel. This is the channel just above channel 1. In Figure 4.1, sprite channels beginning with 1 appear, as does the Script channel. This is the normal position of the score when you start Director: row 1 at the top, with the Script channel the only channel showing above it.

But notice the position of the right-hand scroll bar. It shows that there is more of the score both above and below what you see displayed. Below these rows are additional sprite channels, numbered up to 48. Above are some channels specially designated for effects.

Use the right-hand **scroll bar** to scroll up and display the effects channels above channel 1 (Figure 4.2).

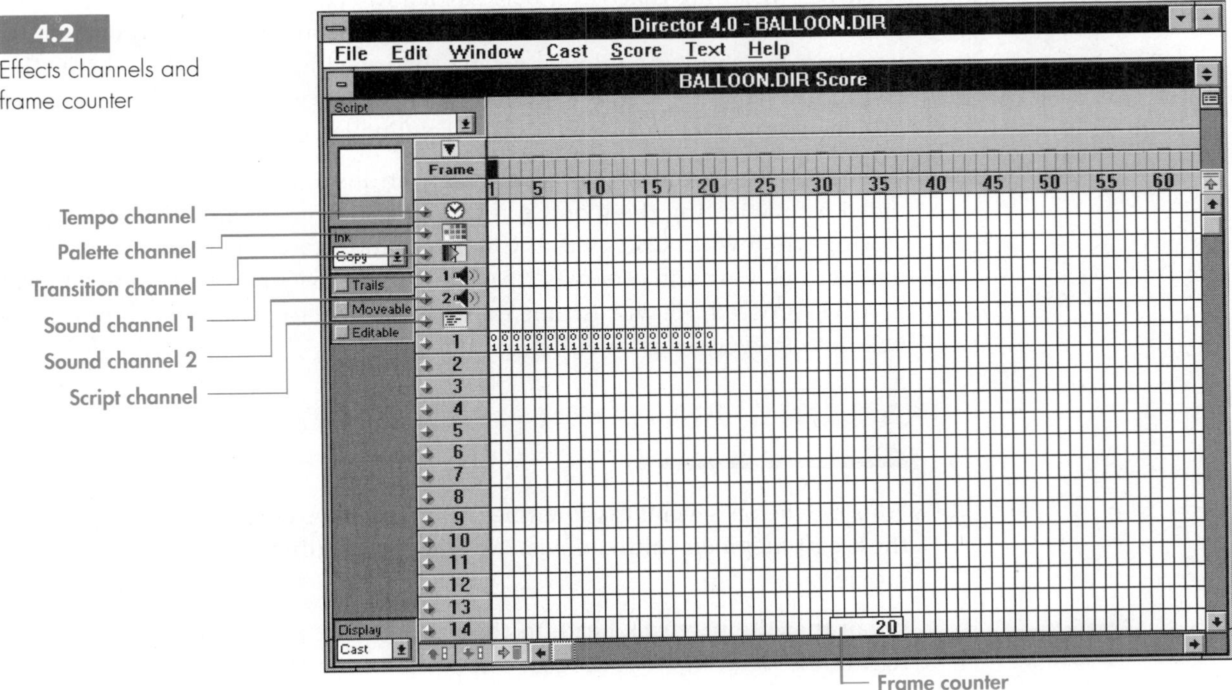

4.2

Effects channels and frame counter

Scroll down in the score and display higher-numbered channels.

When the score isn't in its original location (that is, with the Script channel and channel 1 at the top), you can click the ***Jump To Top button*** (shown in color at the right in Figure 4.2) one time to reposition it there. When the score is in its original position, clicking the Jump To Top button repositions the score at the *very* top; that is, with the effects channels displayed as they are in Figure 4.2.

With higher-numbered channels showing, click the **Jump To Top** button once.

The Script channel and channel 1 reappear.

Now with the Script channel and channel 1 showing at the top of the score, click the **Jump To Top** button again.

The effects channels above channel 1 reappear. We'll be working with effects channels later in this chapter.

A related button for navigating the score is the ***Jump button***, shown in color at the bottom in Figure 4.2. You know that you can select a cell by clicking the cell. Should you select a cell and then scroll the score so that the selected cell is no longer visible in the Score window, you can click the Jump button. Doing so will position the score so that the selected cell is again visible in the Score window.

Click a cell to select it.

Scroll so that the cell is no longer visible.

Click the **Jump** button to bring the cell back in view.

Another tool that's helpful for navigating the score is the ***frame counter***. This is a box with a number in it that appears above the horizontal (left/right) scroll bar when you drag that scroll bar (labeled in Figure 4.2). The number represents the frame centered (left to right) in the Score window and changes as you drag, but shows no number greater than the highest frame number with a cell in use. Thus the highest number you'd see in your movie now would be 20. The frame counter is useful when scrolling large movies.

Be sure you feel comfortable using the buttons and other instruments provided for navigating the score. You should also be familiar with opening and closing windows as discussed in Chapter 1 and stretching them as necessary, and with playing and otherwise manipulating movies as discussed in Chapter 2. As we proceed, we will assume that you are able to perform such basics; we will not list every step for doing so.

ADDING AND SHUFFLING SPRITES

Your movie has several cast members that you have created. Let's begin using these cast members in the movie. We'll start by adding the gradient sky to the movie.

Recall that the playback head, in the row labeled "Frame," indicates the current frame. That frame is the one displayed on the stage.

With the playback head at frame 1, drag the **Sky** cast member to the stage.

The cast number of the Sky, 03, appears in channel 2, frame 1. It is selected as indicated by reverse highlighting. The cast member of the selected cell appears as a thumbnail in the top left of the score, where the cast member's number and name also appear. Also, the balloon disappears; it is behind the sky. We'll fix that in a bit.

Drag the sky as necessary to center it on the stage.

Right now the sky is only in frame 1, the current frame. Should you play the movie, it would disappear immediately, as soon as the playback head moves past frame 1. To keep this from happening, we can use in-betweening to create copies of the sky in additional frames. (Because the sky will not move, we do not need to create a final copy of it first, as we had to with the balloon in Chapter 1.)

> With sky's cell selected, **Shift-click** the channel **2**, frame **20** cell.
>
> Use **Score**, **In-Between Linear** or Ctrl+B to generate sprites in frames 2 to 20.

The channel is filled and the generated sprites are indicated with dots that appear at the tops of their cells. The results are shown in Figure 4.3. Also in this figure you can see that the sky has a black frame around it. Create one for your movie as well:

4.3

Placing gradient sky on the stage

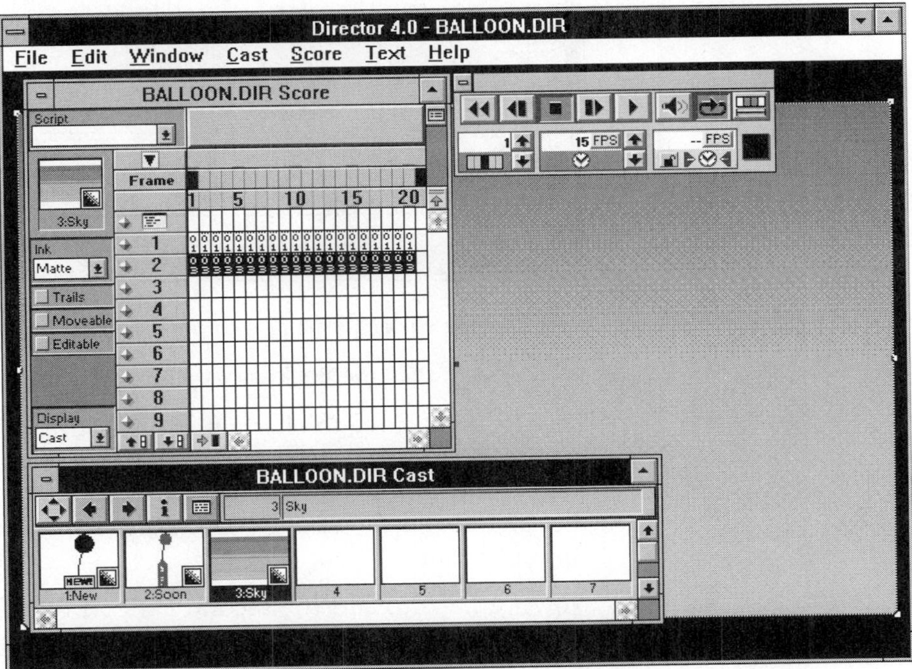

> Use the Control Panel's **Stage Background** color chip to change the stage background to black. (Changing the color of the stage background is discussed in Chapter 2.)

The balloon, however, is still behind the sky. Were you to play the movie now, you would see only sky for the entire movie.

Items you place on the stage are laid down in the order in which you create them, just as if you were laying down successive sheets of paper on a desk. Because you created the balloon first, it was laid down first and placed in channel 1. You laid down the sky next, and it was placed on top of, and hence in front of, the balloon and was assigned to channel 2. Later we'll add the second balloon and it will be in front of both of these, in channel 3.

Fortunately, you can use ***shuffling*** to correct this problem. Shuffling is the process of moving the contents of one or more cells forward (down) or backward (up) by one channel in the score. To shuffle, you use the Shuffle Backward and Shuffle Forward buttons, shown in color in Figure 4.4.

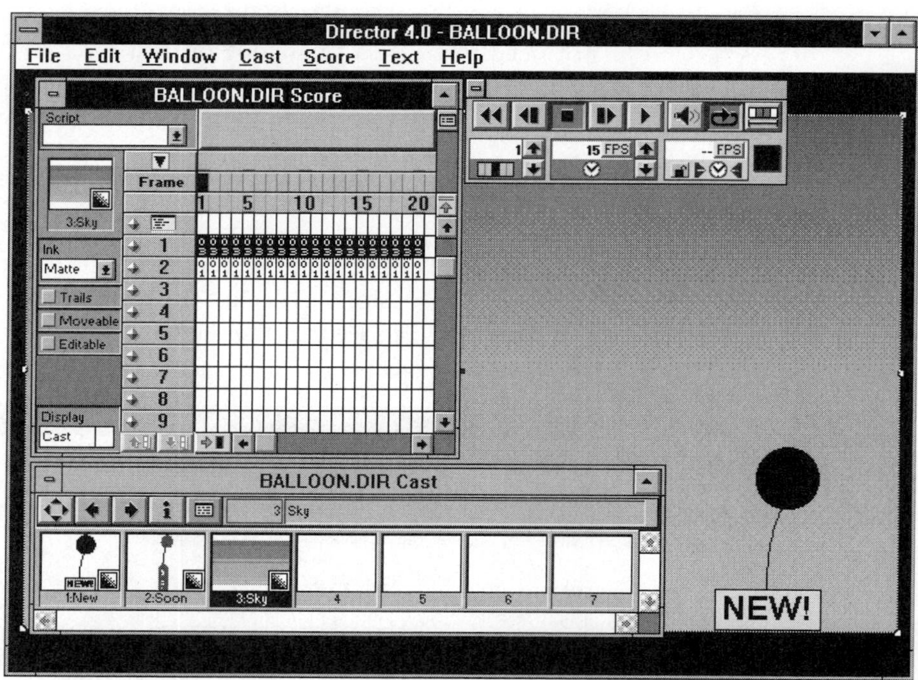

4.4

Shuffle Backward and Shuffle Forward buttons

Double-click channel **2**'s channel number to select all the cells for the sky.

Click the **Shuffle Backward** button, the left color button in Figure 4.4.

The sky cells move to channel 1, displacing the balloon cells, which are bumped to channel 2. On the stage, the balloon comes forward and appears in front of the sky, as shown in Figure 4.4. Alternatively, you could have achieved the same results by selecting the *balloon's* sprites and then using the Shuffle *Forward* button.

Now we need to add the second balloon to the movie. When it initially appears, we want to position it so that it is just beginning to peek out at the bottom of the screen, as shown at the bottom of Figure 4.5. To have its rising overlap the animation of the first balloon, let's make it appear in frame 11, when the first balloon is halfway up. We'll have it reach the top at frame 30. As with the first balloon, we'll place it at its initial position and its final position and use in-betweening to create the intervening sprites.

Before placing the first sprite on the stage, recall that there are three ways you can do that. You can move the playback head to frame 11 and then drag the sprite from the Cast window to the proper position on the stage. Or you can drag the cast member from the Cast window to the score's cell (channel 3, frame 11). This creates a sprite in the center of the stage and you can then move it to the appropriate position—or you can drag from the Place button.

Use one of these techniques to create the beginning sprite in channel 3, frame 11, positioned as shown in Figure 4.5.

Similarly, create the ending sprite at the top-left corner of the stage, in channel 3, frame 30.

Select the channel and use in-betweening to generate the intervening sprites, as shown in reverse highlighting in Figure 4.5.

Play the movie.

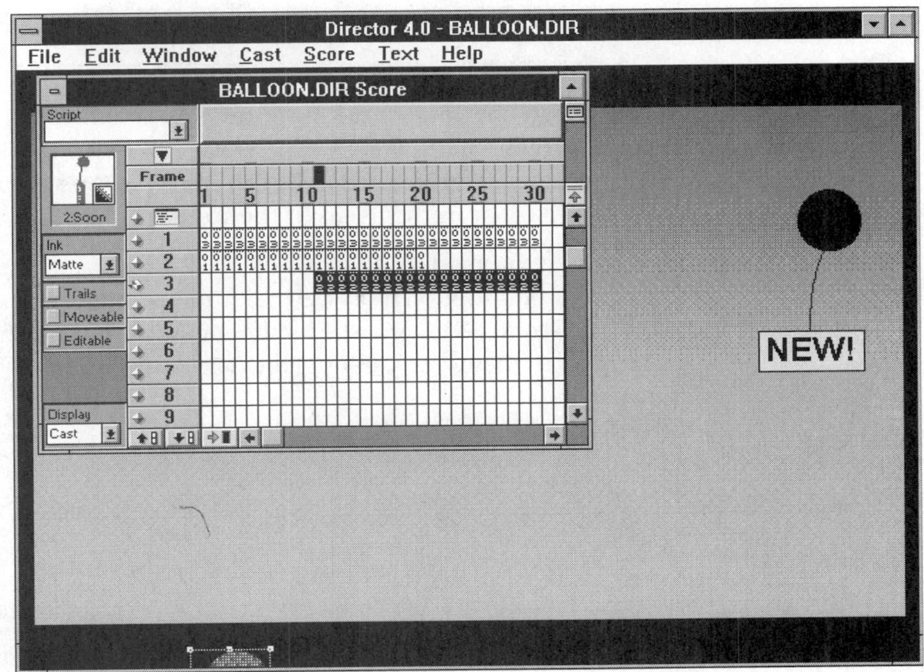

4.5
Adding second balloon

The balloons should rise smoothly, first one and then the other. However, you'll see the sky disappear at the same time that the first balloon does. We need to create additional sprites of the sky for the new frames used by the second balloon, frames 21 to 30.

> Click the channel 1, frame 1 cell and **Shift-click** the channel 1, frame 30 cell.
>
> Use in-betweening to generate the intervening sprites.

Figure 4.5 shows the results.

> Play the movie to check the results.

TURNING OFF CHANNELS

As you get more sprites on the stage it could become difficult to view specific activity. Director provides a way to isolate channels. You can turn channels off and their contents won't appear as you run the movie. Turning off is temporary; it's not saved with the movie or once you quit Director. Each channel has a ***channel button*** to turn channels off and on with. Try turning off the second balloon (channel 3):

> Point the **channel button** for channel **3** (shown in color in Figure 4.5) and click.

The channel button darkens, indicating that the channel is turned off.

> Play the movie.

Now the second balloon doesn't appear.

> Turn channel 3 back on and play the movie.

Once again the second balloon appears.

SELECTING MULTIPLE CELLS

As you continue creating sprites, you often need to move them around and otherwise manipulate them, as we did with shuffling when the balloon disappeared behind the sky. To manipulate sprites, you first must select them on the stage or in their cells in the score.

You've been selecting individual cells by clicking and you've done some selecting of multiple cells as well. Let's look at more ways to select multiple cells in the score. Figure 4.6 shows the methods for selecting multiple cells. In addition to these, you can use Edit, Select All (or Ctrl+A) to select all the cells of all frames in use.

4.6 Selecting multiple cells in the score

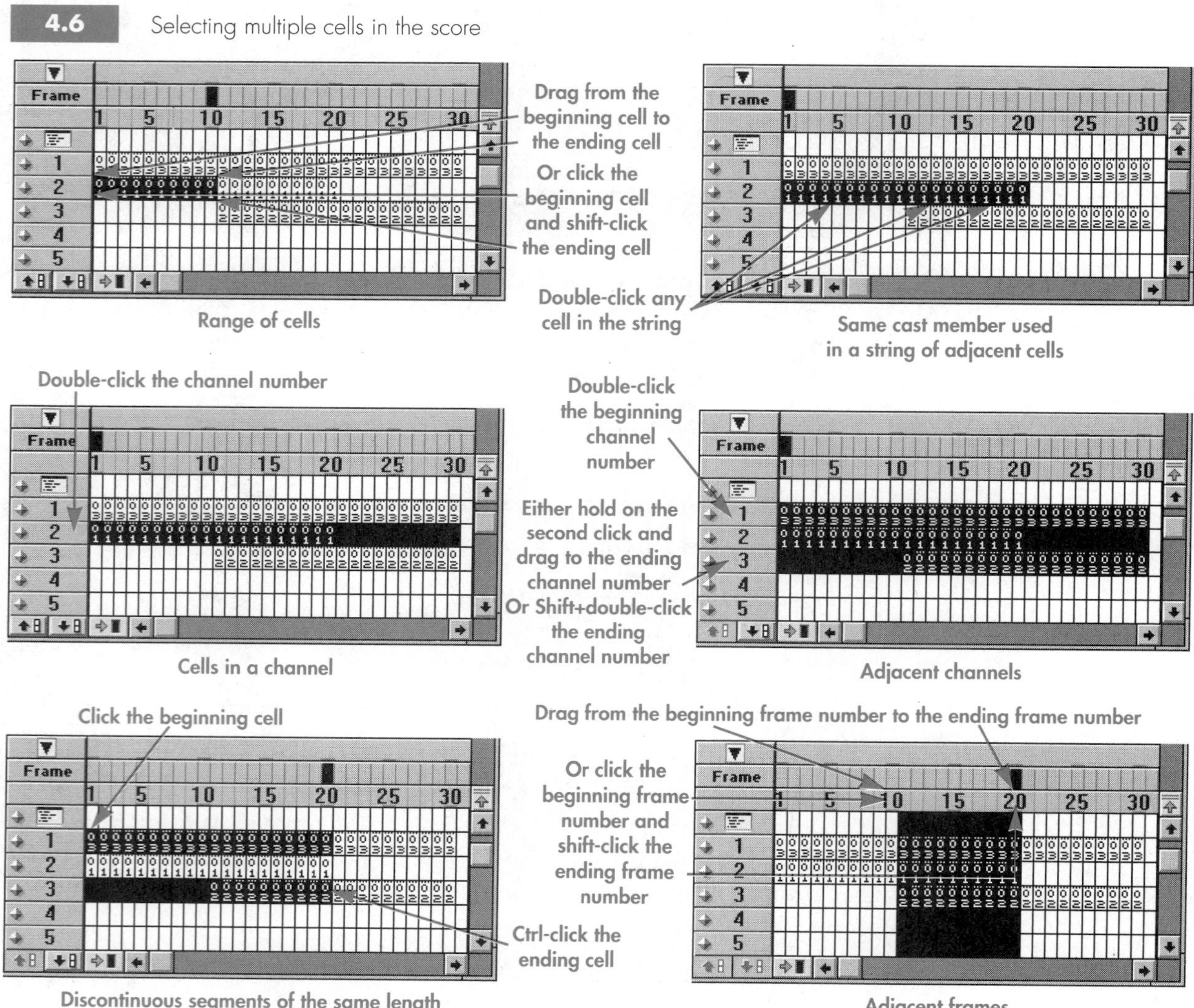

➡ *Important*: There's a point to consider when you drag to select cells. Normally for this to work, the first cell must *not* be selected before you begin dragging. If it is selected, dragging moves the contents of the selected cell(s). This is the case when the Score, Score Window Options, Drag And Drop check box is turned on (more Score Window Options at the end of this chapter). Before dragging, take your clues from the shape of the mouse cursor. When the cursor is shaped like an arrow, dragging will select cells. When the cursor is in the shape of a flat hand, dragging moves the cell contents.

> **Practice selecting multiple cells, using the techniques shown in Figure 4.6, as well as selecting all cells.**

You can also select by clicking actual sprites as they appear on the stage. Multiple sprites are selected by holding down the Shift key as you click. Sometimes it's difficult to select a particular sprite. For example, when the sky is selected, you'll find it difficult to select one of the balloons. However, if you click away from the sky by clicking the black background, you can then click one of the balloons.

> **Move the playback head to frame 15.**
>
> **Click one of the balloons within the sky.**

The balloon is selected.

> **Click within the sky, but not within one of the balloon's bounding boxes.**

The sky is selected.

> **Attempt to click one of the balloons within the sky.**

The sky remains selected.

> **Click the black background (black frame around the sky).**

The sky is no longer selected.

> **Click one of the balloons within the sky.**

Now, with this action you are able to select the balloon.

> **Shift-click the other balloon.**

Both balloons are now selected.

MANIPULATING SPRITES AND FRAMES

Once cells are selected, you can move their sprites to different cells. Some of the methods for doing so we've already examined:

- Shuffling cells to adjacent channels with the Shuffle Forward and Shuffle Backward buttons.
- Dragging selected cells with the flat hand. (See ***Important*** note in the previous section.)
- Using the Edit menu to cut, copy, paste, and clear cells.

➡ *Warning and Tip*: If one or more cells are selected when you paste with Edit, Paste Cells (or equivalent), Director deletes sprites in the score (as many as necessary) and replaces them with the pasted sprites. To avoid this, click the frame number where you want to insert the sprites; a flashing insertion bar appears immediately to the left of the frame and pasting then inserts sprites in that frame, moving the sprites that were previously in that frame ahead (to the right) in the movie.

In addition, you can manipulate sprites with these commands on the Score menu:

- **Delete Sprites** or **Delete key** or **Backspace key** Deletes all selected sprites (without sending them to the clipboard). Effect is the same as Edit, Cut Cells.
- **Insert Frame** or **Ctrl+]** Adds a frame by making a copy of the sprites at the playback head and inserting that copy in the next frame, advancing the playback head there, and pushing existing frames forward. The result is two frames with duplicate sprites, one at the playback head (in its new position) and the other at the frame preceding the playback head. If more than one frame has been selected, this command makes a copy of the final selected frame only.
- **Delete Frame** or **Ctrl+[** Deletes the frame at the playback head.
- **Paste Relative** or **Ctrl+Shift+V** Positions the first pasted sprite in the same position as the sprite in the cell just before it. This command is useful for repeating animation sequences (Chapter 5).
- **Switch Cast Members** or **Ctrl+E** Replaces all the selected sprites with the cast member selected in the Cast window.

Let's try moving some items around. But if you make a mistake, it's important to be able to return the movie to its current condition.

Before proceeding, save the movie.

Now, if you make a mistake you can use File, Revert to return to the saved version of the movie.

Double-click one of the cells in channel 3 that contains sprites created from the Soon (02) cast member.

This selects all the 02 sprites.

Cut the selected sprites to the clipboard.

Select the channel 3, frame 1 cell.

Paste the sprites from the clipboard to that position.

Play the movie.

Both balloons rise simultaneously at the beginning of the movie.

Double-click one of the cells in channel 2 that contains sprites created from the New (01) cast member.

All 01 sprites are selected.

Check that the Score, Score Window Options, Drag And Drop check box is turned on. (If not, turn it on.)

Drag the selected channel 2 sprites so that they begin in channel 2, frame 11.

The result is shown in Figure 4.7.

Play the movie.

4.7
Moving cells

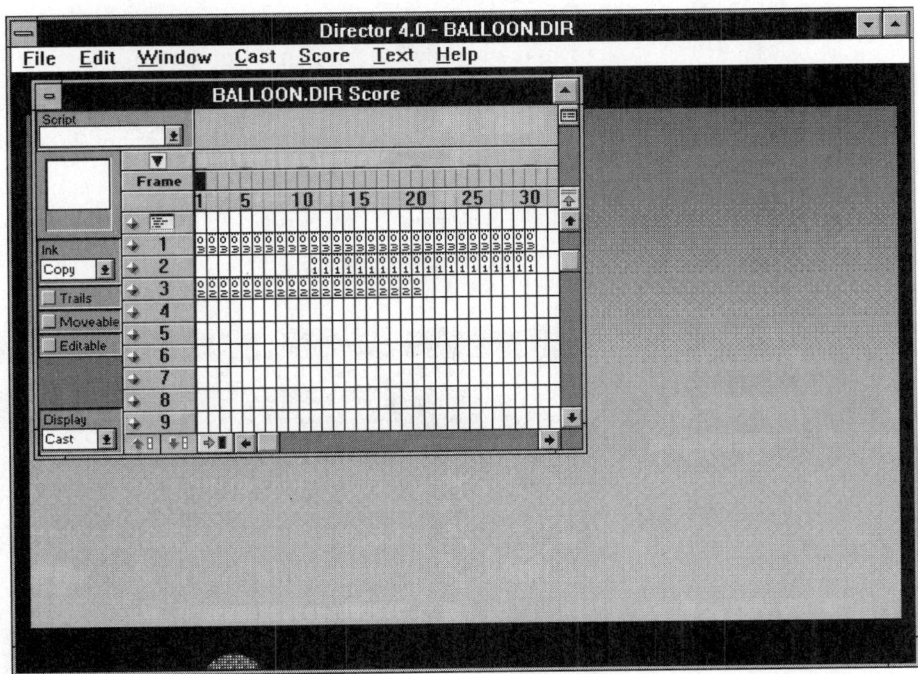

Now the Soon balloon rises first, then the New balloon. Now let's make both balloons New balloons.

Select the string of **01** sprites.

In the Cast window, select the **2:Soon** cast member.

Open the **Score** menu and select **Switch Cast Members** or press Ctrl+E.

Test the movie.

You should see two New balloons rise in succession on either side of the stage.

Position the playback head at frame **20**.

Use **Score**, **Insert Frame** or Ctrl+] to insert a copy of frame 20 following it (at frame 21).

The playback head is now at frame 21.

Print the movie if and as directed by your instructor.

With the playback head at frame 21, use **Score**, **Delete Frame** or Ctrl+[to remove that new frame.

Use these various procedures to return the score to its original condition, as shown earlier in Figure 4.5.

CHANGING THE SIZE OF SPRITES

Once a sprite is on the stage, not only can you move it as we've been doing but you can resize it as well. Be aware that, when you resize a sprite on the stage, only the sprite is affected. The cast member it is associated with remains the same size, and you can quickly return the sprite to that size, as we'll see shortly. This is very different from resizing with the Paint window, which does indeed affect actual cast members.

You can use resizing to create animated effects. For example, proceed as follows to make a New balloon that appears to grow rather than float to the top of the screen.

Copy the **New** sprite from the channel 2, frame 1 cell to channel 2, frame 20.

With frame 20 displayed on the stage, click the **New** sprite and use its top, center handle to stretch the top of the sprite upward, as shown in Figure 4.8.

4.8
Using handles to resize a sprite

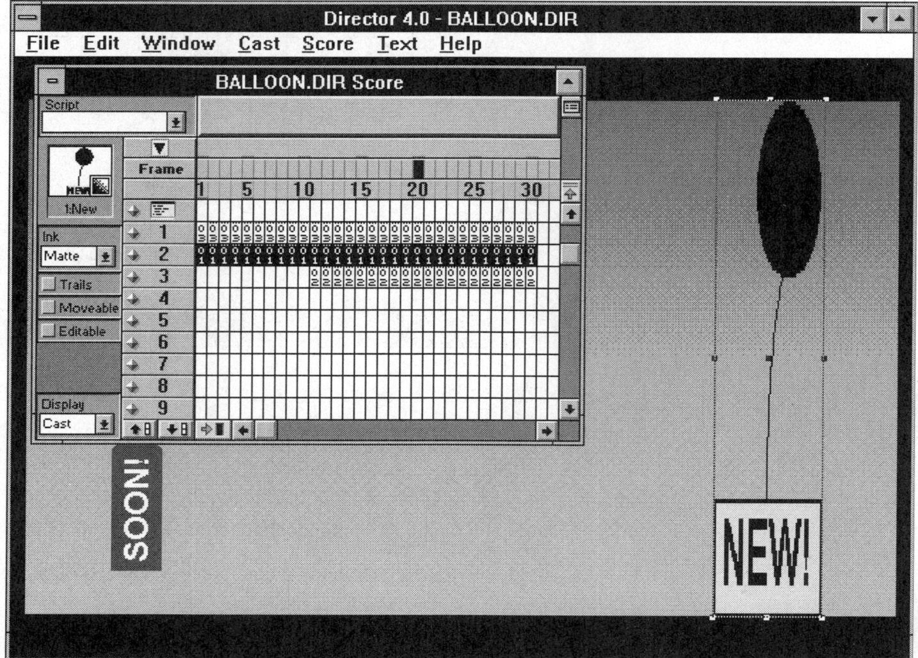

As already mentioned, you can shift-click to select multiple objects. Once selected, you can move the objects as a unit by pointing inside one of them and dragging. You can also adjust the size of multiple objects in like proportions by dragging an object's handle.

Now that you have the original and stretched versions of the New balloon you must re-do the in-between sprites to show the stretching. In addition, you don't want the sprite to just disappear after frame 20 (when it's at its full height), so you need to create in-between sprites following frame 20. Each of the subsequent sprites will show the balloon at its full height. Proceed as follows to do all this.

Double-click channel 2's channel number.

This selects all cells from frame 1 to frame 30, as shown in Figure 4.8.

Use **Score, In-Between Linear** or Ctrl+B to generate the sprites.

Play the movie.

The balloon and its sign grow, reaching full height in frame 20 and remaining there to the end of the movie.

Use **File, Save As** to save this movie as GROW.DIR and print it as directed by your instructor.

Retrieve the BALLOON.DIR movie from disk, which is the movie in its original condition (without the growing balloon).

FINE-TUNING SIZE AND PLACEMENT

Besides dragging and stretching sprites, you can also set their size and location in a variety of ways.

Nudging with the Arrow Keys

One method for fine-tuning placement is by ***nudging*** with the arrow keys. Pressing an arrow key moves the selected sprite(s) by one pixel in the direction of the key, just as we saw with paint art in Chapter 3. The arrow keys operate in this fashion as long as the Tweak window, discussed below, is not open.

Setting Sprite Info

Both size and location of sprites can be set by providing numeric values. Pixels are used for the measurements so you can indicate precise values. You can use these methods to ensure exact consistency among sprites in size and placement when necessary. Display the dialog box for setting these values as follows.

With the stretched sprite in channel 2, frame 20 selected, open the Score menu and select Sprite Info.

The dialog box in Figure 4.9 appears. Of course, the pixel values for yours will probably differ.

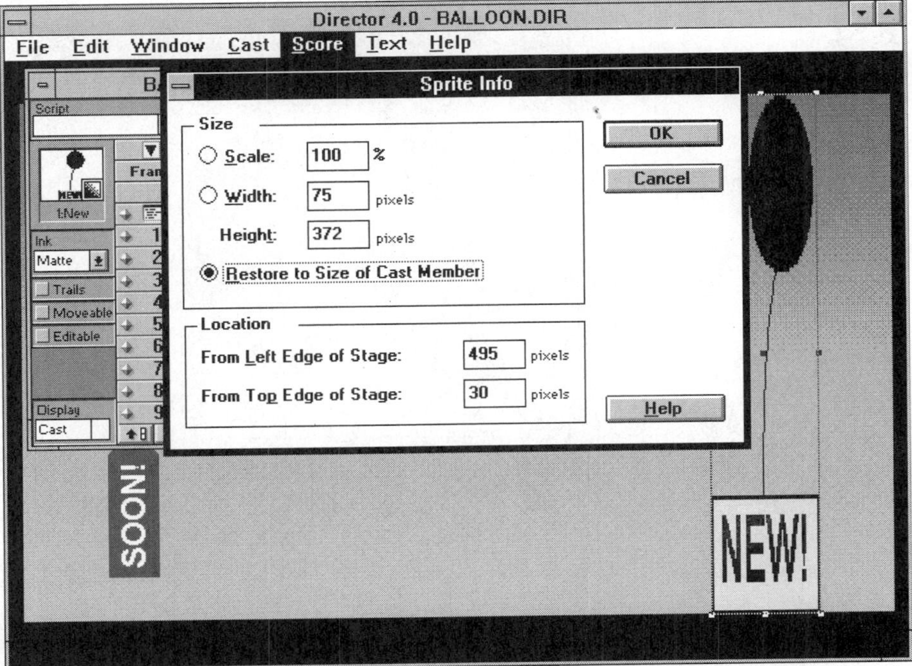

4.9
Score menu's Sprite Info dialog box

Size can be set to one of three buttons. *Scale* adjusts the selected sprite with regard to its present size (*not* the size of the sprite's cast member). Because it's based on the sprite's current size, this value is always at 100% when you open the dialog box. Changing it to 200%, for example, will double the sprite in size. The *Width/Height* boxes initially show how wide and tall the current sprite is; change one or both and the sprite is adjusted accordingly. *Restore To Size Of Cast Member* makes the sprite the size of the cast member. However, you may find it necessary to adjust the position on the stage.

Sidelight: You can also change the size of a cast member in a similar position. To do that, you use the Cast window or Paint window to select the cast member and use Cast, Transform Bitmap. This dialog box, like the one for Sprite Info, has a Size group you can use to set Scale and Width/Height.

Location has two boxes you can use to provide values for positioning the sprite. *From Left Edge Of Stage* is for providing a value to the left edge of the sprite's bounding box. *From Top Edge Of Stage* is measured to the top edge of the sprite's bounding box. For values you enter into either of these boxes to take hold, you must not have the Restore To Size Of Cast Member button turned on; be sure to switch the Size group to one of the other two buttons (Scale or Width/Height) before using OK. For example, if you only wanted to adjust a sprite's location, you could first click the Scale button, set at 100%.

Caution: The Restore To Size Of Cast Member button may be initially turned on when you open this dialog box. If you don't want to reset the sprite to the size of its cast member, be sure to change the Size setting before using OK.

Click the Cancel button or press the Esc key or Alt+F4 or double-click the Control-menu box.

Tweaking

Another process that can assist in precise placement is ***tweaking***. It uses a curious little window called the Tweak window (Figure 4.10). Display it this way.

4.10
Tweak window

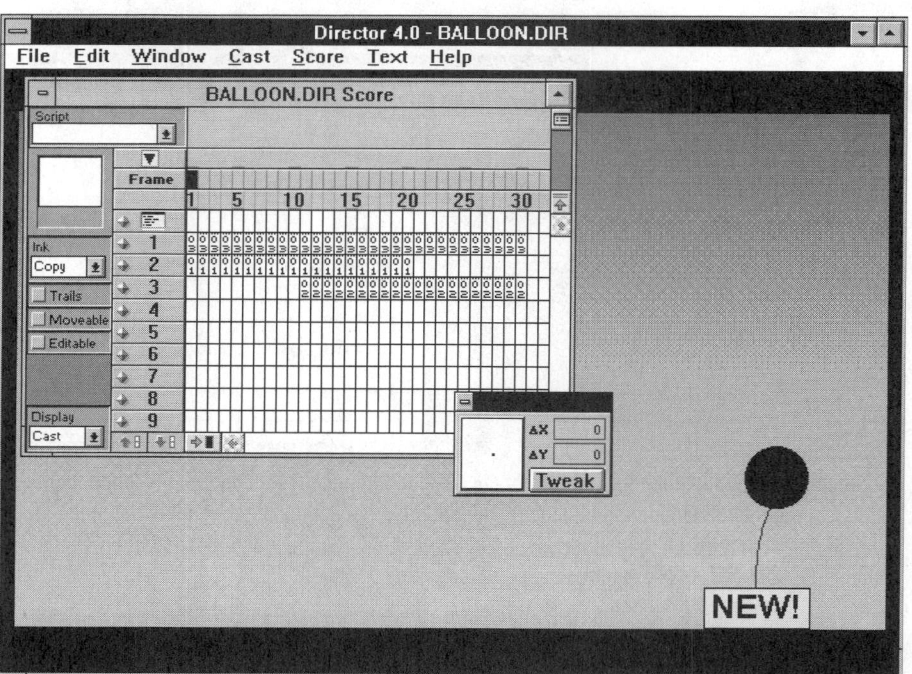

Open the Window menu and select Tweak or press Ctrl+Shift+T.

This window allows you to move the selected sprite(s) by horizontal and vertical amounts, repeatedly if necessary. To use it, you first set the tweak values in the window. You do this by dragging from the dot in the window in the direction and amount you wish the sprite displaced; a line appears from the dot as you do. (You can drag beyond the Tweak window itself, if necessary.) Alternatively, you can click beside the dot or line to create or adjust the line. You can also use the arrow keys.

As you adjust the line, X changes to reflect the left (positive) or right (negative) number of pixels for displacement; Y changes to indicate the down (positive) or up (negative) number of pixels. Each press of an arrow key adjusts the appropriate value (X or Y) in the direction of the key by one pixel.

Once the values are set, you click the Tweak button, which adjusts the selected sprite(s) accordingly. You can again click the Tweak button to adjust by the identical amount repeatedly, selecting other sprites between clicks if desired.

Use these methods (nudging, Sprite Info, or tweaking) to fine-tune placement of your sprites where needed. (Be sure to in-between again if necessary.)

CREATING MARKERS

Once your sprites are in place, you may want to document their appearance and other activities that occur in the score. The implement Director provides for doing this is the ***marker***. You were introduced to markers in Chapter 1; now let's see how to create them. To create a marker you use the ***marker well*** (shown in color in Figure 4.11). This item in the score provides a supply of markers that you use by dragging into position. Create the two markers shown in the figure like this:

4.11

Markers and Markers window

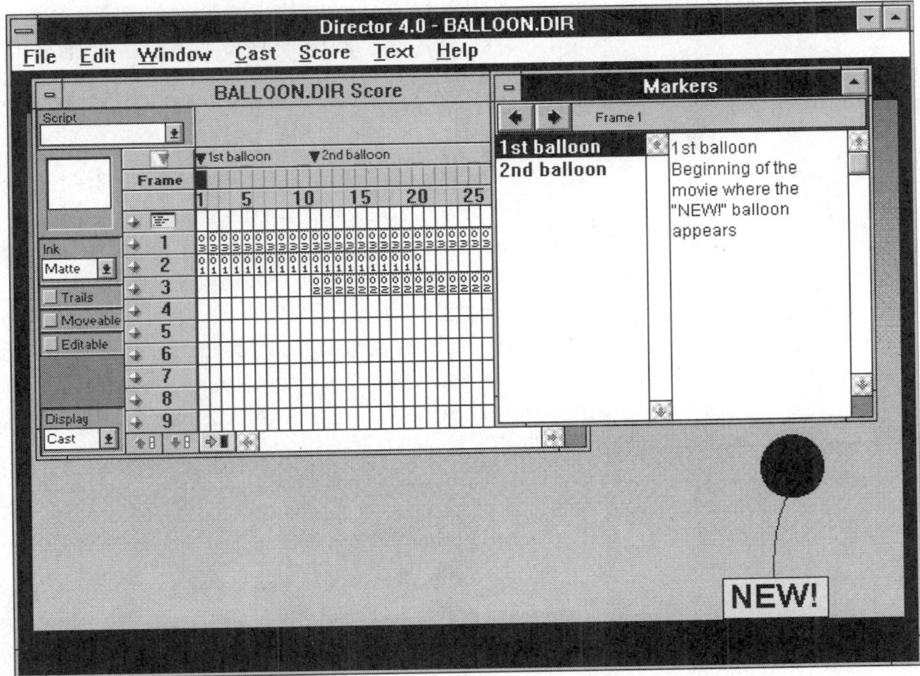

Drag from the marker well to a position in the same row as the marker well in frame 1.

A dotted-line version of a marker appears as you drag. When you release, the marker appears, along with an insertion point. You can use the insertion point then to provide a label for the marker.

White highlighting appears around the name as you type; you can click elsewhere to make the highlighting go away. If you later need to change the marker label, you can click it. This causes the highlighting and insertion point to reappear so you can edit.

You edit marker labels by using the standard editing utensils:

- **Arrow, Home, End keys**, or **clicking** Move the cursor
- **Delete** or **Backspace keys** Delete/erase text
- **Dragging** Selects text

Drag from the marker well to create a marker in frame 1. Label it **1st balloon**, as shown in Figure 4.11.

Repeat the process for frame 11, labeling it **2nd balloon**, as in the figure.

To delete a marker, you drag the marker up, into the Script Preview button (or the score's Title bar if the script area of the score isn't showing, as discussed earlier in this chapter). The deletion of markers cannot be undone.

When you move cells, markers don't normally move with them. However, if you select one or more frames (by dragging across frame numbers or clicking and shift-clicking frame numbers as described earlier in the chapter), you can use the Edit menu (or equivalent techniques) to cut (or copy) and paste the frames along with their markers. Note that markers do not move with the selected frames if you drag the frames with the flat-hand cursor; you must cut (or copy) and paste the frames.

Figure 4.11 also shows the Markers window. Display the window as follows:

Open the **Window** menu and select **Markers** or press Ctrl+Shift+M or double-click one of the markers you created.

The Markers window has two scroll areas. The left area lists the marker labels as set in the score. You cannot edit these labels in the left section. The right area initially shows a copy of whichever label is selected in the left half. You can edit the label here and your change is effected when you go to a different label or close or deactivate the Markers window. Labels are selected by clicking the list in the left area or by clicking the arrow buttons toward the top of the Markers window: left for previous marker and right for next marker. The frame number of the selected marker appears to the right of these arrows.

You can also use the right section to insert additional text below the label. This text does not show in the score but it remains available for viewing in this window. Proceed to add such a marker comment as follows:

With **1st balloon** selected in the left section, press the **End** key or the → key or click to the right of the label in the right section.

Press **Enter**.

Add the comment as shown in Figure 4.11.

Not only are the marker comments available for viewing in the Markers window; you can also print them with File, Print, Marker Comments. Additionally, as discussed in Chapter 2, you can use the storyboard format to print marker comments alongside the stage. Do this by turning on File, Print, Stage, Options, 1/2 or 1/4, Storyboard Format, Marker Comment.

Add your own marker comment for **2nd balloon**.

Print the movie in storyboard format showing marker comments as directed by your instructor.

USING TOOLS ON THE STAGE

Now that you've learned how to create sprites, select and manipulate those sprites, and document them with markers, let's look at another way you can dress the stage. You used the Paint window to create bitmap cast members that became sprites. Director also provides a means of placing text, shapes, and other items directly on the stage. To do this you can use the Tools window. Display it as follows:

Open the **Window** menu and select **Tools** or press Ctrl+7.

The Tools window appears. It's shown in Figure 4.12; the position of yours may differ. (Other items we'll examine shortly are also shown.)

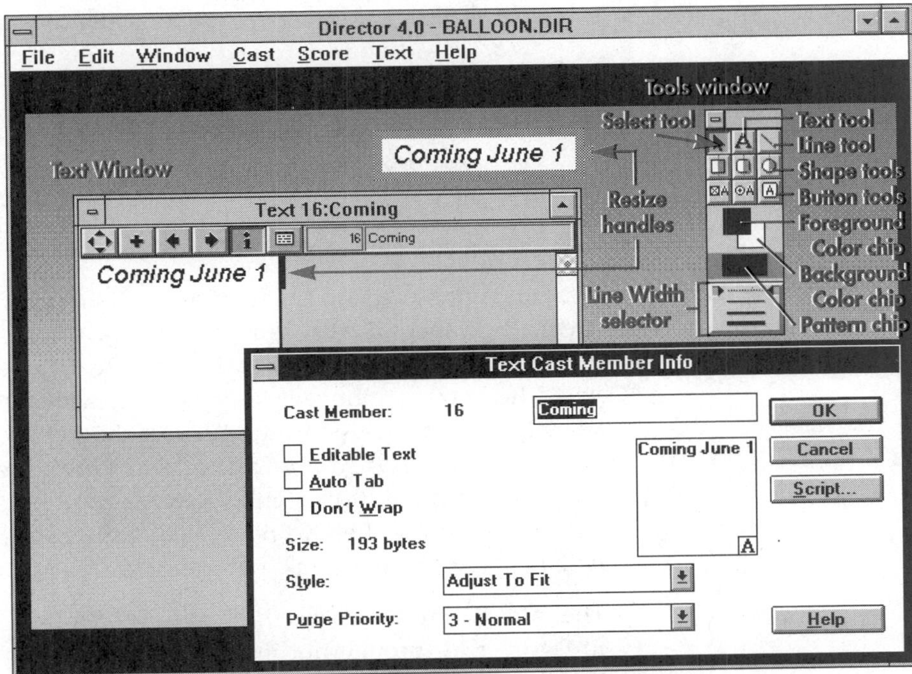

4.12
Tools window, Text window, and Text Cast Member Info dialog box

In the Tools window are some tools that are similar to those in the Paint window. Available are the Text (A) tool, Line tool (\), and Shape tools (rectangle, oval, and round rectangle, in hollow and filled versions). You can also use this window to create buttons (Chapter 6). The arrow-shaped Select tool is for changing the mouse cursor back to its standard shape for selecting.

The Tools window's Foreground Color chip is used to change the color of black pixels in the selected sprite(s). With the Background Color chip you can change the color of white pixels. (Other colors may change unpredictably as well. This occurs with tools that are designed primarily for use with black-and-white objects.) There is also a Pattern chip for assigning patterns to objects drawn with the Shape tools. With the Line Width selector you can control the width of lines drawn with the Line tool (\). It also controls the width of lines that appear along the perimeter of objects drawn with the Shape tools.

➡ *Careful*: Before drawing with the Line tool or with hollow versions of the Shape tools, be sure to set the Line Width selector to some setting other than the first one, dots (···). That setting makes lines invisible. Invisible lines could be desirable when you are working with filled versions of the Shape tools, but they amount to nothing when you are drawing with the Line tool or with hollow Shape tools.

As with the Paint window, you can hold the Shift key to constrain directions or shapes as you drag.

Proceed as follows to create the "Coming June 1" text at the top of the sky:

Using the **Tools** window's **Text** tool, click toward the top of the sky.

Use the resulting text box to enter the text, as shown toward the top in Figure 4.12.

Use the **Text** menu to set its size to **18** points, its style to **Italic**, and its alignment to **Center**.

If you wish, add other Text menu enhancements, such as a border, margin, or shadow. You can also use Text, Font to change the font (typeface) assigned to the text.

Use the text box's middle-right handle to adjust the size of the text box as necessary, and drag with the box's borders to position the text box as shown.

When you are satisfied with the results, save the movie.

You can edit directly on the stage as we did or by using the Text window (Figure 4.12), displayed with Window, Text or Ctrl+6. The Title bar of this window gives the Cast number to which the Text cast member is assigned. (Yours will differ; you can move it to 16 to agree with the figure if you wish.) Additionally, for some revisions, the Title bar shows the Cast name, Coming, which is derived from the text itself and assigned to the Text cast member automatically. Below are buttons similar to their counterparts in the Paint and Cast windows; you use them to place, add, and navigate Text cast members (and *only* Text cast members).

The Info (i) button displays the Text Cast Member Info dialog box, also shown in Figure 4.12 (though not in its normal position). With a Text cast member selected, you can also display this dialog box by using Cast, Cast Member Info or Ctrl+I—or you can point to a cast member or sprite and click the right mouse button.

Display the **Text** window and the **Text Cast Member Info** dialog box.

Cast Member shows the number and name of the cast member. You can adjust the cast name here; however, you must use the Cast window to adjust the cast number (by moving the cast member to a different position).

Editable Text lets you allow users to change the text while the movie is running. In the next section we'll experiment with editable text. **Auto Tab** is for use with multiple Text cast members that are editable; it allows the user to press the Tab key to advance among such items. **Don't Wrap**, like the other check boxes, is normally turned off and, if the text is wider than the Text box, the text wraps down, lengthening (but not widening) the Text box as necessary. When this check box is turned on, the Text box shows only as much of the text as its width allows; text does not wrap down (although you can still use the Enter key to force text to a new line) and you cannot scroll to the right to see the additional text.

Style has four settings. *Adjust To Fit* is the normal setting; the Text box automatically lengthens as necessary to accommodate the text it holds. *Scrolling* causes a scroll bar to appear at the right of the Text box; it provides a means for scrolling up and down the text box as necessary to view text. *Fixed* keeps the Text box at the size that you set and does not allow for scrolling. *Limit to Field Size* is for use with Lingo.

With the first setting, Adjust To Fit, only a right handle is necessary as Director determines the length of the Text box automatically. With the other settings, additional handles appear below and at the bottom-right corner so you can adjust the Text box's length, width, or both.

Purge Priority is for providing the movies with guidelines for dealing with low memory, as discussed in reference to cast members in Chapter 3.

You can convert text created with the Tools window to a bitmap (paint) cast member. To do that you use the Cast window to select the cast member you wish to change. Then you select Cast, Convert To Bitmap. Be careful with this command: You can't undo it and there's no warning to that effect.

EDITING WHILE A MOVIE IS PLAYING

Text you create with the Paint window, such as the "NEW!" sign, cannot truly be edited. On the other hand, as you work on a movie, you can easily edit text created with the Tool window's Text tool. (Standard text editing doesn't always operate, however. For example, the arrow keys nudge the sprite in their respective directions rather than moving the text cursor.)

In addition, should you specifically designate Text-tool text as ***editable text***, the text can be changed by a user *while the movie is playing*. For example, you can make the Coming text editable so that, should delays occur, the date can be changed, even while you are viewing the movie. (Of course, if this were for actual use, you probably wouldn't want a user to be able to make such a change, but it will do for demonstration purposes.)

Editable text can be changed by the user with the standard editing utensils:

- **Arrow, Home, End keys**, or **clicking** Move the cursor
- **Delete** or **Backspace keys** Delete/erase text
- **Dragging** Selects text

Try creating editable text as follows:

> **In the Text Cast Member Info dialog box for the Coming text you entered with the Text tool, turn on the Editable Text check box.**

Click the **OK** button or press the Enter key.

With looping turned on, play the movie.

Change the text to **Coming July 1**. Then return it to the original date.

Stop the movie.

You can also designate particular cells containing Text cast members as editable. To do that, you would use the score to select the cells corresponding to when and for what Text-tool text you'll allow text editing. Then, in the left portion of the score, you would turn on the score's Editable check box.

GENERATING ANIMATION TRAILS

So far we have accounted for one of the three check boxes on the left side of the score. Let's examine the other two, Trails and Moveable. First, we'll look at Trails. Normally, sprites have this check box turned off and each sprite disappears once the playback head moves to the next frame. Sprites with this check box turned on remain on the screen after being displayed, creating ***trails*** (although all or part of the sprite could be overlaid in subsequent frames). Try creating trails.

Select both channel 1 and channel 2.

Turn on the **Trails** check box.

Play the movie.

Your results should look something like Figure 4.13 (except for the balloons and the "HUGE MALL!" sign, which we'll create shortly).

4.13
Trails

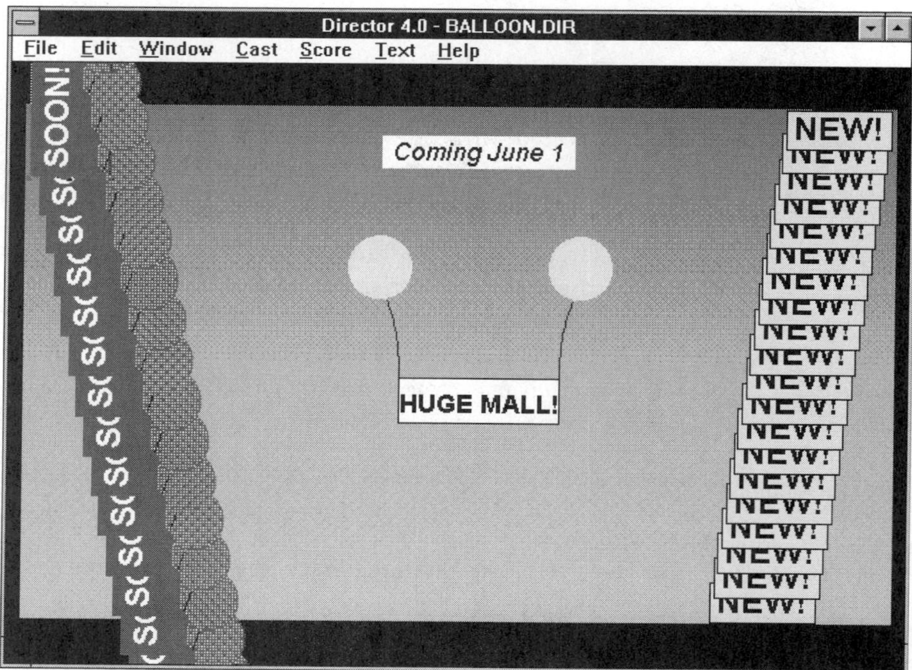

Note: The Trails check box displays the status of the selected cell. If multiple cells are selected, this check box shows a status, on (check) or off (unchecked), only if all the selected cells share the same status. If the statuses of selected cells differ, the check box is darkened. In that case, you can change the status of all selected cells by clicking once (for on) or twice (for off). This note applies to the other check boxes below Trails as well—namely, Moveable and Editable.

Select cells of both kinds, some that have trails turned on and some that have trails turned off.

Notice the Trails check box.

Select channels 2 and 3 and turn off trails for their sprites.

CREATING MOVEABLE SPRITES

The Moveable check box creates ***moveable sprites***, sprites that the user can drag around the stage while the movie is running. Create them like this:

Use the Paint window to create the HUGE MALL! banner with yellow balloons, shown in Figure 4.13. (Use a shrink selection rectangle and the Paint window's Effects, Flip Horizontal command to flip the graphic horizontally.)

Similarly there is an Effects, Flip Vertical command to flip paint graphics vertically.

Insert the balloons and their banner into the score and onto the stage.

Now you need to apply an ink effect, as you did to create the matted balloon in Chapter 2. You'll use the pop-up arrow shown in color in Figure 4.14. There will be more on the various score ink effects shortly.

4.14

Cloud cover, ghost text, and Ink pop-up arrow

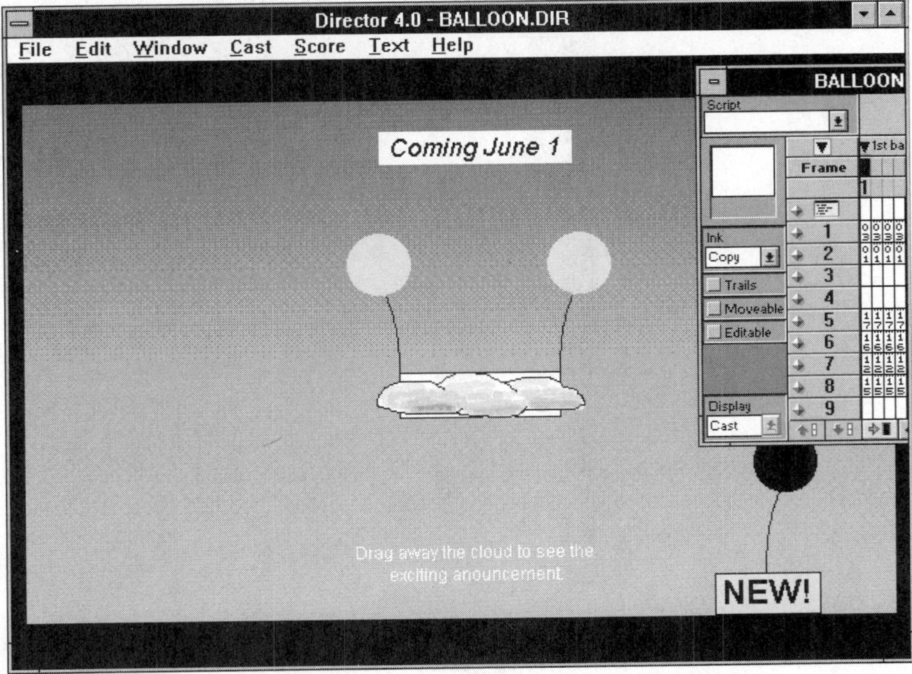

With the new art selected, apply the score's Matte ink effect.

Place one of your clouds on the score so that it covers the banner, as shown in Figure 4.14.

Duplicate all these sprites for the entire movie.

With the sprites selected, turn on the score's Moveable check box.

Now use the Tools window's Text tool.

Toward the bottom of the screen, create the text shown in Figure 4.14. To create the white text, set the score's ink effect to Ghost

Turn on looping for the movie.

Play the movie.

With the movie running, experiment with dragging the cloud out of the way. Then, since we will not be using this effect until later, remove the instructional text.

CREATING INK EFFECTS IN THE SCORE

Now that we've examined the Trails, Moveable, and Editable check boxes, let's study the item that appears just above these: the Ink Effects pop-up menu. Figure 4.15 shows this menu, displayed by clicking its pop-up arrow. Once an object is selected on the stage, you can also display this menu by pointing to the object, holding down the Ctrl key, and pressing the mouse (highlighting and then releasing to select a menu item). Displayed this way, the menu appears right at the object, rather than in the score.

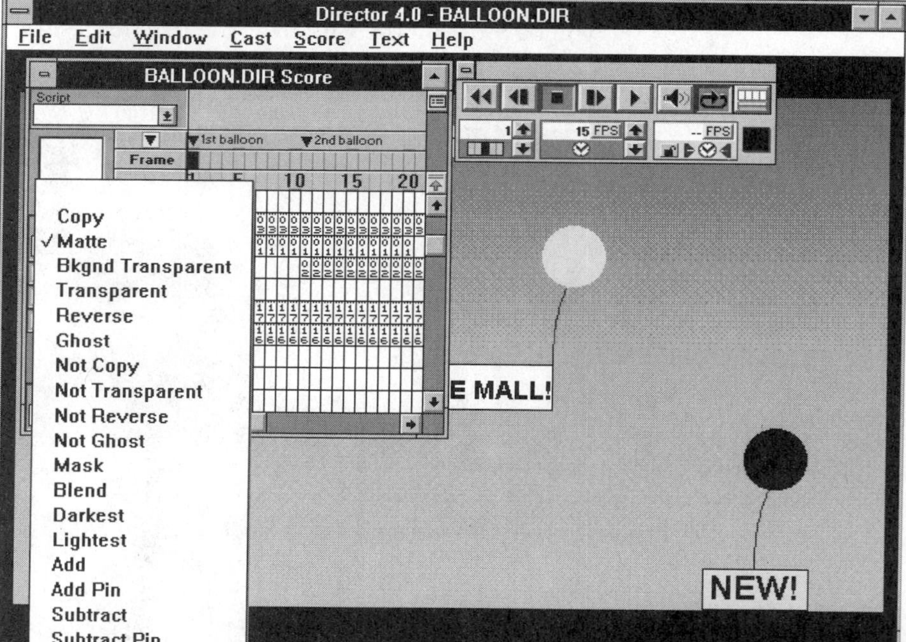

4.15
Menu of ink effects available in the score

Copy is the standard score ink effect, and so far you've changed this to two other ink effects, Matte and Ghost. Figure 4.16 shows examples of these and other Score ink effects when applied to the Soon balloon placed against a black-and-white background.

You can see the ink effects demonstrated in motion by opening the c:\director\tutorial\learning\ink_fx.dir movie. To be able to see all the instructions at

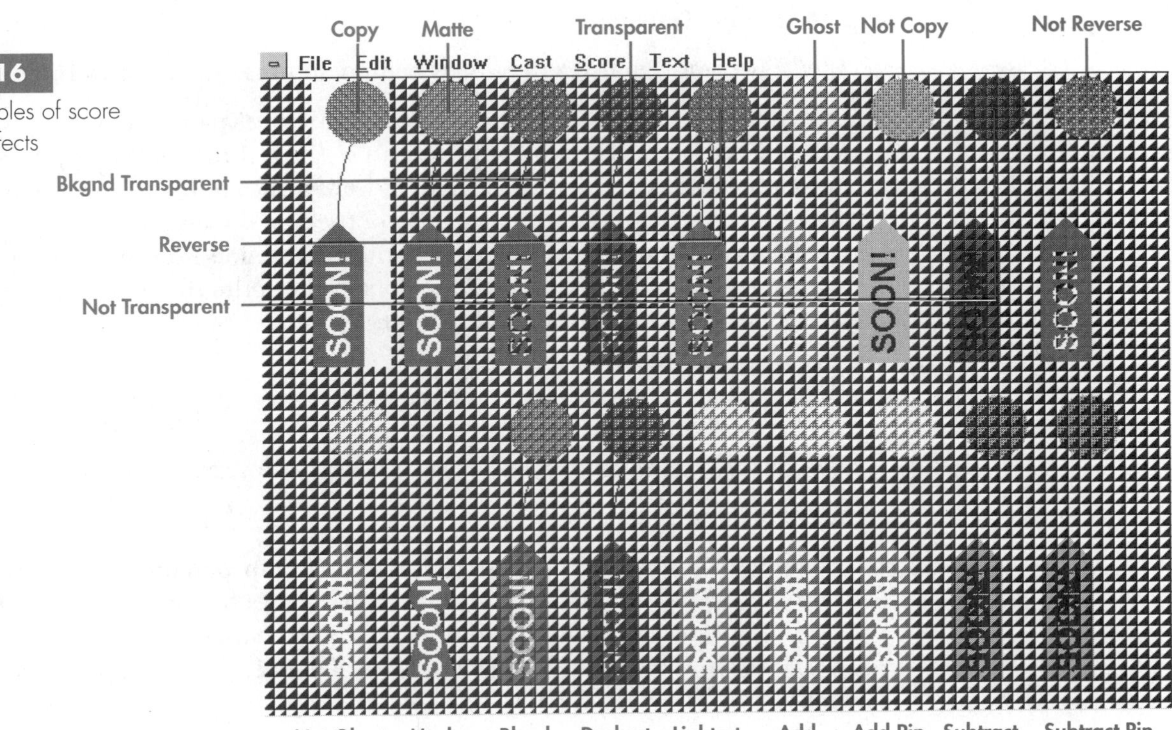

4.16

Examples of score ink effects

the bottom of the screen while viewing, maximize the Director window (bearing in mind the maximizing precautions discussed in Chapter 1). Play the movie and use Ctrl+. (Ctrl with the >. key) to stop it. Refer to Figure 4.16 as you study this list.

Here's a list of the score's ink effects. Refer to Figure 4.16 as you study this list.

- **Copy**

All colors: Remain the same.

This is the standard ink effect. Generally the sprite is simply a copy of its cast member, including the white bounding box around it. However, if you select a sprite and use the Tools window to change the Foreground or Background Color chip, the following occur:

Black: Becomes the color of the Tools window's Foreground Color chip.

White: Becomes the color of the Tools window's Background Color chip.

Colors: Vary unpredictably.

- **Matte**

All colors: Remain the same.

The object's bounding box disappears and what's behind shows around the object. If you select a sprite and use the Tools window to change the Foreground or Background Color chip, the following occur:

Black: Becomes the color of the Tools window's Foreground Color chip.

White: Becomes the color of the Tools window's Background Color chip.

Colors: Vary unpredictably.

- **Bkgnd Transparent**

White: Becomes transparent (what's behind appears rather than white).

Generally, white areas of the object are made transparent, allowing what's behind them (objects or the background) to show through. White pixels that make up patterns become transparent as well. Notice how the background not only shows through the white lettering of the sign but also through the white pixels in the balloon. If you select a sprite and then use the Tools window to change its Background Color chip, colors in the sprite that match that color, rather than white, are made transparent.

- **Transparent**

White: Becomes transparent.

Black: Normally remains black (or becomes other foreground color).

Colors: Vary unpredictably.

Generally, white areas of the object are made transparent, allowing what's behind to show through. This includes white pixels that make up patterns. If you select a sprite and use the Tools window to change its Foreground Color chip, black in the sprite is changed to that color. In Figure 4.16, the red is made transparent, allowing the black to show through.

- **Reverse**

Black in front of black: Becomes white.

Black in front of white: Remains black.

White: Becomes transparent.

Colors: Vary unpredictably.

Notice how the black string in the figure switches between black and white as it crosses over white and black areas, respectively.

- **Ghost**

Black: Becomes white (or other background color).

White: Becomes transparent.

Colors: Vary unpredictably.

Generally, black areas of the object become white. If you select a sprite and use the Tools window to change its Background Color chip, black in the sprite is changed to that color.

- **Not Copy**

All colors: Remain the same.

Like copy, generally the sprite is simply a copy of its cast member, including the white bounding box around it. If you select a sprite and use the Tools window to change the Foreground or Background Color chip, the following occur:

Black: Becomes the color of the Tools window's Background Color chip.

White: Becomes the color of the Tools window's Foreground Color chip.

Colors: Vary unpredictably.

- **Not Transparent**

Black: Becomes transparent (what's behind appears rather than black).

White: Becomes black (or other foreground color).

Colors: Vary unpredictably.

Generally, black areas of the object are made transparent, allowing what's behind to show through. If you select a sprite and use the Tools window to change its Foreground Color chip, white in the sprite is changed to that color.

- **Not Reverse**

Black: Becomes transparent.

White in front of white: Becomes black.

White in front of black: Remains white.

Other Colors: Vary unpredictably.

- **Not Ghost**

Black: Becomes transparent (what's behind appears rather than black).

White: Remains white (or becomes other background color).

Colors: Vary unpredictably.

Generally, white areas of the object remain white. If you select a sprite and use the Tools window to change its Background Color chip, white in the sprite is changed to that color.

- **Mask** Allows you to create a custom cut-out that masks certain parts of a sprite while allowing other parts to remain visible. The figure uses a mask with a keyhole cut-out.

You must create the mask as a cast member (but not necessarily as a sprite) immediately following the cast member you wish to mask (whose sprite must have its ink effect set to Mask). For the mask, use black to create the design you want for the visible portion; leave other areas white. Thus, to create the figure, there is a black keyhole shape against a white background. Then, for this masking cast member, you must set Cast, Transform Bitmap, Color Depth to 1 Bit. (Reducing color depth can also save memory and disk space and speed animation.) You may need to move your masking art around in the Paint window for precise placement; as you do, you may need to drag and remove a window from in front of the sprite before your changes take effect.

- **Blend** Makes the sprite partially transparent depending on how the Score menu's Set Sprite Blend (Ctrl+Alt+B) dialog box (Figure 4.17) is set for the selected sprite. Range is from 1% (completely transparent and hence invisible) to 100% (no transparency and hence opaque). You can change the percentage in this dialog box by clicking the bar (10% for each click) or the arrows (1% for each click) or by dragging the sliding box. In Figure 4.16, the sprite labeled "Blend" is set for 75%.

- **Darkest** For each pixel in the sprite, compares the color of the sprite with whatever color is behind it and displays the darker color.

- **Lightest** For each pixel in the sprite, compares the color of the sprite with whatever color is behind it and displays the lighter color.

4.17

Score menu's Set Sprite Blend dialog box

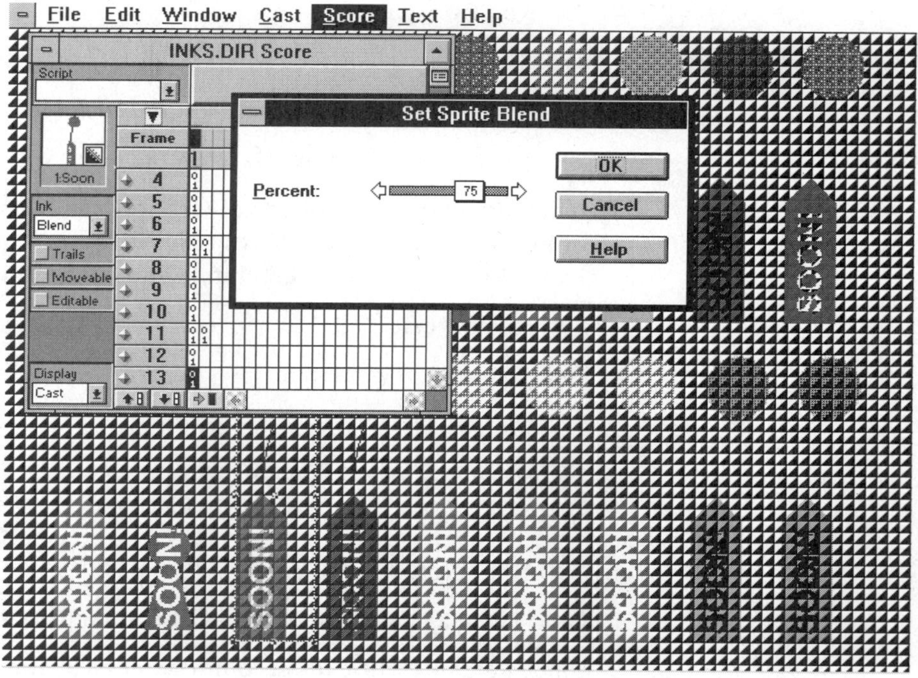

- **Add, Add Pin, Subtract, Subtract Pin** These ink effects deal with the mathematics of color, an advanced use we won't examine.

CHANGING CELL DISPLAYS IN THE SCORE

As you know from your work throughout this and other chapters, cells in the score normally display the number of the cast member assigned to the cell. However, you can also display a variety of other information in the cells. Let's look at what can be displayed and how you can set the score to do so.

Figure 4.18 shows other ways the score can look. In color, each score in the figure shows the setting of the Display pop-up menu, which is the menu you use to set the score's display.

Displaying Cast Members

Cast is the standard setting for the Display pop-up menu. As mentioned, it usually displays the cast numbers. (For cast numbers over 99 the score shows the last two digits; "24" for cast member 124, for example.) You can instead make this display show the first two letters of the cast member's name. Try that with your movie now.

> Open the **Cast** menu's **Cast Window Options** dialog box.

We examined this dialog box in Chapter 3.

> Set the **Cast ID Style** pop-up menu to **Name**.

The score changes and cells now indicate cast names. (When a cast member does not have a name assigned, cells show the cast number instead.)

> Change **Cast, Cast Window Options, Cast ID Style** back to **Number:Name**, the default.

Cast numbers reappear in the score.

4.18
Score displays

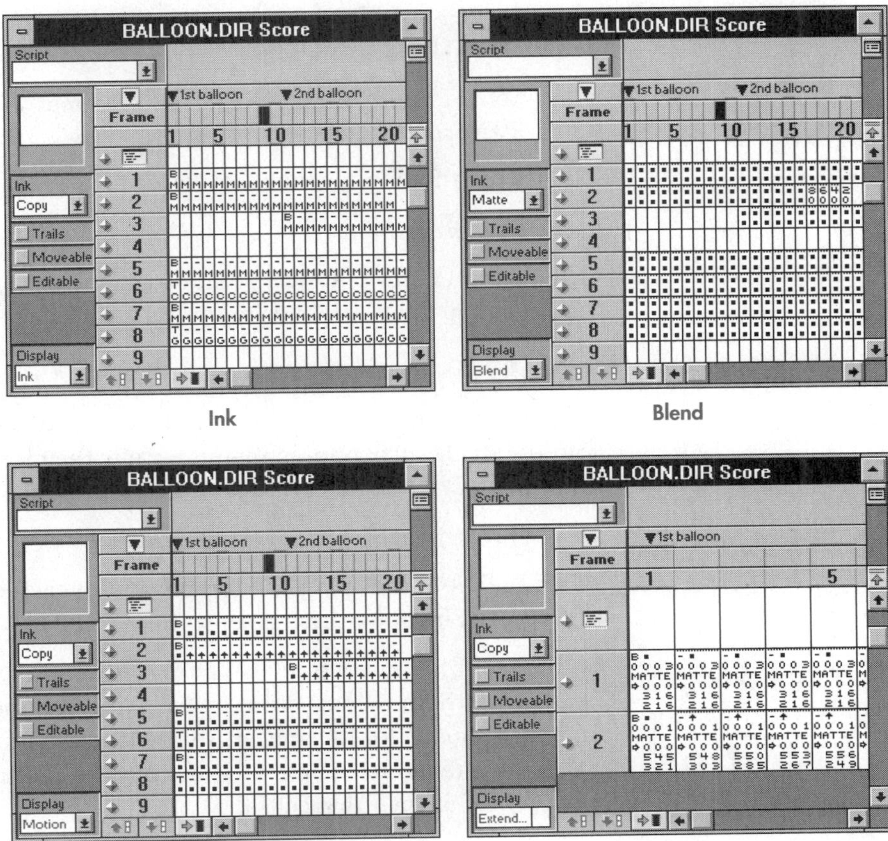

Displaying Ink Effects

The first item on the Display pop-up menu is Extended. We'll return to that item later, but now let's discuss the second item, Ink.

Set the score's Display pop-up menu to Ink.

When you select the Ink display, each cell shows the Ink effect assigned to it. These letters appear at the bottom of the cell. Generally, mnemonic lettering indicates the ink as follows: Copy (C), Matte (M), Transparent (T), Reverse (R), Ghost (G), Blend (B), Darkest (D), Lightest (L), Add (A), and Subtract (S). Bkgnd Transparent's letter (W) reminds you that white is normally made transparent. A graphic indicates Mask (▣). Not and Subtract versions of ink effects display the letter corresponding to their standard counterparts with triple dots underneath.

Additionally, letters at the top of each cell indicate the type of sprite. They appear when the cell contains a bitmap (B), text (T), shape (Q), buttons (X, Y, or Z), or Macintosh PICT file (P). A dot indicates film, video, or movie (•). A hyphen (-) appears at the top if the sprite was created from the same Cast member.

Displaying Blends

In Figure 4.17, you saw the Score menu's Set Sprite Blend dialog box and learned that you assign a blend by providing a percentage. With Blend, you can have the score show the percentage at which this dialog box is set. Normally, the cells show two square dots (⁚), which indicates 100% (no blend).

You can create a blend to make the first balloon fade away as it reaches the top of the stage:

> **Set the blend for cells in channel 2, frames 17 to 20 at 80, 60, 40, and 20, respectively.**

Your score should now look like Figure 4.18's Blend score.

> **Play the movie.**

The balloon fades as it nears the top. In the next chapter you'll see how you can assign graduated blends to multiple cells like this automatically.

Displaying Motion

The next setting is Cast, the default, which we've discussed. After that, you can use the Display pop-up menu to show the motion in your movie. Do that as follows:

> **Set the Display pop-up menu to Motion.**

With the Motion display, the top portion of each cell is similar to that of the Ink display. It shows the type of sprite.

In the lower half of each cell, an arrow indicates the position of the cell's sprite relative to the previous sprite in the same channel. If the sprites' positions match, a square dot (■) appears in the lower half of the cell. Our balloons go up, so in the figure their cells show upward pointing arrows, except for the square dots in their first cells.

Extended Display

Finally, the top item on the Display pop-up menu is Extended. This shows a lot of information about each cell, including information that appears in other displays.

- **First line** Shows the type, motion, and an indicator for blends (B).
- **Second line** Shows the cast member's name or number.
- **Third line** Shows the ink effect (for example, MATTE).
- **Fourth line** Shows a script number, if any; otherwise, 0's appear.
- **Fifth and sixth lines** Show the X and Y coordinates, measuring the top-left corner of the object from the top-left corner of the stage. (When you are using objects created with the Tools window, these numbers match the Score, Sprite Info, Location values, discussed earlier in this chapter. This is not the case with bitmap [paint] cast members, which calculate the X/Y values for Sprite Info by using the cast member's registration point, discussed in Chapter 2.)

At the end of this chapter, we'll look at the Score menu's Score Window Options dialog box and how you can customize the Extended display. For example, you can also have the Extended display show the difference in X and Y values from the previous sprite, in a seventh and eighth line.

SETTING EFFECTS

Now we'll examine the ***effects channels***, special channels that are positioned above channel 1 in the score. You displayed these channels earlier in this chapter (shown labeled earlier in Figure 4.2).

Display the effects channels.

We'll discuss the Tempo, Palette, and Transition channels. We won't examine the Sound or Script channels at this time (see Chapter 6).

Setting Tempos

The first channel is the Tempo channel. It's indicated with a clock-type symbol (shown in color in Figure 4.19). You can change the speed of a movie at a particular frame, or assign other tempo effects. You do this by assigning a tempo to a particular cell in the Tempo channel. The tempo you've set takes effect when the playback head reaches the frame with that cell. For example, let's create a tempo setting for frame 30. With looping turned on, the effect will take place each time the movie reaches the end.

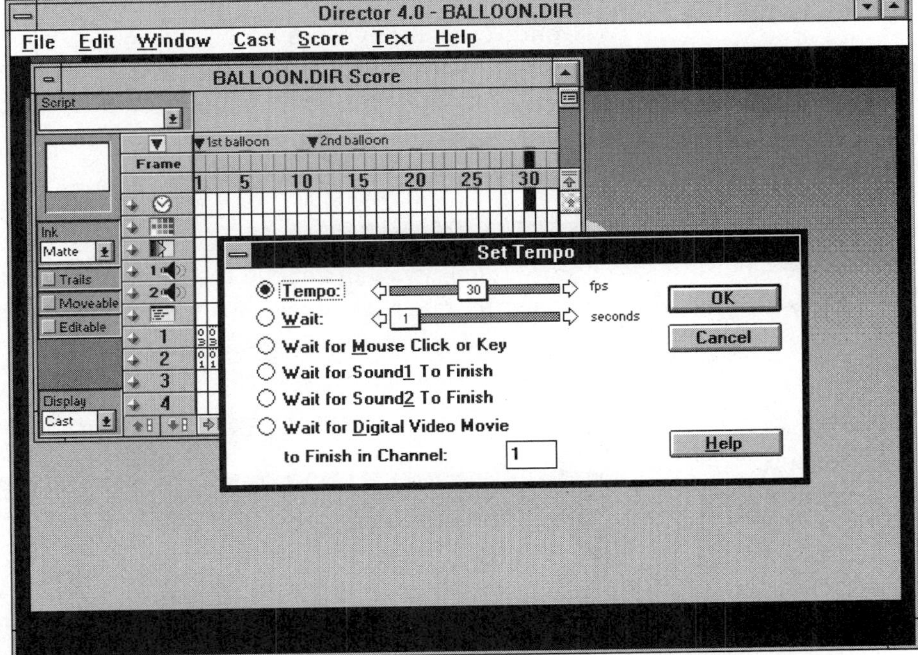

4.19

Score menu's Set Tempo dialog box

To set a tempo, you use the dialog box shown in Figure 4.19. You can display this dialog box for frame 30 in either of two ways:

Click the Tempo channel's frame 30 cell and select Score, Set Tempo, or combine these steps by double-clicking the cell.

The **Tempo** slider is for changing the frames per second. Its normal setting is 30 fps; you could decrease it to slow the movie at the frame position. **Wait** allows you to make the movie pause for the number of seconds you indicate. **Wait For Mouse Click Or Key** makes the movie stop until the user clicks the mouse or presses a key. Additional buttons are for use with sound and video (Chapter 6).

Click the Wait button and set its slider to 5 seconds.

Click the OK button or press the Enter key.

With looping turned on, play the movie.

At the end of each cycle the movie pauses for 5 seconds.

At the same frame, open the Score, Set Tempo dialog box again.

Turn on Wait for Mouse Click or Key.

Click the OK button or press the Enter key.

Rewind and play the movie.

When the movie reaches the end, it stops, and the mouse cursor changes into the shape of a mouse.

Click the mouse or press a key.

The movie repeats.

Remove the tempo setting by selecting its cell and using Edit, Clear Cells or Score, Delete sprites or by pressing the Delete key.

With most displays, cells assigned a tempo show a number that indicates the seconds or FPS assigned by the Score, Set Tempo dialog box. (00 means the Wait For Mouse Click Or Key button is selected.) In Extended display, codes show which button is selected and numbers indicate amounts; for example, TEMPO 5 FPS (Tempo, 5 fps), DELAY 5 SECS (Wait, 5 seconds), WAIT 0 CLICK (Wait For Mouse Click Or Key).

Setting Palettes

At any frame you can change the color palette that a movie uses. To do so, you use the Palette channel (shown in color in Figure 4.20) and the Set Palette dialog box (also in that figure). Director provides several color palettes for you to choose from.

4.20

Score menu's Set Palette dialog box

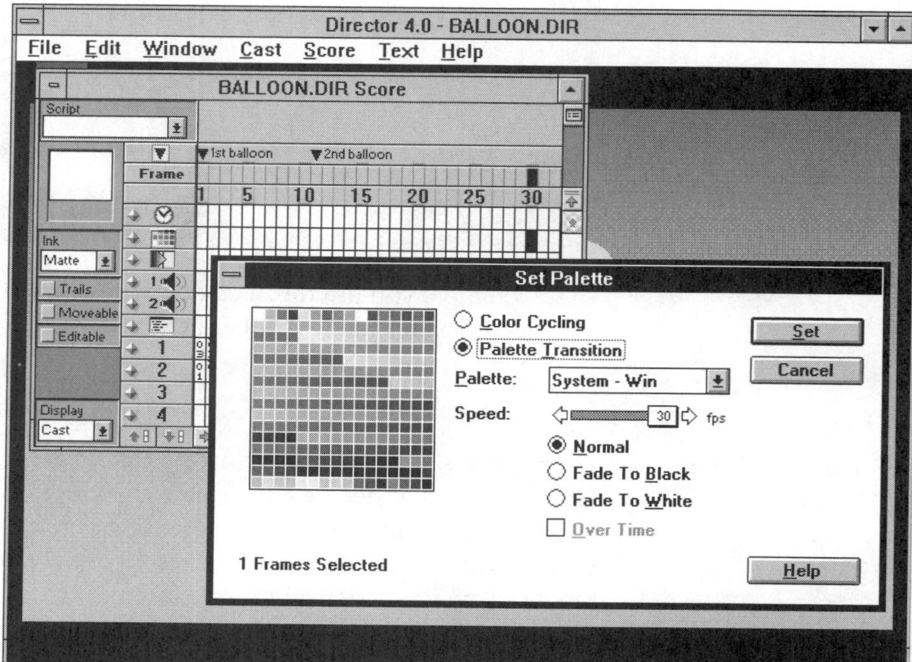

➡ *Important*: Working with color palettes can be disconcerting. When you change the color palette, Director's interface changes too. In fact, colors throughout Windows may change as well. Turn on the File, Preferences, Black And White User Interface check box if necessary, as discussed in Chapter 2.

Let's make the movie change to rainbow colors at the end.

> Click the Palette channel's frame 30 cell and select **Score**, **Set Palette**, or combine these steps by double-clicking the cell.

The **Palette Transition** button is initially turned on. The **Palette** pop-up menu is used to select the new palette the movie will now use; the palette at the left in the dialog box changes to reflect your choice. With **Speed**, you can determine how quickly the colors change. With **Normal**, the colors change directly from one palette to the other. With the **Fade To** buttons, you can make the colors fade to black or white before the new colors fade in. The **Over Time** check box is available when you have more than one Palette cell selected. It will cause the transition to occur over the span of the selected cells.

When **Color Cycling** is turned on, you can drag or you can click and shift-click colors in the palette to indicate a range of colors. Sprites with a color in your selection will rotate among the range of colors you've selected.

With most displays, cells in the Palette channel that have been assigned a palette show a number that represents the type of palette. (The numbers follow the Score, Set Palette, Palette pop-up list, starting with 0 for the first item in this list.) In Extended display, a code indicates color cycling (CYCLE) or palette transition (COLORS) and a number gives the speed and number of cycles. Text also appears for check boxes that are turned on.

➡ *Sidelight*: You can change the palette that a particular bitmap (paint) cast member uses. To do that, you use the Cast window or Paint window to select the cast member and use the Cast, Transform Bitmap, Palette pop-up menu.

Or you can temporarily change it with Cast, Cast Member Info, Palette (Chapter 3).

Setting Transitions

Director provides many built-in methods for changing the screen from one scene to the next. These are called ***transitions*** and they are available through the Transition channel (shown in color in Figure 4.21) and the Set Transition dialog box (also in that figure). Director is generous in the many transitions you can choose from.

For example, we can use a transition at the end of the movie to indicate clearly that the movie is starting over when looping occurs. Let's do that.

> Click the Transition channel's frame 30 cell and select **Score**, **Set Transition**, or combine these steps by double-clicking the cell.

On the left of the dialog box is the scroll list of transitions. In the list, transitions are both spelled out and depicted. There are more than four times the transitions you see in the figure.

4.21

Score menu's Set Transition dialog box

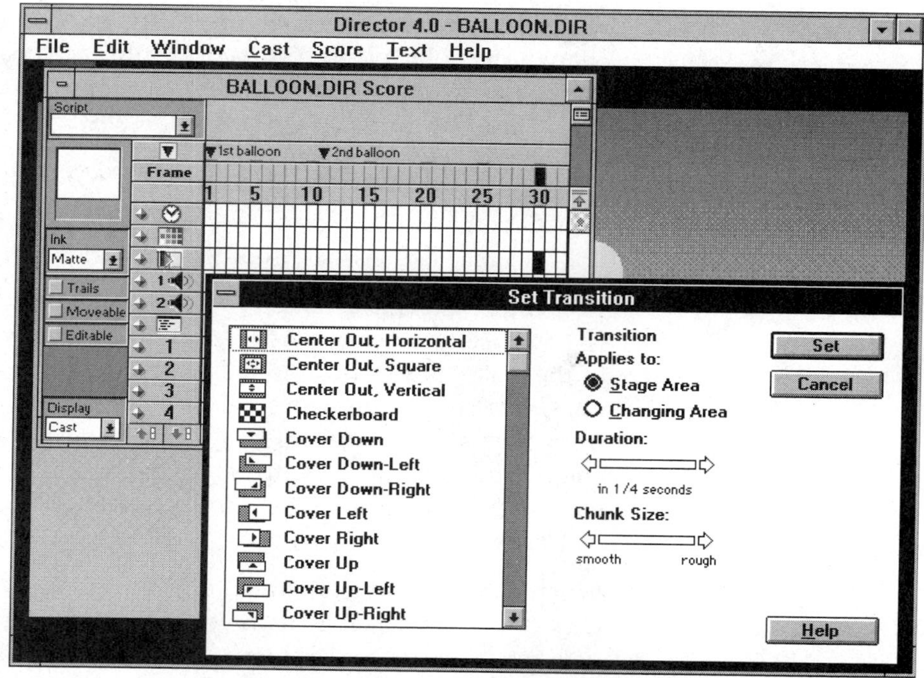

Scroll and examine the list of transitions.

Select the **Push Up** transition.

Turn on the **Stage Area** button.

This is important to do, since most of our stage remains the same when the last frame changes to the first frame. **Stage Area** causes the transition to take place over the entire stage. **Changing Area** shows the transition only on those parts of the stage that differ from one frame to the next.

Careful: Settings on the right side of this dialog box are retained for each transition. So, for example, should you select Stage Area and then change the type of transition, you may need to select Stage Area once again. Be sure the settings are as you want them before you OK the dialog box.

Click the **Set** button or press the Enter key.

Rewind the movie and, with looping turned on, play it.

The **Duration** slider is used for setting the amount of time it takes to complete the transition. It's set in increments of one-fourth of a second and ranges from 0 to 120 (30 seconds). With the **Chunk Size** slider you control how rough or smooth you want the transition to be and determine how much screen changes at a time.

Use the same cell to experiment with the **Set Transition** dialog box's two sliders.

With most displays, cells assigned a transition show a number that represents the type of transition. (You can see a listing of these code numbers with their transitions by going to Help, Contents, Search, puppetTransition. Puppet-Transition is a Lingo command.) In Extended display, a graphic indicates the type of transition (like graphics in the Score, Set Transition dialog box), numbers give the duration and chunk size, and a code indicates whether the transition applies to the stage (STGE) or the changing (CHNG) area.

CUSTOMIZING THE SCORE

Let's round out our examination of the score by looking at ways that you can customize it.

Open the Score menu and select Score Window Options.

The dialog box in Figure 4.22 appears.

4.22

Score menu's Score Window Options dialog box

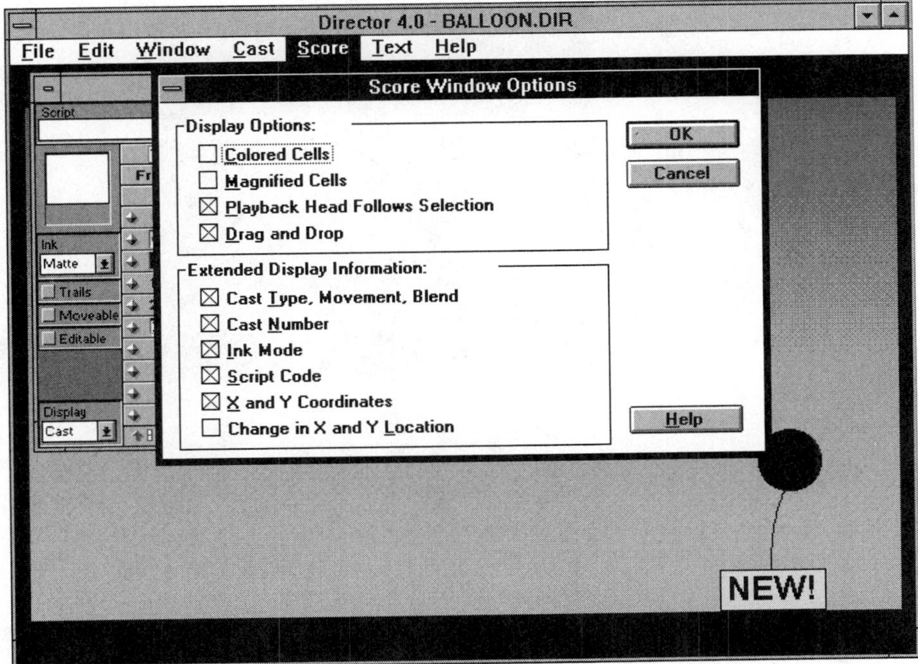

Setting Score Window Options

Colored Cells is the first check box in this dialog box. When this check box is turned on, a small palette of colored chips appears in the left part of the score (as shown in color in Figure 4.23). You can use these chips to color cells, just for the purpose of marking the cells. For example, as you work with this movie you may want to indicate the cells in frame 11, where the second balloon appears. That way you can more easily keep your bearings when you scroll the movie as you work.

Turn on the Colored Cells check box.

Click the OK button or press the Enter key.

Select the cells in frame 11, channels 1, 2, and 3.

Click one of the Colored Cells chips to color the cells, as shown in the figure.

Should you turn off the Colored Cells check box, the coloring goes away but the movie records its location. When the Colored Cells check box is turned on again, the coloring returns, correctly placed.

4.23
Colored cells

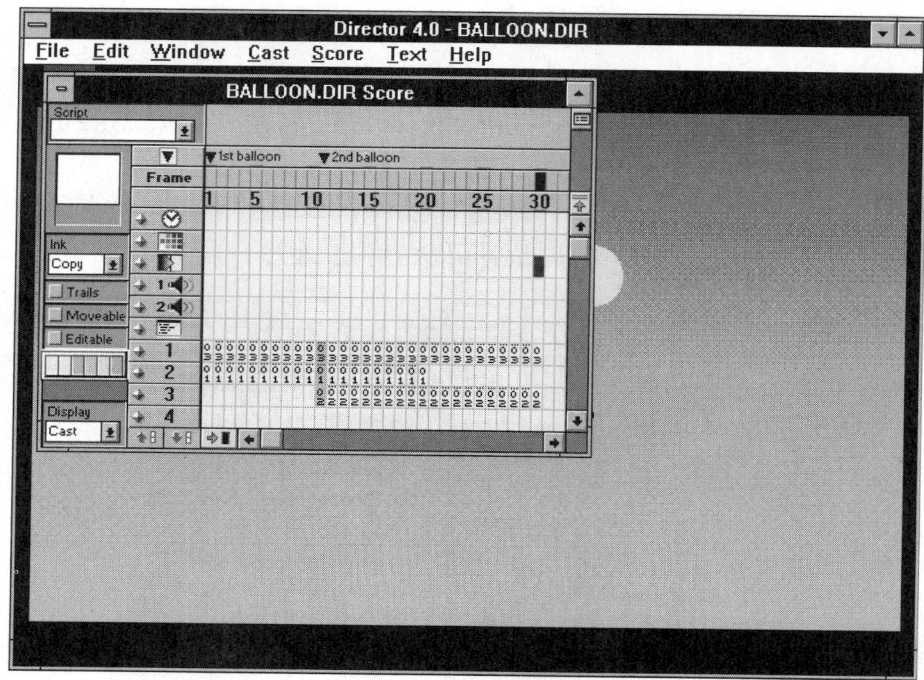

Magnified Cells causes the score to display larger versions of the cells, a display that can be helpful for viewing with some video drivers. **Playback Head Follows Selection** is normally turned on, so the playback head relocates to the frame with the cell you select. (Alternatively, you can switch by holding the Alt key as you click.) **Drag And Drop** allows you to drag selected cells to new locations; when this checkbox is turned off, dragging in the score selects cells instead. (Alternatively, you can switch by holding down the Spacebar as you drag.)

Setting Extended Display Information

The Extended Display Information group controls what appears when the score's Display pop-up menu is set to Extended, as discussed earlier in conjunction with Figure 4.18. In Figure 4.22 the defaults are checked. You can turn on the **Change in X and Y Location** check box to show the amount of sprite movement, as mentioned earlier in this chapter. Or you can turn off settings that you don't need to view, thereby increasing the number of cells that can be displayed in a given area.

CHAPTER REVIEW

KEY TERMS

sprite channels
Jump To Top button
Jump button
frame counter
shuffling
channel button
nudging
tweaking
marker
marker well
editable text
trails
moveable sprites
effects channels
transitions

REVIEW QUESTIONS

1. **T F** The Jump To Top button always makes the score go to the same place, the score's top channel.
2. **T F** Dragging across cells doesn't always select them, though it can.
3. **T F** Score, Insert Frame inserts an empty frame at the playback head.
4. Pressing an arrow key moves the selected sprite(s) by one pixel as long as which window is not open?
5. Before creating lines and hollow shapes with the Tools window, what should you check about the Tools window's Line Width selector?
6. Which ink effect do you use if you want the white areas of the selected sprite to disappear, allowing items behind to show through?
7. Which channel do you use to have the movie pause for the user to click the mouse or press a key?
8. Which type of display provides the most information, information that you can customize?

PROJECTS

1. Using the cast members you've created, make balloons in a variety of shapes and sizes and have them rise, stretch, and otherwise change, demonstrating techniques you've studied in this chapter. (Save this new version of the movie under a different name.)
2. Create some signs that remain in place and are aligned precisely with one another.
3. Make the signs editable so the user can tab from one to another to change them.
4. Apply trails and various ink effects to different balloons. Use markers to document your work.
5. Slow the rise of some balloons and make the signs change with transitions.

5

Animation and File Procedures

THIS CHAPTER WILL TEACH YOU HOW TO

- **Use in-between techniques to animate changes in size, position, blend, and other characteristics.**
- **Record animation, frame by frame or in real time.**
- **Make wholesale changes in sprites and cast members with regard to time and location.**
- **Distort a cast member and animate the distorting.**
- **Automatically automate text with various effects and create items for presentations (bar charts and bulleted lists).**
- **Manipulate files, by using such procedures as importing and exporting.**

In this chapter we'll be performing a variety of advanced animation applications. In addition, we'll examine procedures that apply to entire movies, such as importing, exporting, and compacting.

As we work through this chapter we'll use existing and new cast members. Figure 5.1 shows the current cast members. You may have additional cast members depending on the projects you have completed. In the figure, the cast members are somewhat organized by rows, with seven cast members per row.

It's not vital to have your cast members organized in this fashion but that is the convention followed in this book. Cast numbers need not match as long as cast members are named and placed in the correct cells in the score, and procedures refer to the cast members by name rather than number.

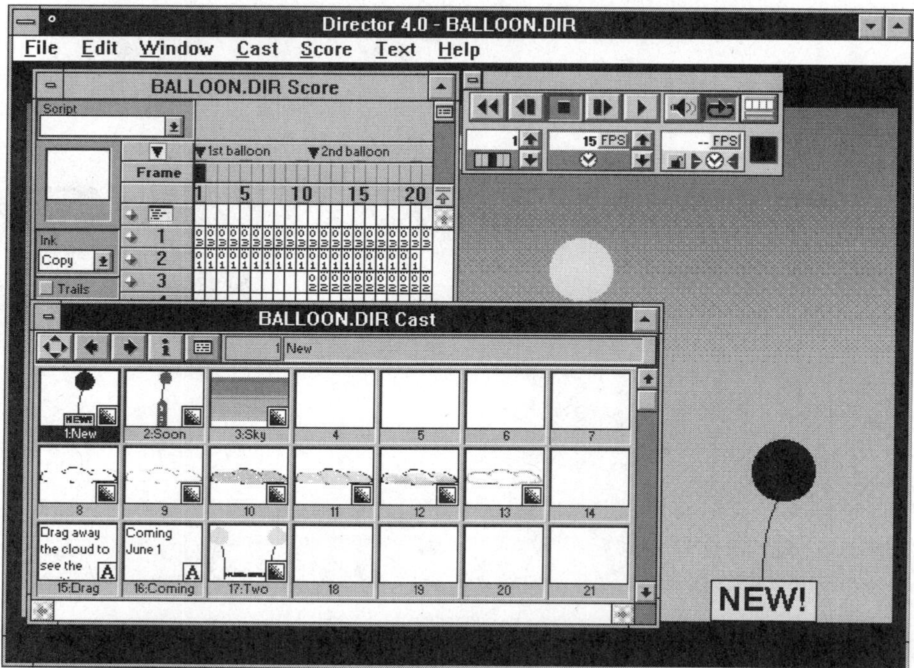

5.1
Cast members in the score

Sidelight: You can sort your cast members to organize them by name, size, and other criteria. To do that, you use the Cast window to select the cast members you want sorted. (Use Edit, Select All or Ctrl+A to sort all cast members.) Then open the Cast menu's Sort Cast Members dialog box, select the appropriate criteria, and click the Sort button.

Also as we continue, we'll be working with a white background.

Change the background color of the BALLOON.DIR movie to white (discussed in Chapter 2).

ADDITIONAL IN-BETWEENING TECHNIQUES

You've used in-betweening to move an object from one location to another. You can also use in-betweening to generate sprites that handle changes in characteristics other than position. For example, you can change the size of a sprite and have Director automatically change its size gradually. Or you can in-between both size and position.

In-Betweening Size and Multiple Positions

First, let's change the size of a sprite. Then you'll see how you can change the position simultaneously.

To show the exercises clearly in the figures, a new cast member with just a balloon and no sign is used. You can create such a cast member (by using the Paint window to copy an existing cast member and remove the sign) or you can just use an existing cast member with a sign. We'll be making changes in the size of the sprite but not in the cast member.

Place a sprite of the cast member into frame **30**.

Add three more sprites of the same cast member to every fifth frame.

In the first sprite (frame 30), use the sprite's handles to enlarge the sprite as shown in Figure 5.2.

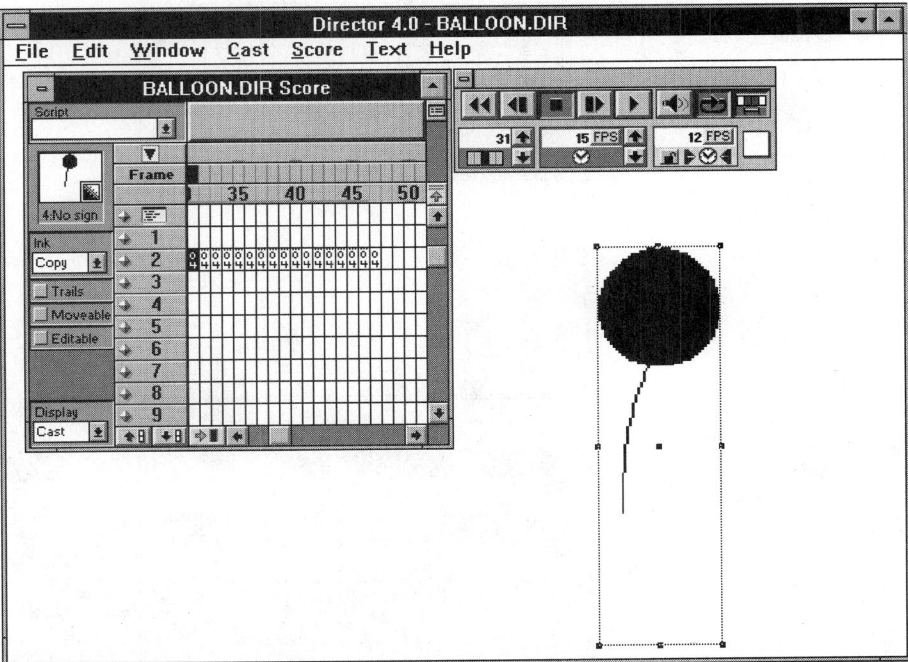

5.2
First position for in-betweening size

Keep the next sprite the same size as the cast member (Figure 5.3) but make the one after that smaller than the original (Figure 5.4), and reduce the fourth sprite as much as possible.

If we were to change the size of the sprite and/or its position in a strictly ***linear*** (straight line) fashion, you would need to create only the first and final sprites; Director could generate all the ones that appear in between. However, by placing the additional sprites, you can create a curving path for the balloon to follow, as we will do shortly. First, though, we'll simply create the shrinking.

With the first through last cells of the sprite's channel selected, use **Score, In-Between Linear** or Ctrl+B to generate the intervening sprites.

Select these frames and play only them (as discussed in Chapter 2).

As you do this, the balloon shrinks in size, appearing to float off in the distance. To give you an idea of what you should obtain, Figure 5.5 shows the result of turning on trails (discussed in Chapter 4) for these cells and playing the frames. (Only the left edge of the balloon appears in this figure as the rest is covered in each succeeding frame.) You needn't have trails turned on; it's only done here for the purpose of creating the figure.

As balloons drift off, of course, they seldom rise in a straight line. You can make the balloon move in a meandering fashion as it goes away.

5.3

Second position for in-betweening size

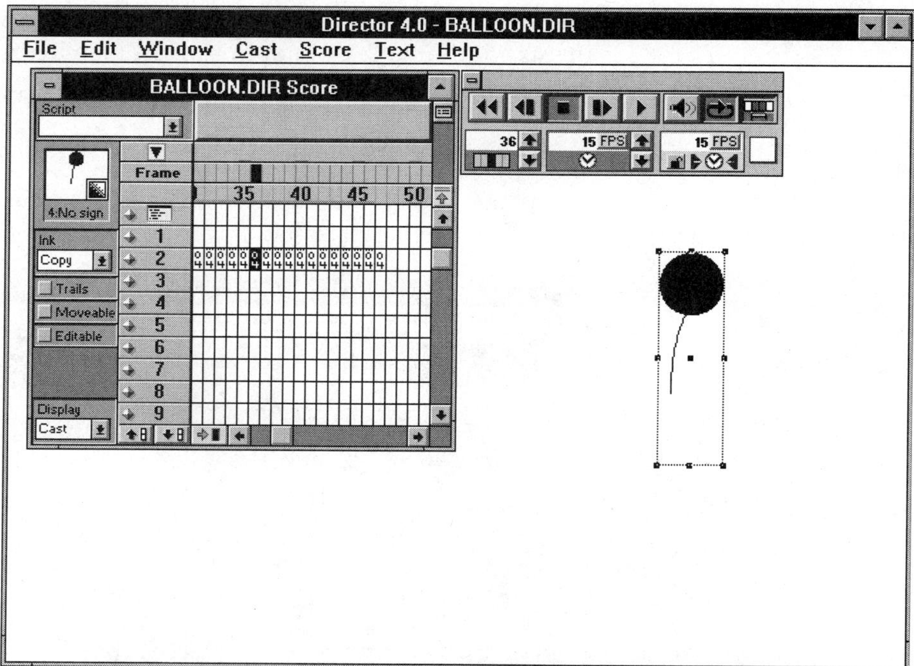

5.4

Third position for in-betweening size

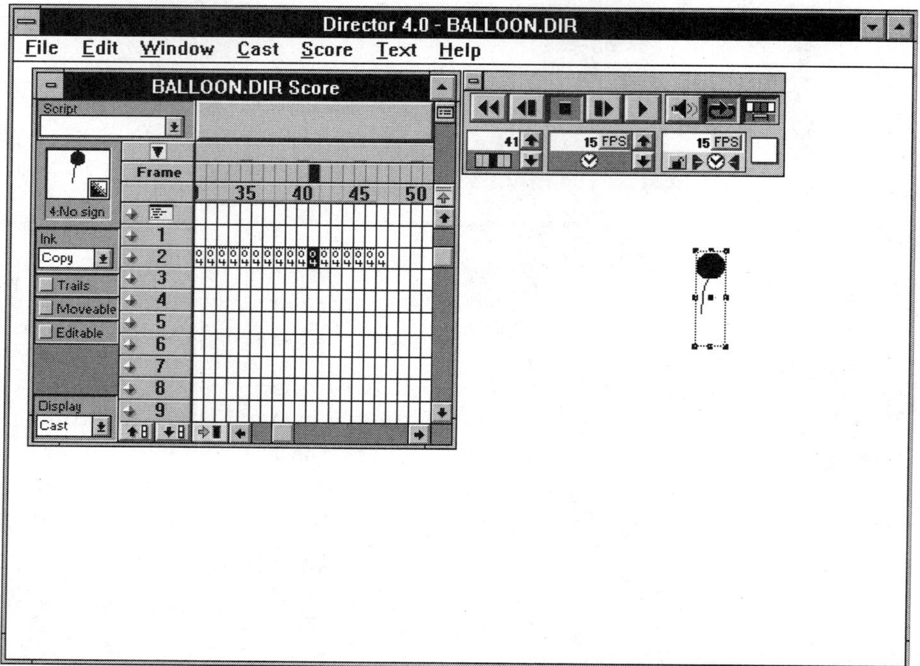

Reminder: As you proceed, remember that cells with generated sprites have dots above their cast number. Cells with sprites you created do not have dots.

Select the cell with the sprite you created that's the same size as the cast member.

On the stage, drag its corresponding sprite to the right.

Select the cell with the balloon sprite you created that's smaller than the cast member.

On the stage, drag its corresponding sprite to the left.

5.5

Balloon trails showing diminishing size

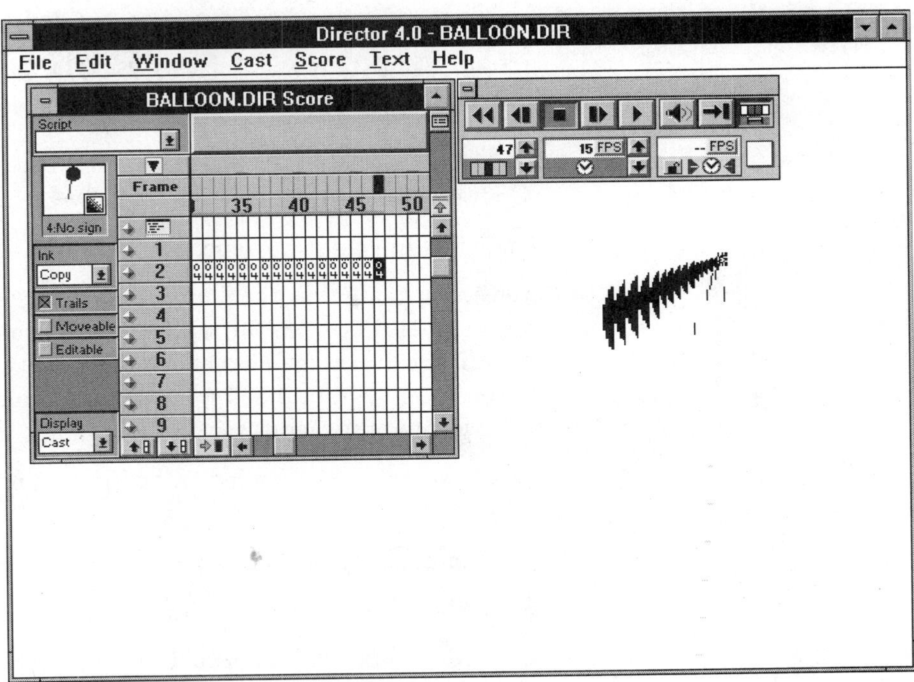

Regenerate the in-between sprites and play the frames.

The balloon wavers as it shrinks.

Special In-Betweening

Director provides a method for in-betweening other aspects of sprites—blends and speed, for example. To create such ***special in-betweening***—that is, in-betweening other than size and linear position—you use the dialog box shown in Figure 5.6. The following examples, which demonstrate this, use the same sprites with which we've been working. However, all are the same size as the cast member. Prepare to continue as follows:

5.6

Score menu's In-Between Special dialog box

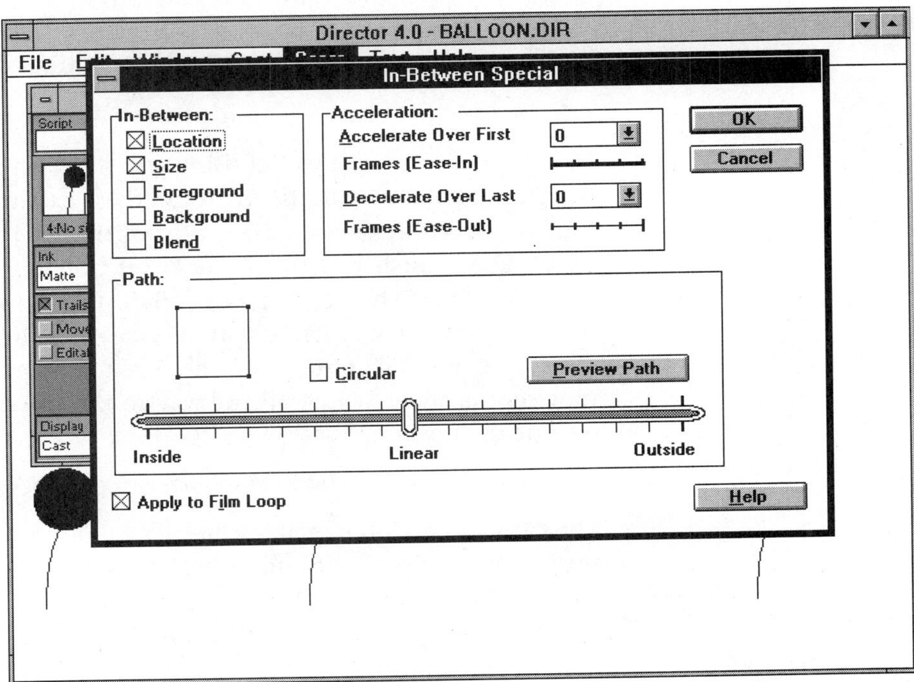

In turn, select each of the bigger and smaller sprites you created and return them to their initial size by using the **Score**, **Sprite Info**, **Restore to Size of Cast Member** check box.

Regenerate the in-between sprites.

Open the **Score** menu and select **In-Between Special**.

The dialog box in Figure 5.6 appears.

In-Between normally has the *Location* and *Size* check boxes turned on. Left like this, the dialog box has the same effect as using Score, In-Between Linear or Ctrl+B. You can use the *Foreground*, *Background*, and *Blend* check boxes to in-between the foreground color, background color, or percentage of blend. Try in-betweening the blend.

Select the cell corresponding to the last sprite in this series, which should be a standard (not in-between) sprite.

Use **Score**, **Set Sprite Blend** to set its blend to **20%**.

Select the third and fourth standard sprites and all sprites in between.

Use **Score**, **In-Between Special**, **Blend** on these cells.

Play the movie.

The balloon should fade out over the last few frames.

The **Acceleration** section can be used to speed up (***accelerate***) the animation or slow it down (***decelerate***). All you need do is set the corresponding drop-down list to the number of final frames in the sequence over which the change should occur (or you can use *Other* to provide your own number of frames).

Experiment with changing the acceleration of the balloon.

The **Path** section of this dialog box is rather curious. In it, a slider switch can be set to *Inside*, *Linear*, *Outside*, or positions in between. As you drag the switch, the rectangular (Path) box in this section changes to correspond to the slider, showing a curved path inside the dots or outside them.

Adjust the slider switch and observe the effect on the Path box.

Figure 5.7 shows the effect of using this slider on sprites in a path. Again for the purpose of clarity in the figure, all these examples were created with trails turned on. The first shows the sprite positions before in-betweening. The second is accomplished with the slider set to Linear; the result is the same as using Score, In-Between Linear or Ctrl+B. The third example shows what happens with the slider switch set all the way to the Inside setting; curving occurs inside the original sprite positions. The fourth example shows the result of moving the slider switch all the way to the Outside setting; curving occurs outside the positions.

Generate these examples in turn in the frames that follow (frames 31–46).

The *Circular* check box makes Director attempt to create a circular path from the starting sprite to the ending sprite. To accomplish this, both sprites must be in the *same position*. (You can ensure that this is the case by positioning one of the sprites and then copying and pasting it to the second location.)

5.7

Linear and special in-betweening

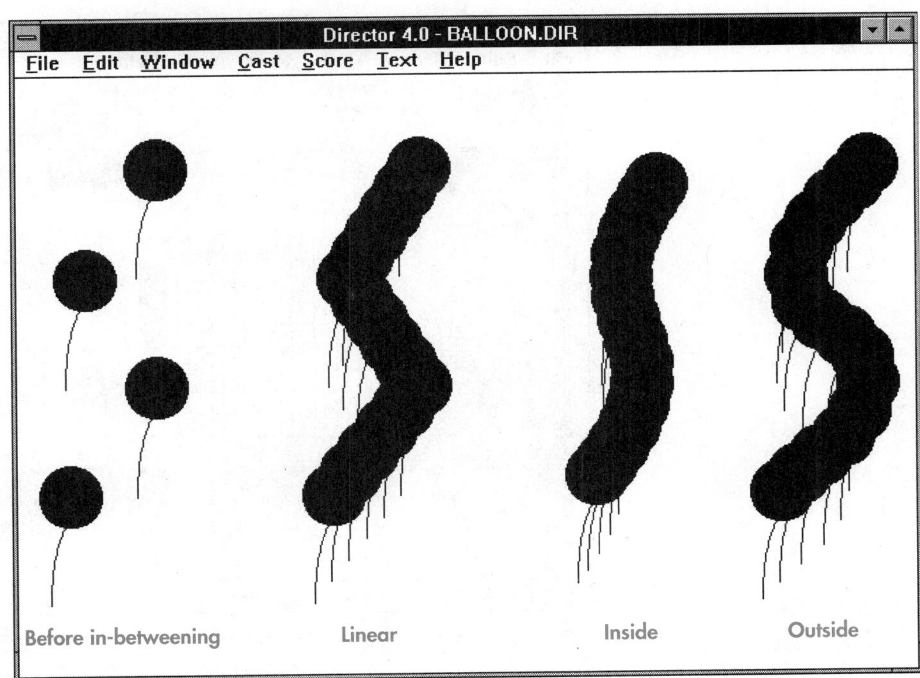

The *Preview Path* button displays a line on the stage that shows the path the sprites will take. You can use it before generating the sprites to see whether they will accomplish the effect you need.

RECORDING ANIMATION

Another way to create animations is by recording them. There are two methods of recording: ***step recording*** (recording one frame at a time) and ***real-time recording*** (recording your movements as you make them). Neither of these methods uses in-betweening; they both create standard sprites in each frame. We'll begin with step recording.

Step Recording

Step recording begins automatically, as soon as you place a sprite. Once begun, you simply advance the movie, frame by frame, repositioning the sprite as desired for each frame. Because step recording allows you to control the sprite in each frame of the animation, it's useful in situations that demand precise placement. Use step recording to animate a balloon rising in frames 47 to 67.

Drag a cast member to frame **47** to create a sprite there.

The red step-recording indicator, which shows that step recording has been activated, appears next to the channel number, as shown in color at the left in Figure 5.8.

Important: At this point, it's vital not to play, rewind, or otherwise manipulate the movie except as follows. Such actions will turn off step recording. Step recording cannot be turned back on except by creating the sprite again.

Use **Edit, Step Forward** or an equivalent such as Ctrl+→ (Ctrl with the right-arrow key) or the keypad 3 key or the keypad 6 key or the Control Panel's Step Forward button, shown in color at the right in Figure 5.8.

5.8
Using step recording and the step-recording indicator

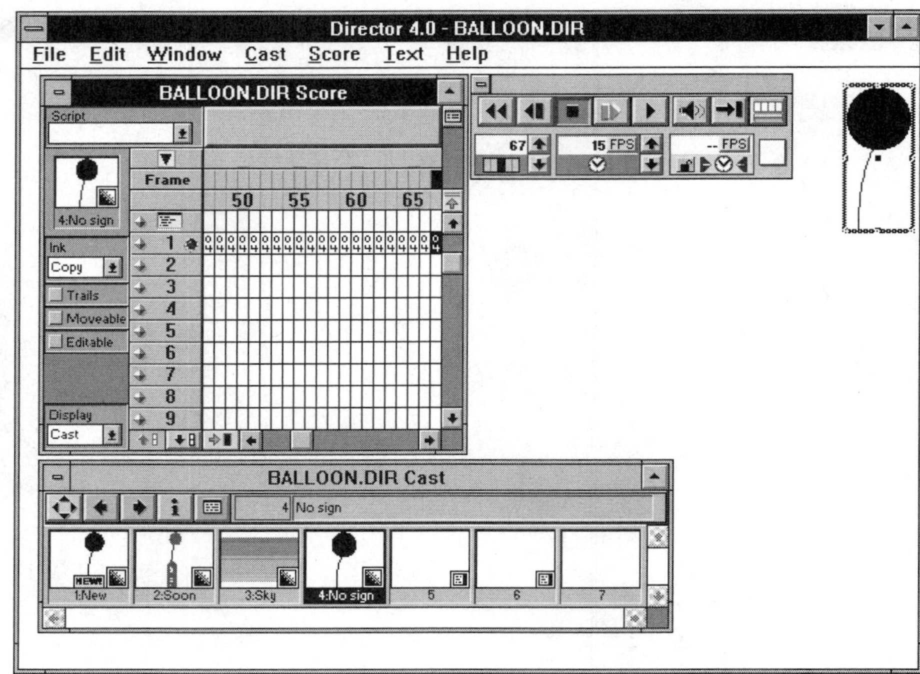

The movie advances to the next frame and step recording remains active, as evidenced by the step-recording indicator that still appears next to the channel number.

Move the sprite to its new position for the second frame of the animation.

Repeat the process (step forward, move sprite) for each remaining frame of the animation.

Play these frames of the movie.

The results are probably jerkier than they are with in-betweening.

Real-Time Recording

With real-time recording, Director simply records your motions as you drag a sprite about on the stage. It creates additional sprites that, when played back, exactly duplicate the motions you made while recording. In this section, you'll create another rising balloon by using real-time recording.

Real-time recording is tricky. You may want to read all the following steps before attempting it. Also, be prepared to do more than one take, as you will probably need practice to create animation that begins and ends smoothly.

Place the balloon in frame **67** and move the playback head to that frame.

Press and hold **Ctrl+Spacebar**.

Still holding Ctrl+Spacebar, **click** the cell in the score where you want the real-time recording to begin. Keep holding Ctrl+Spacebar.

The red real-time recording indicator appears next to the number of the channel that you've selected, as shown in color in Figure 5.9. In the next step, when you release Ctrl+Spacebar, recording begins and you should immediately begin dragging the object.

5.9

Real-time recording and the real-time recording indicator

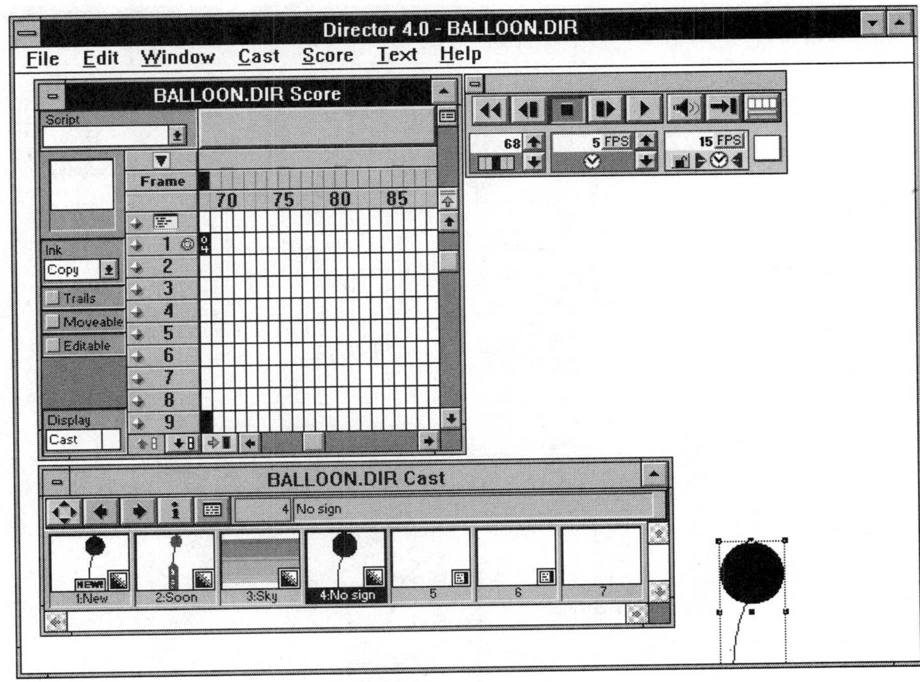

Still holding Ctrl+Spacebar, **point** within the object (at the registration point, discussed later in this chapter, to be exact), **press** the mouse, then **release** Ctrl+Spacebar and **drag** to create the animation.

If you watch the score as you do this, you'll see the playback head move, showing the recording operation as it occurs.

Play these frames of the movie and try again if necessary.

MANIPULATING SPRITES TOGETHER

Now that you can create sprites, let's examine ways that you can manipulate them in the score. For example, you can change sprites from channels to frames, or from cast positions to channels or frames.

Using Space To Time

You can use these procedures to create animation. For example, you can position sprites at various locations in one frame and lay out an animation path with them. Then you can use Space To Time to assign the sprites to different frames, thereby creating the animation. Try that as follows:

Assign four sprites from the same Cast member to four channels in the same frame, as shown in Figure 5.10.

Select the four cells with the sprites, as shown in the figure, and open the **Score** menu and select **Space To Time**.

The dialog box that appears suggests:

```
Spread sprites 1 frame(s) apart.
```

Change this setting to **5** frames and click the **OK** button or press the Enter key.

5.10

Sprites positioned for Score, Space To Time

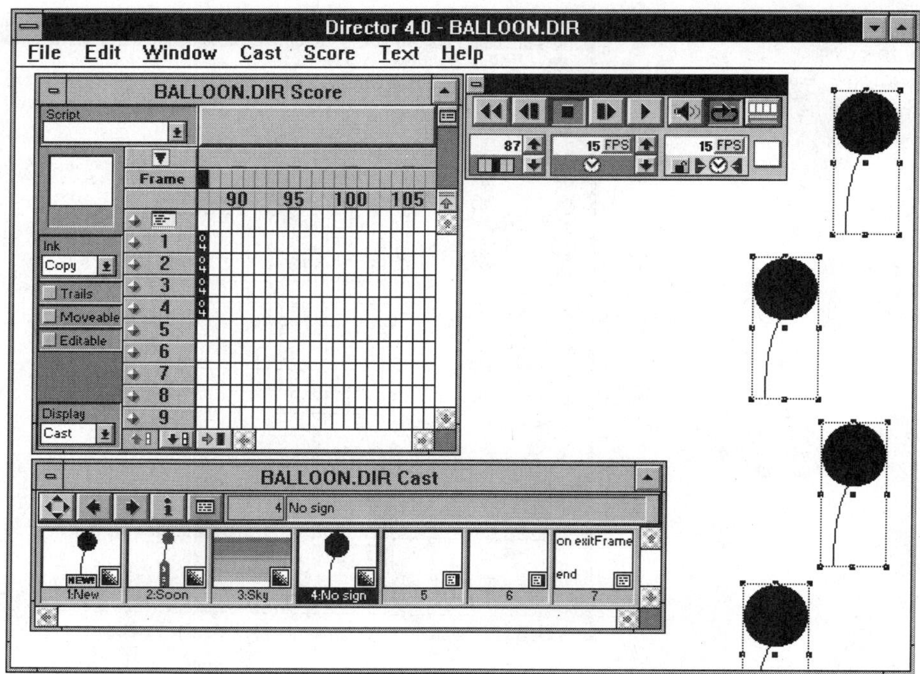

This moves the sprites from channels 2, 3, and 4 in the same frame to positions in every fifth cell in the first channel.

Use in-betweening to fill in the intervening cells.

Play these frames of the movie.

Using Cast To Time

You can also move multiple cast members to the score to create sprites in different ways. We'll try that in this section.

With this exercise we'll begin building our movie so that after the introduction there are various sequences that show the different kinds of shops and merchandise to be available in the huge mall. Prepare for that as follows.

Save the **BALLOON.DIR** movie and make a copy of it by saving it under a new name.

The copy you create shows your work on the various methods of creating animation in this chapter so far.

Print out or provide copies of this file to your instructor as directed.

Open the **BALLOON.DIR** movie again.

Now you'll make changes to this file to begin creating the movie as described.

Move the animation you have created in this chapter so far to channels in the first 30 frames. Change colors or patterns, add signs, or simply remove them to create your own individual display.

Now we'll create a marquee for a fictitious theatre that will have a space at the mall. To do that, we'll use cast members already created and provided with Director.

Open and play the movie **\director\clips\animatn\marquee1.dir**.

It shows a marquee with operating chaser lights.

Select the three cast members that make up this movie and copy them to the clipboard.

Open your **BALLOON.DIR** movie.

In the Cast window, select cast position **22** and there paste the three cast members from the clipboard.

The three cast members from the marquee1.dir movie are now cast members in your movie. Now to add them to your score.

Select the starting cell for the marquee (frame 35, channel 1).

Select the three cast members.

Select **Cast**, **Cast to Time**, or hold down the Alt key and drag the selected cast members to the score (Figure 5.11).

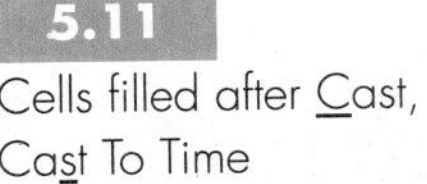

5.11

Cells filled after Cast, Cast To Time

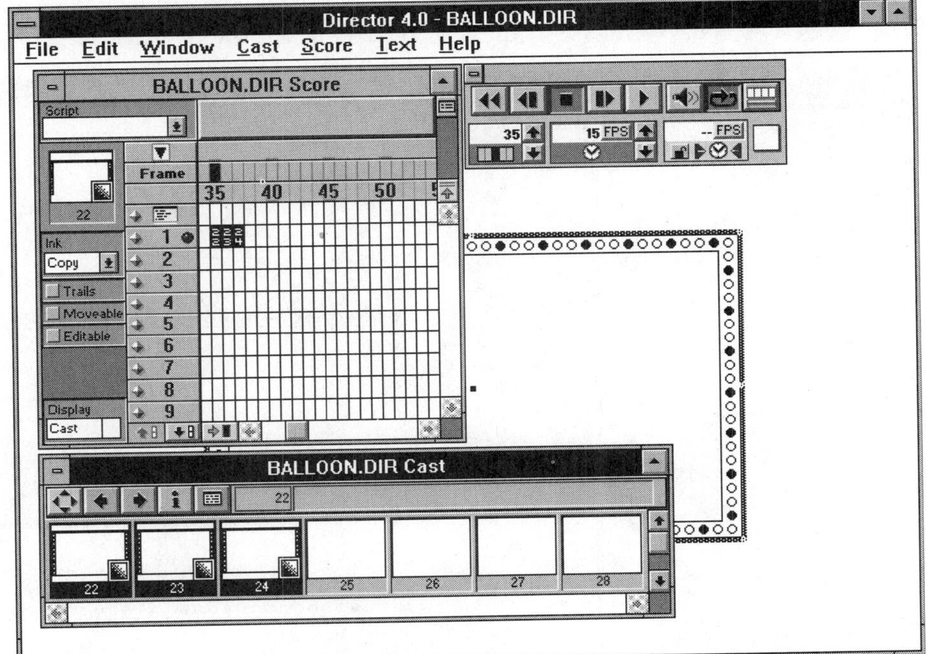

Normally, when you drag cast members to the score they all head for the same frame. Holding the Alt key makes them occupy separate, though sequential, frames. (If you did drag without holding the Alt key you could then use Score, Space To Time to achieve the same result.)

With looping turned on, play these frames of the movie.

In each frame a different set of chaser lights is lit. Playing the movie makes the lights appear to travel in a counterclockwise direction.

Once an animated sequence has been created you can assign that sequence to a single cast member, called a ***film loop***. To do that you select the cells that make up the sequence and drag them to a position in the Cast window. The Film Loop cast member can then be placed in the movie to show the animation when the movie is played. What's more, the film loop itself can be moved about the screen. Thus if you created a film loop of the marquee, you could record movement of the film loop's sprite on the stage. The result is a marquee sliding across the stage whose chaser lights are moving as well.

Reversing a Sequence of Cells

You can reverse a sequence of cells in the score as well. Let's reverse these three cells to change the direction of the lights.

With the three cells selected as in Figure 5.11, open the **Score** menu and select **Reverse Sequence**.

Play these frames of the movie.

Now the chaser lights appear to travel clockwise.

Copy this sequence three times so you have a total of four sets.

You may wish to slow the tempo for this portion of the movie (Chapter 4).

Finally, use the **Tools** window and in-betweening to create the boxed "Theatre" display as shown in Figure 5.12.

5.12
Marquee created

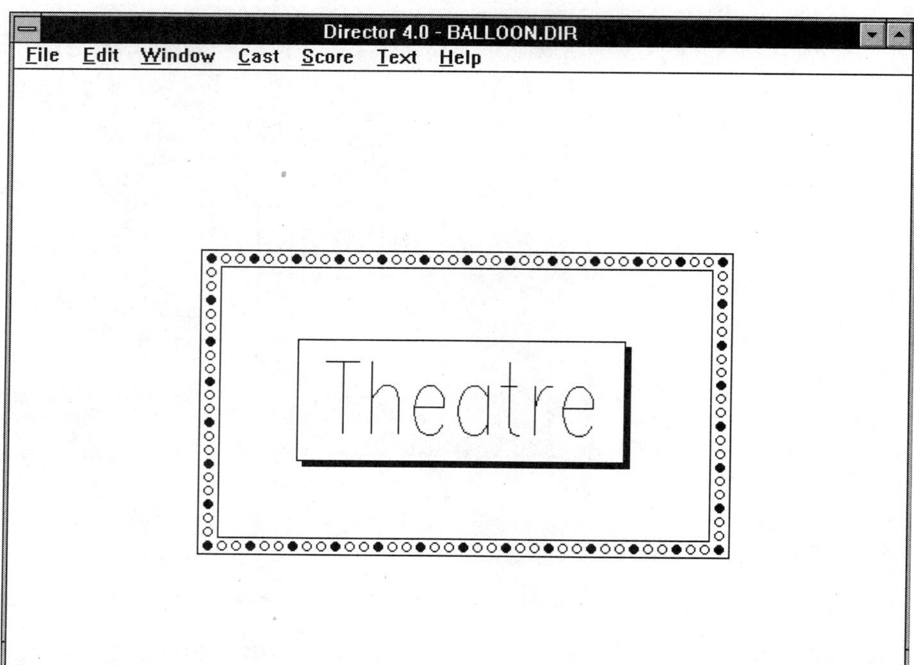

AUTO DISTORT

Auto distort is another important animation instrument. The process uses an existing cast member that you modify with one of several specific effects. It automatically creates cast members that reflect a progression from the original shape to the modified shape. You can then assign the new cast members to the score and thereby create animation that changes the shape of an image on the screen.

We'll create a box that turns on its side. Begin by creating the original cast member.

Open the **Paint** window and create the box in Figure 5.13.

5.13
Paint art created to be rotated

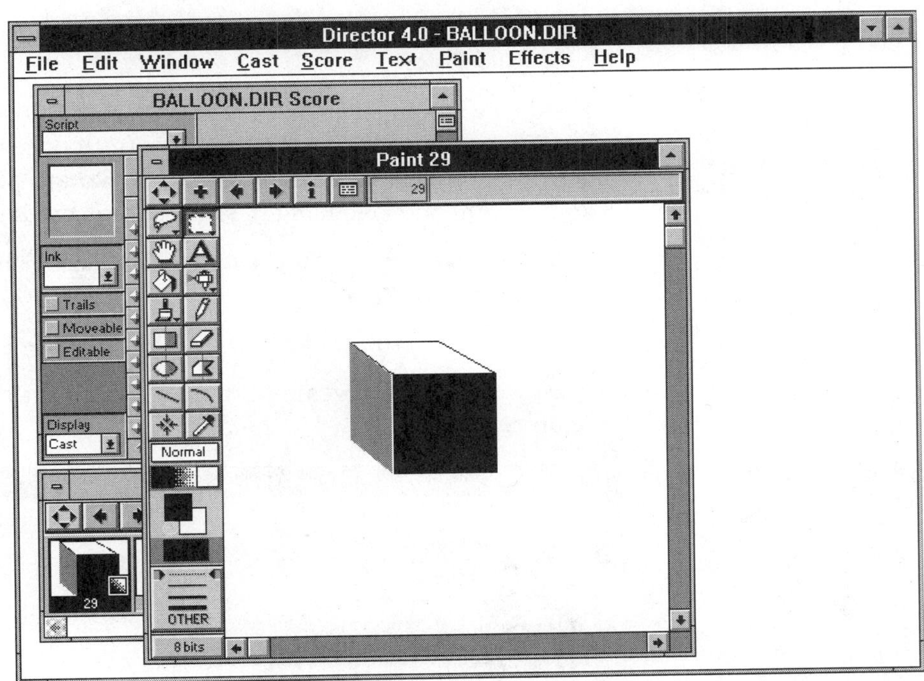

In the example the box is assigned to cast number 29.

Use a shrink-style Selection Rectangle to select the box.

A no-shrink selection rectangle will also allow you to use an effect. Lasso selecting will not.

Open the Paint window's **Effects** menu and select **Rotate Right**.

The box rotates 90 degrees to the position shown in Figure 5.14, surrounded by moving dashes. Leave the selection rectangle in place.

5.14
Effects menu's Auto Distort dialog box

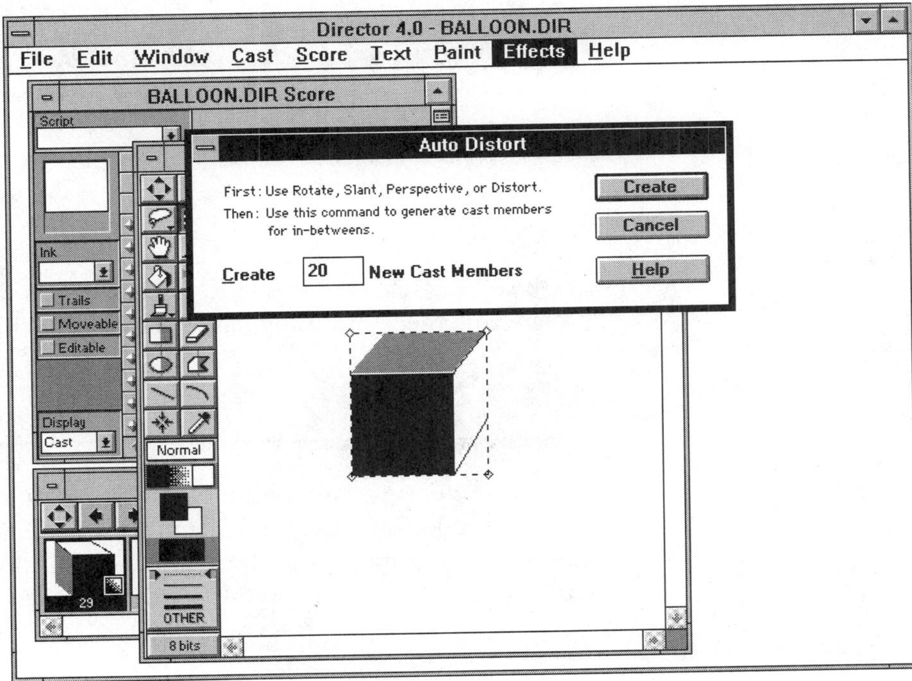

With the moving dashes still showing, open the **Effects** menu and select **Auto Distort**.

The dialog box in Figure 5.14 appears. Note the instructions that appear at the top. They point out Effects commands (introduced in Chapter 3) you can use before opening this dialog box, namely Rotate (which includes Rotate Left, Rotate Right and Free Rotate), Slant, Perspective, and Distort.

Set the dialog box to **Create 20 New Cast Members**, as shown in the figure.

Click the **Create** button or press the Enter key and watch the screen.

One by one, the intervening cast members are created in the cast, as shown in Figure 5.15.

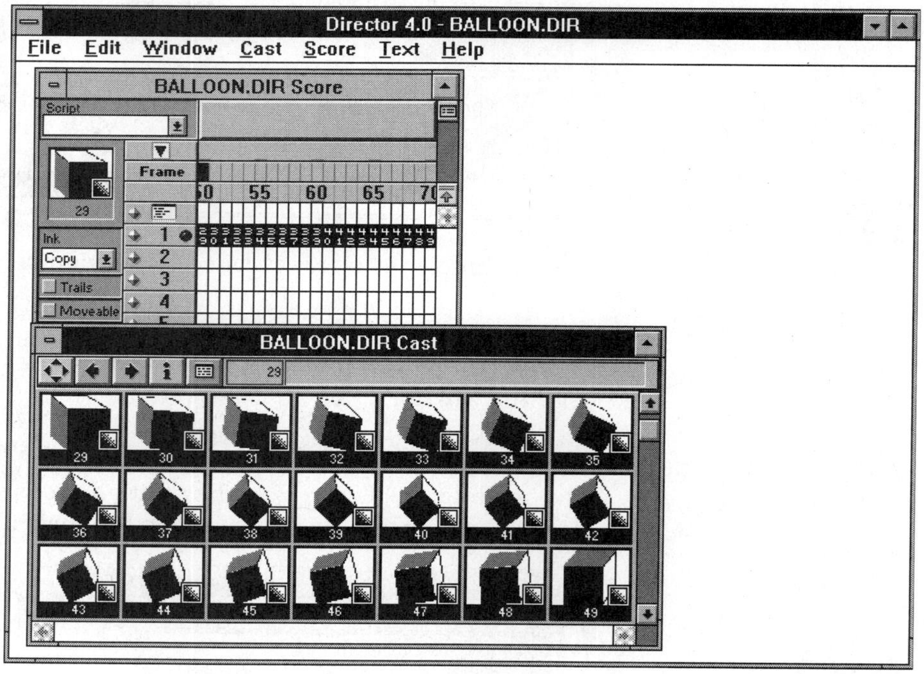

5.15

Auto-distort art added to score

Using one of the techniques recently described, select all the box's cast members and add them to a channel in the score, as shown in the figure.

Play these frames of the movie.

The box rotates. Should you make a mistake, you can remove the cast member by selecting them and using Edit, Clear Cast Member.

AUTO ANIMATE

Auto animate is yet another important animation implement. It is available through six items on the Score menu's Auto Animate submenu. As you'll see, auto animation items are related to automatically creating a variety of text effects and items that are useful in presentations.

Banners

A banner is auto animated text that travels across the screen, from right to left. Let's use auto animation to create a banner that says "TOYS!" It will begin appearing as the box begins rotating and will travel across the screen.

Save the movie.

This procedure creates numerous cast members that cannot easily be changed. Saving allows you to revert to the saved version if necessary, a move that can be easier than clearing cast members.

Move the playback head to the frame that begins rotating the box.

Select Score, Auto Animate, Banner.

The dialog box in Figure 5.16 appears.

5.16

Score, Auto Animate, Banner dialog box

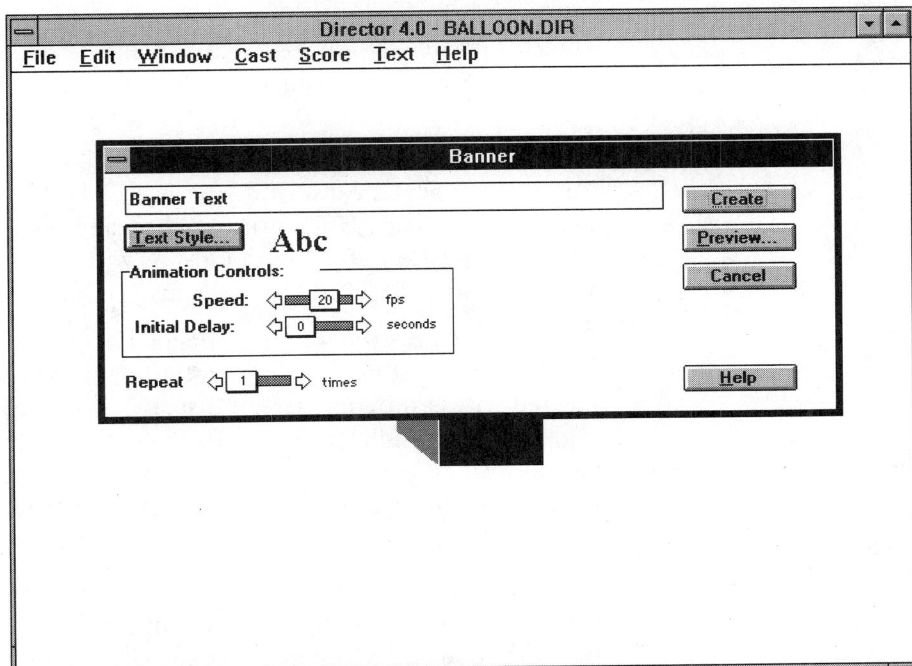

In the box at the top, replace the words "Banner Text" with TOYS!

The "Abc" indicator displays the text style currently in effect for the banner.

Select the Text Style button and use the resulting dialog box to select the Fixedsys font, 24-point Bold; then OK the Text Style dialog box.

Back at the Banner dialog box, the other settings should be as they are in Figure 5.16. However, you can check your choices before committing to inserting them in the movie.

Select the Preview button.

In the Banner Preview screen that appears you should see the text "TOYS!" appear and move across the center of the screen. At the bottom of the screen are four buttons. The **Play** button will trigger the traveling text once again. If you don't like it centered, you can reposition the text so that it travels across a different part of the screen. You do that by simply clicking a point on the screen that you want the text to cross. Should you later decide that you want the text back at the center you can click the **Center** button to reset it there. The **Cancel** button (or Esc key) leaves the banner as it was. Use the **OK** button to effect a change you've made in placement.

In Banner Preview, click a spot about a quarter of the way from the top.

The text travels across, repositioned where you clicked. Notice the speed of the text. (Use the Play button to watch again if necessary.)

When the text is properly positioned, click the OK button.

The Banner dialog box (Figure 5.16) reappears.

If the speed of the text was inappropriate, adjust the corresponding slide switch. Use the Preview button again if necessary.

Once you consider the display to be satisfactory, select the Banner dialog box's Create button.

Director creates the necessary cast members following the last cast member you have. Sprites are created as well.

Bar Charts

You can use Score, Auto Animate, Bar Chart to create a bar chart with animated vertical bars. This auto animation and the next, Bullet Chart, are useful in the preparation of presentations. As with banner text, they both have Preview buttons you can use for test runs.

Figure 5.17 shows the Bar Chart dialog box with its default settings and a display of the chart that these default settings create. (This figure and the next are created with a different screen display.) The settings are rather self-evident; you just substitute your values for the default values to make them appear at the corresponding position in the chart. For example, replace "Title" in the dialog box with your title to make your title appear on the chart where "Title" appears in the chart in the figure.

When you run the frames this dialog box creates, the bars grow from the bottom of the chart at the speed you've provided (normally 20 fps). The bars can be set for one of five different bar styles, including stacking coins and a hand with a growing arm.

Save the movie and then use a new movie to experiment with creating bar charts.

Bullet Charts

The other presentation instrument that Director provides is the Bullet Chart. Figure 5.18 shows the Score, Auto Animate, Bullet Chart dialog box. For the most part, it shows the default settings, except that the Bullet Type is set to Dot rather than None.

Again the settings are rather self-explanatory; substitute your values where desired. Several **Bullet Type** settings have both static and animated versions. For example, there's both Hand (hands appear in place of the dots in the figure) and Flying Hand (same idea, except the hands slide into place).

Motion controls the bullet text. It can be stationary or it can appear in various ways from various directions. Normally the title is stationary; turning on the **Animate Title** check box makes it appear in the same fashion as the bullet

5.17

Score, Auto Animate, Bar Chart dialog box

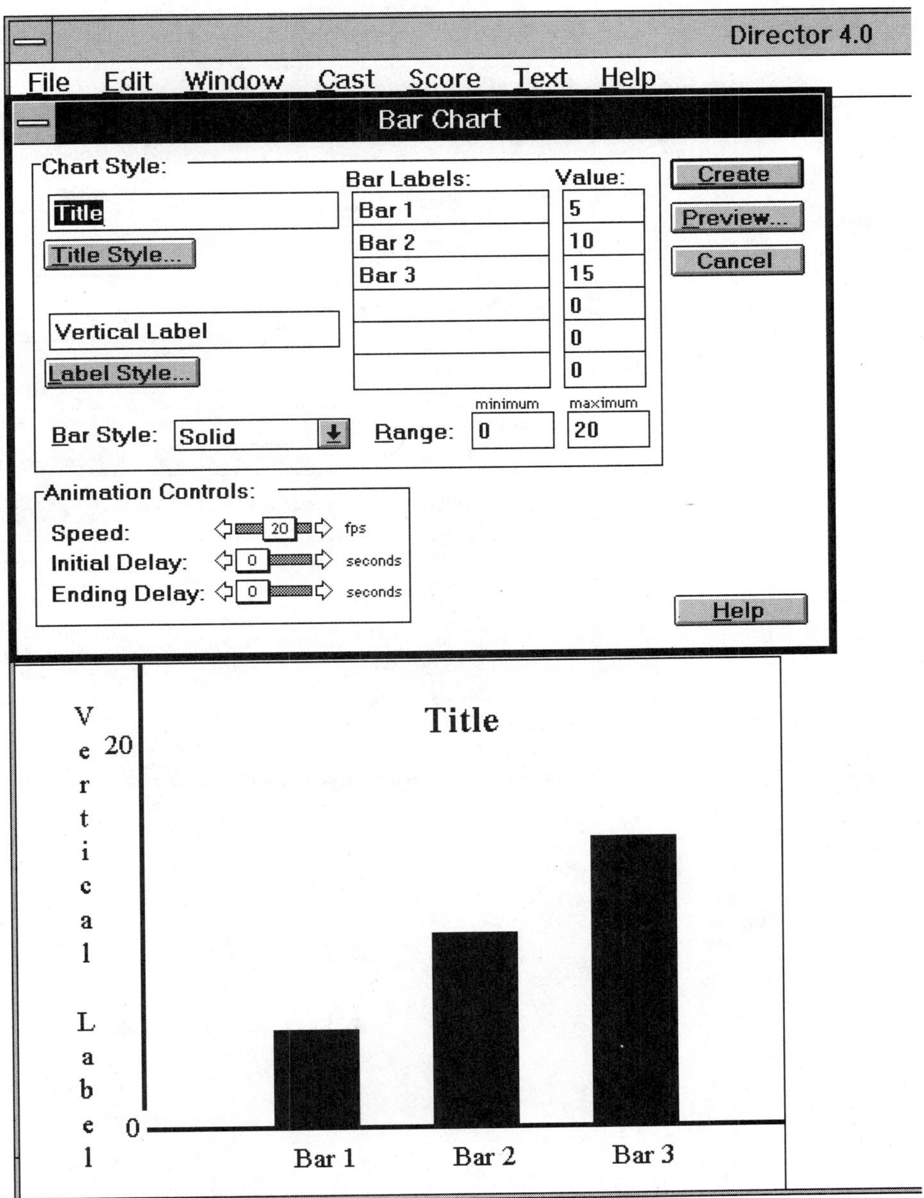

text. If **Advance At Mouse Click** is turned on, the movie pauses before each bullet text until the mouse is clicked—a very useful feature if you're giving a presentation. However, you can't preview this particular capability as clicking in preview relocates the position of the title of the chart to the point clicked.

Use the same new movie to experiment with bullet charts.

Rolling Credits

With the Score, Auto Animate, Credits dialog box (Figure 5.19) you can create rolling credits, like those that typically appear at the end of a film. Just replace the text shown in reverse highlighting in the figure with a list of the credits you want in the order in which you want them to appear.

Justification can be set for Left, Center, or Right. Regardless of the setting you choose, the list will always appear left justified within this dialog box. When

5.18

Score, Auto Animate, Bullet Chart dialog box

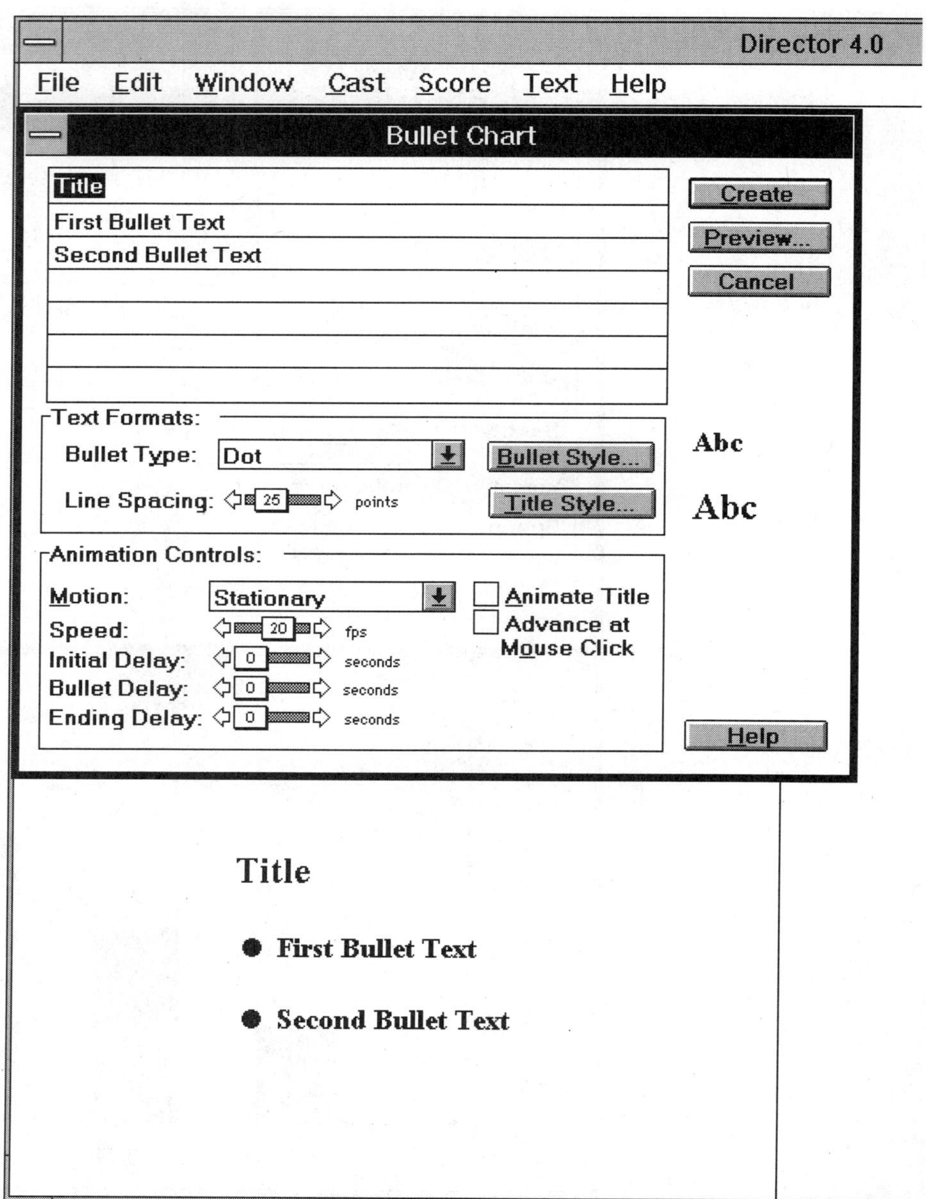

you preview or create the credits, however, Director shows the text with the justification you've selected.

Sparkle, Letter Slide, and Typewriter Text Effects

The Score, Auto Animate, Text Effects dialog box can be set to one of three effects. **Sparkle** animates the text to shimmer with star shine as shown in Figure 5.20, which also displays the dialog box. With **Letter Slide** the characters that make up the text travel across the screen to fall into place one by one. **Typewriter** makes the characters appear in place individually, as if they were being typed.

In your BALLOON.DIR movie, use the **Sparkle** text effect to preview and create a sequence that says **Jewelry**. Make the font big enough to create an impression.

5.19

Score, Auto Animate, Credits dialog box

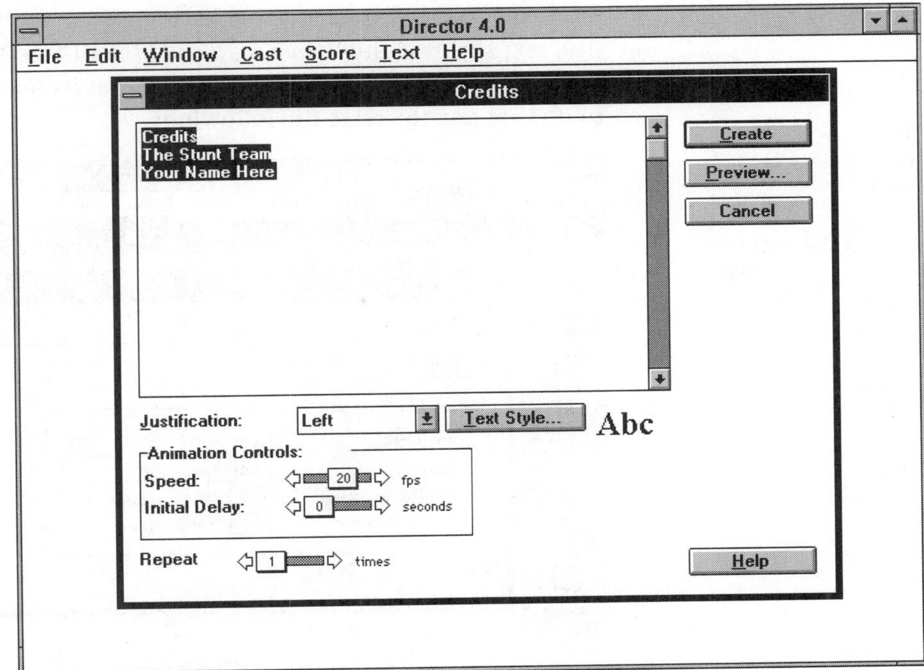

5.20

Score, Auto Animate, Text Effects dialog box and Sparkle text effect

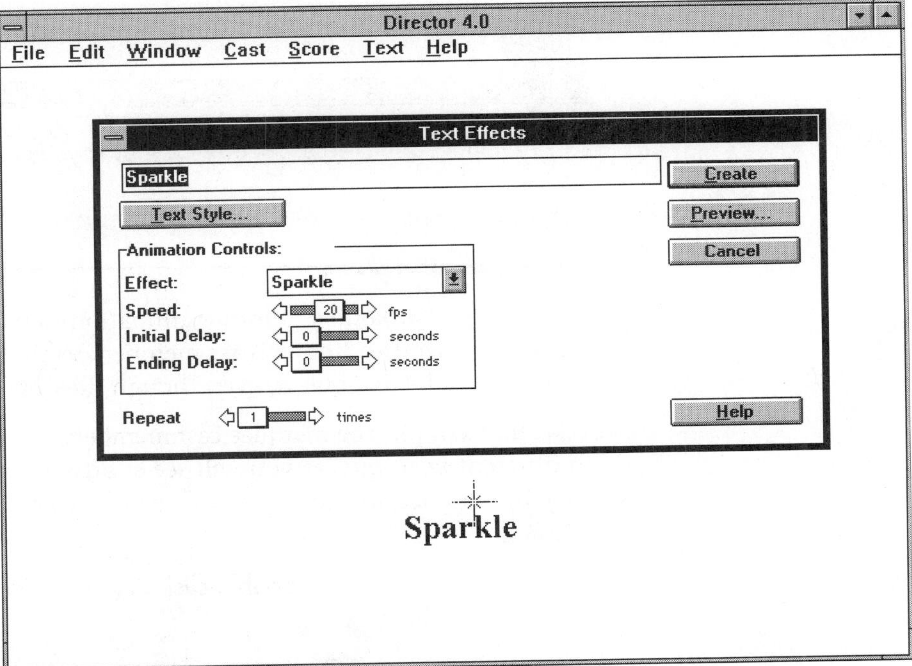

Use the **Typewriter** text effect to preview and create a sequence that says **Office Supplies**. Use a font that looks like it could come from a typewriter.

Preview: In the next chapter we'll add sound to the typewriter text, making it sound as though it were being produced on a typewriter.

Zoom Text

Zoom text is text animated to expand, contract, or do both in succession. Figure 5.21 shows the Score, Auto Animate, Zoom Text dialog box used to create such an effect. (Ignore the Paint window behind the dialog box for the moment.) **Zoom Type** has three settings: *Zoom in* (the text enlarges), *Zoom out* (the text shrinks), and *Zoom in, then out*. **Full-Size Duration** can be increased to give users enough time to read the text at its maximum size; you may need to do that as you create the following:

5.21

Score, Auto Animate, Zoom Text dialog box and Registration tool

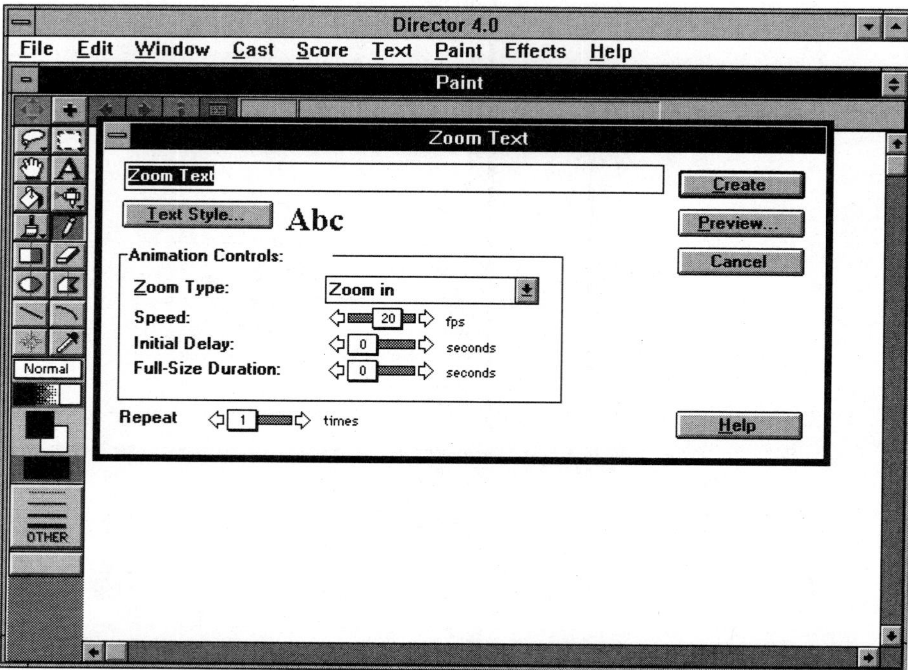

Preview and create a sequence that says **Sports Equipment**.

ALIGNING CAST MEMBERS

The ***registration point*** is another animation implement you should be aware of. It allows you to line up cast members so that, when they are animated, they seem to be one object, even though they may not actually be the same.

Take, for example, the marquee cast members. These cast members are actually in different positions, as you will see shortly in the Paint window. However, they line up because they have the same registration point. Observe that as follows:

In the Cast window, **double-click** the first marquee cast member to open it in the Paint window.

Maximize the Paint window.

Notice the art's position in the window.

Advance to the next marquee by clicking the Paint window's **Next Cast Member** (right arrow) button or press Ctrl+Shift+→.

Notice that this marquee cast member is in a different position.

Advance to the next marquee cast member.

Notice that the third marquee cast member is in a different position as well. Now look at the registration points of these cast members.

Click the Paint window's **Registration** tool, shown in color in Figure 5.21.

Cross hairs appear, marking the registration point in the center of the art.

Advance to the next two marquee cast members.

Notice that the registration point in these is in the same position relative to the art.

Flipping through cast members in the Paint window like this is one way to check your animation. But if the cast members are not aligned (as these are not), you can't effectively check the animation. It is possible, however, to correct the alignment. You can do that with the marquee:

Restore the **Paint** window to its reduced size.

Activate the **Cast** window and select the three marquee cast members.

Select **Cast**, **Align Bitmaps**.

Now use the **Paint** window to flip through the marquee cast members.

The cast members are correctly aligned in the Paint window.

The registration point is initially in the center of the bitmap cast members. To relocate the registration point, you use the Registration tool to click or drag the registration point to a different location. You can return the registration point to its initial position in the center of the art by double-clicking the Registration tool in the Paint window's Tool palette.

The registration point of items created with the Tools window is at the top left of the item. For these items it cannot be changed.

SAVING AND OTHER FILE PROCEDURES

To close out this chapter, we'll examine some commands and dialog boxes that affect entire movies.

- **File, Save And Compact or Ctrl+Alt+S** ***Compacting*** a movie saves the movie in its most compact form to create the smallest possible size for the file. Its use is recommended before distributing a movie. With larger movies it may take longer to save with this command than it does with the standard save commands.
- **File, Update Movies** This command displays a dialog box for selecting a movie from the disk. It allows you to compact and save a movie on disk. The dialog box has a **Protect Movies** check box. Turning on this check box secures the movie against alteration, as Director can no longer be used to open it. However, the movie can be played from a projector, discussed next. Protected movies are assigned the .DXR extension. The dialog box also has a **Select All** button that allows you to update all the movies that are in the selected directory. Or you can use shift-clicking to select a range of adjacent file names or Ctrl-clicking to select multiple files individually.
- **File, Create Projector** This command displays the dialog box at the top in Figure 5.22; its **Options** button displays the dialog box at the bottom in the figure. With it you create a ***projector***, an executable (.EXE)

movie that can be played (but not edited) on any Windows computer, even without Director. When you open this dialog box, movies may appear under **Movies** (depending on the directory), but the **Movie Play Order** list is empty. You use the **Add** or **Add All** buttons to add movies to the play-order list, **Remove** to take them off it, and **Move Up** and **Move Down** to rearrange the list. In the Projector Options dialog box, be sure to turn on the Play Every Movie check box if you want the movies to be played one after another as indicated by their order on the list. Otherwise, Director plays only the first movie; others must be launched by the first movie with Lingo script.

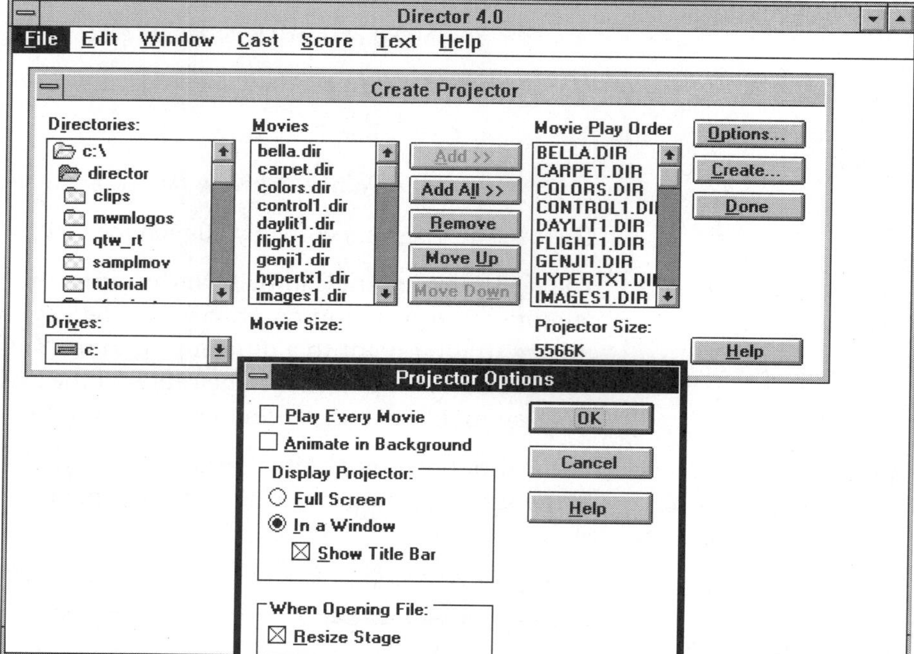

5.22

File menu's Create Projector dialog box

- **File, Import or Ctrl+J** This command displays a dialog box that allows you to ***import***—that is, to bring various files into Director. For example, you can bring in sounds, graphics, video, and other Director movies. Imported items become cast members. To list only files appropriate to what you want, use the dialog box's **List Files Of Type** command to restrict the file names that appear. You'll do this shortly. The **Linked file** button links the file rather than truly importing it; ***linked files*** do not become a part of the movie, but the movie remembers the file's location on disk so it can refer to the file as necessary.

Let's import a graphic for use in the "TOYS!" sequence of the movie.

Open this dialog box and set **List Files Of Type** to **Windows Bitmaps (*.BMP, *.DIB)**.

Select the **\windows\cars.bmp** file.

Click the **Import** button or press the Enter key.

The Palette Mismatch dialog box will probably appear, as Director will detect a difference in the colors used to create the incoming file from those used by the movie. The color of the car being imported is not vital.

Select the **Remap Colors** button and click **OK** or press the Enter key.

Use the Paint window to move and (free) rotate the car so that it seems to be driving horizontally from left to right. Switch colors to remove the pavement from beneath the car (change gray to white).

Create animations with the cast member to make one or more cars seem to drive out of the overturned box. You can also create additional copies of the cast member, switch colors to create cars in various colors, and add them to the animation.

- **File, Export or Ctrl+Shift+E** This command displays the dialog box in Figure 5.23. You use it to ***export*** frames of the movie—that is, create a new file with the frames. Use the **Range Of Frames** section to specify just which frames to export. You can export them as one of two types, set by **File Type**. *DIB File Sequence* (*.BMP*) transforms the frames into a series of bitmap files. Each file is named with four characters you provide (after selecting Export), plus a four-digit number identifying the frame number and the .BMP extension. The other option is *Video for Windows* (*.AVI*); use it to create a video and use the *Video for Windows Options* button to supply the video's speed in frames per second.

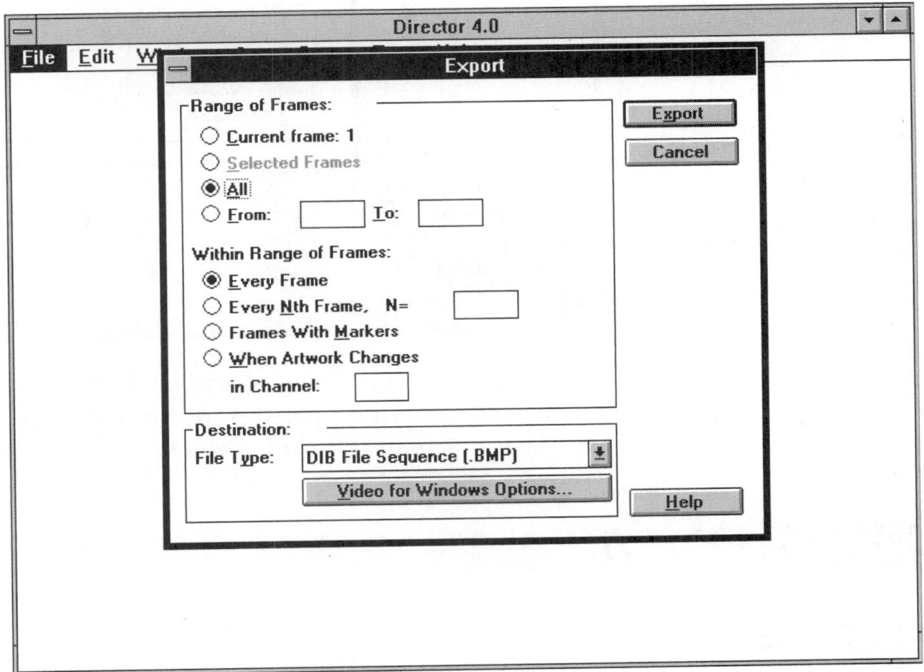

5.23

File menu's Export dialog box

- **File, Movie Info or Ctrl+U** This displays the dialog box shown in the top right of Figure 5.24, which is used to check and change items specific to the movie that's opened. **Load Cast** can be set for *When Needed*, good when you have large-size cast members that can be loaded at various times throughout the movie. *After Frame One* gets the initial image on the screen. That way, the user has something to look at, possibly a sign that says "Please Wait," while cast members are loading. *Before Frame One* gets everything loaded and then launches into the movie; it's an acceptable choice as long as the wait isn't too long. Use **Default Palette** to set the palette that the movie uses (unless otherwise changed during the course of the movie as demonstrated in Chapter 4). You can view palettes with the Color Palettes window, also shown in this figure. In fact, you can use the Color Palettes window and its Palette menu to create your own custom palette; if you do, your custom palette will be available as an option on the Default Palette pop-up menu. **Remap Palettes When Needed** permits Director to automatically deal with situations in which a sprite on the stage does not have access to the colors that its cast members require (due to a palette change). The **Font Mapping Table** section is used to handle differences between Windows and Macintosh fonts.

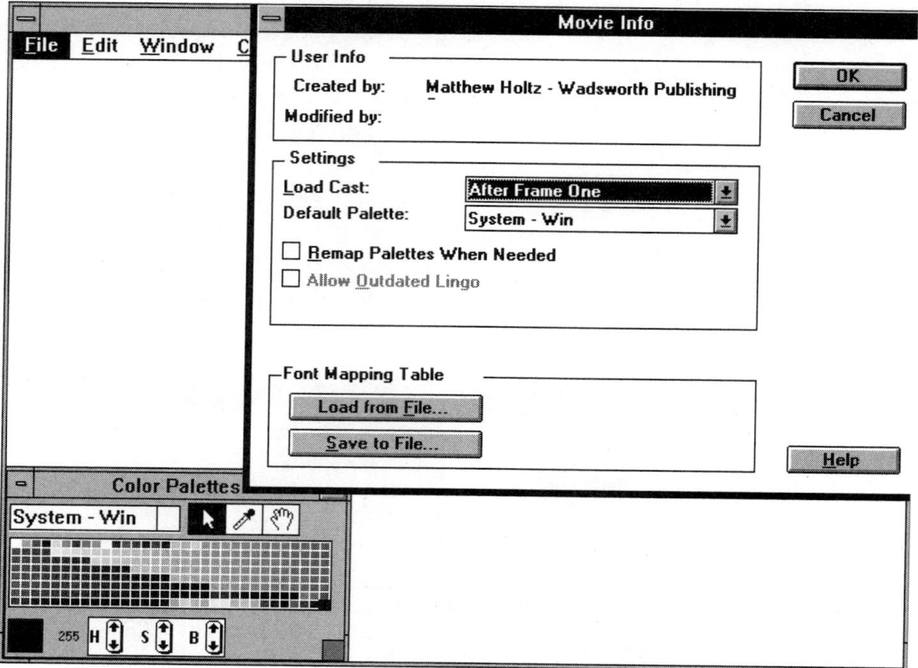

5.24
File menu's Movie Info dialog box and Color Palettes window

As Director provides several color palettes with a wide array of colors, we won't further discuss custom palettes in this text. If you need to create a custom palette, use Help to search for Color Palettes window and Palette menu.

CHAPTER REVIEW

KEY TERMS

linear
special in-betweening
accelerate
decelerate
step recording
real-time recording
film loop
auto distort
auto animate
registration point
compacting
projector
import
linked files
export

REVIEW QUESTIONS

1. **T F** Score, In-Between Linear can create in-between sprites for both size and position.
2. Which Control Panel button works with step recording?
3. Which keystrokes trigger real-time recording?
4. Which menu contains the Cast To Time command? Space To Time?
5. Which window must be active to use auto distort?

PROJECTS

1. Use auto distort with the Paint window text to create an animation for a type of mall store. Reverse the animation so that the text changes from distorted to regular.
2. Create a presentation on a subject of your choice, using bullets and bar charts, and possibly other effects.
3. Use Score, Auto Animate, Credits to add rolling credits to the end of your movie. Be sure to acknowledge this book!
4. Create a projector of your movie thus far. (Create another on its completion at the end of the book.)

6

Video, Sound, Scripts, and Searching

THIS CHAPTER WILL TEACH YOU HOW TO

- **Import digital video and use it in your movie.**
- **Import sound and use it in your movie.**
- **Create scripts with Lingo and use various Director elements related to Lingo.**
- **Create operational buttons, repeating frames, hypertext, and custom menus.**
- **Use Director's various implements for finding and optionally changing an item once found, where appropriate.**

In this chapter, we'll continue to look at importing—specifically, at importing video and sound so you can add these media to your movie. Adding either of these is rather straightforward. Then we'll discuss the creation of scripts with Director's programming language, ***Lingo***. With Lingo you can program buttons, control movie playback (by having the movie repeat the same section of frames, for example), create menus, and more. We'll close with a look at Director's various procedures for finding text and other material.

VIDEO

To use video in a Director movie, you first import the video, which makes it a cast member in the movie. Then you can place the video on the stage and into the score and also control how the video plays.

Let's assume that our huge mall will have gambling. Create a sequence that includes the video of a roulette wheel provided with Director, as follows:

> Open the **File** menu's **Import** dialog box or press Ctrl+J.
>
> Set **List Files of Type** to **Digital Video (*.MOV, *.AVI)**.

Once you do this, notice that the Linked File check box is turned on and cannot be turned off. This is always the case for these types of files; they are always kept as separate linked files and not truly imported into the movie (see Chapter 5).

> Select the **\director\clips\video\rlttwhl.mov** file and use the **Import** button.

The Cast window appears if it is not already showing, and the video is now available as a cast member. To work with the video, open its window as follows:

> Select **Window, Digital Video** or press Ctrl+9 or double-click the video's cast member.

The Digital Video window opens with the roulette wheel in it, as shown at the top left in Figure 6.1. The window has several button with which you are familiar, including the Place, Add, Previous, Next, Info, and Script buttons. The window also shows the cast member's number and name, although at its current size the window is not big enough to display it all. The cast name is assigned automatically; Director uses the name of the file that was imported. Thus this video is named RLTTWHL.MOV.

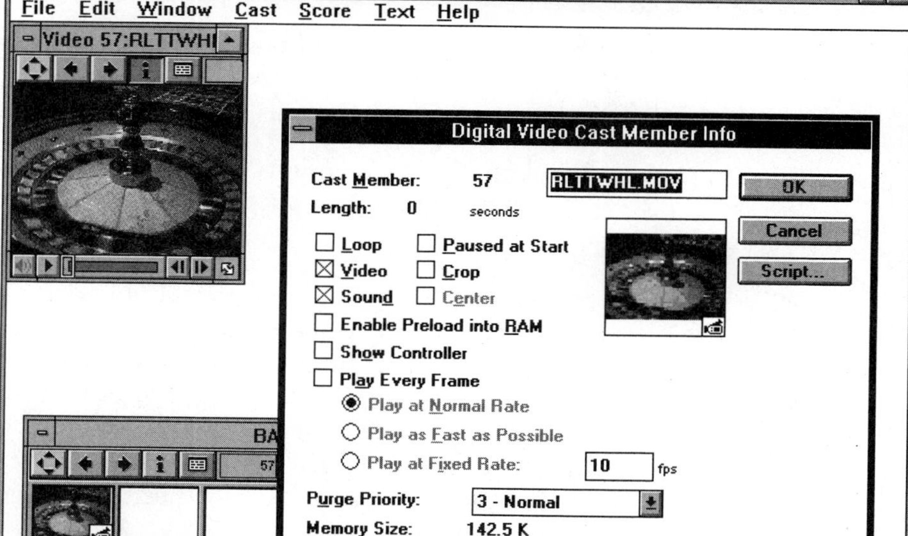

6.1
Digital Video window and Digital Video Cast Member Info dialog box

As you may have noticed from the list of file types, Director imports movies with the .MOV and .AVI extension. Director recognizes two formats, as indicated by these extensions: Microsoft Video for Windows (*.AVI) and QuickTime for Windows (*.MOV). At the bottom of the Digital Video window is an area called the ***controller***. This is the strip with a sound button, a slider switch, and some VCR-type controls. The controller is available only with MOV files, not AVI files.

One way to use a video in a movie is to make the movie wait while the video is playing, and then have the movie continue once the video is finished. The video of the roulette wheel is very short so we won't be using this technique, but here's how it's accomplished. You drag from the cast member to create a sprite on the stage and in a score cell, as usual. Then, at the same frame in which the sprite appears, you select the cell in the Tempo channel (discussed in Chapter 4) and use Score, Set Tempo (or equivalent). In the Set Tempo dialog box that appears (also discussed in Chapter 4) you turn on the Wait For Digital Video Movie To Finish In Channel button and provide the channel number of the video.

Because our video is short, we'll extend its playing time by making the video loop—that is, play itself repeatedly. We'll use the score to control how long it plays. If a video is assigned to a continuous string of adjacent cells in the same channel, it will begin playing and play for the length of the string. Interrupting the string—with an empty cell, for example—and starting another string of cells (to which the video is assigned) causes the video to start again from the beginning.

You can get and set information about the video by displaying its Info box. Do so as follows.

> With the Digital Video window activated, select **Cast**, **Cast Member Info** or Ctrl+I or click the Digital Video window's Info (i) button.

The Digital Video Cast Member Info dialog box, also in Figure 6.1, appears.

> Turn on the **Loop** check box and click the **OK** button or press the Enter key.
>
> Drag this cast member to the score and use in-betweening to make copies for as long as you want the video to play.
>
> Elsewhere on the stage, use the Paint window to add the title "Casino" using Auto Distort (Chapter 5) with an appropriate effect. Adjust the video length as necessary to correspond to the effect.

We won't examine every option in this dialog box in Figure 6.1. However, notice the **Video** and **Sound** check boxes. Some videos have both sound and video and you can use these check boxes to turn on one or the other or both. ***Cropping*** refers to the process of clipping away part of an image. **Crop** is initially turned off and, if you resize the video's sprite, the video will stretch or shrink as necessary to match the size you indicate. With Crop turned on, the video will keep its size the same. Should the sprite be made smaller, Director will show as much of the video as possible (from the video's top left); if a larger area is specified, the video will occupy the top-left corner of the area. **Center** becomes available if Crop is turned on; it causes the video to be centered in its bounding box, whether the box is larger or smaller. **Show Controller** causes the video's sound button, slider switch, and VCR-type buttons to appear at the bottom of the sprite, allowing the user to operate them and so control the video. **File Name** shows the location of the video's file; you can click this box to change the linked file if necessary.

> **Test user operation of the controller by turning on its check box and playing the video's frames with looping turned on (playback looping, that is, using Edit, Loop or equivalent, in addition to looping the video).**

As you add multiple videos to a movie, you may find it helpful to take advantage of Director's ability to open additional Digital Video windows. By opening more than one Digital Video window, you can work with each video in its own window. To do this, you activate the Digital Video window and simply select Window, Duplicate Window. Alternatively, you can hold down the Alt key while selecting both Window and then Digital Video. Also, recall that Ctrl+9 is the keyboard shortcut for activating the Digital Video window; once it is activated, you can press Alt+Ctrl+9 to open a second Digital Video window. Double-clicking the digital video cast member in the Cast window opens the Digital Video window; if there is one Digital Video window open and you hold the Alt key as you double-click the digital video cast member, a second Digital Video window opens.

Techniques similar to these also work with the Text and Script windows. Simply adjust the procedures as appropriate to those windows.

SOUND

Director's use of sounds is similar in some ways to its use of digital videos. You begin by importing the sound to make it a cast member. To assign a sound to the score, however, you must use one of the two Sound channels, shown in color in Figure 6.2.

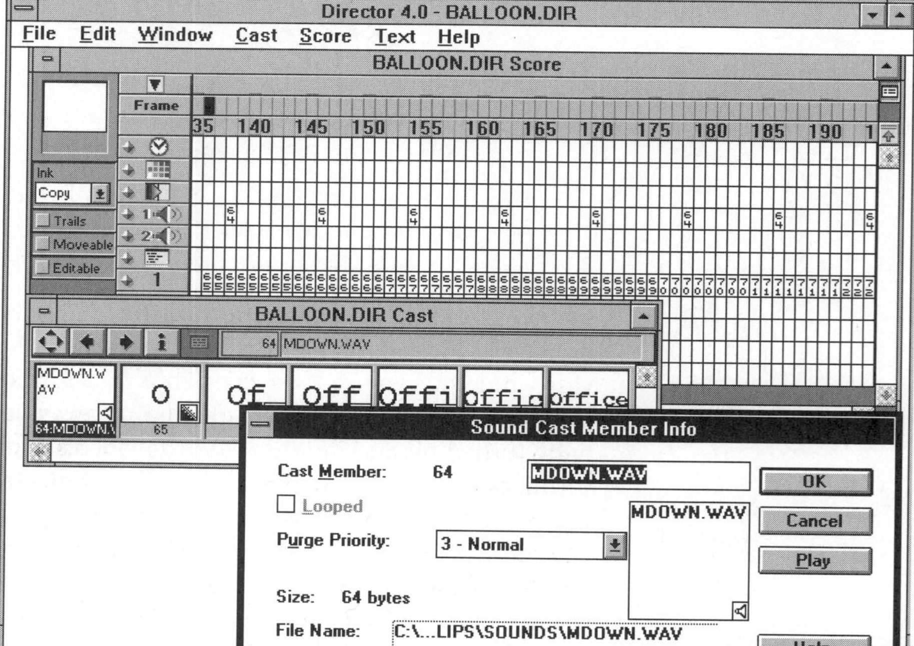

6.2
Sound channels and Sound Cast Member Info dialog box

Like all cast members, sound cast members have a dialog box of information. You select the sound cast member and use Cast, Cast Member Info or equivalent to open the dialog box shown in Figure 6.2. There is a **Looped** check box that can be turned on to have the sound play repeatedly; it is available only if the sound is fully imported into the movie rather than linked (see Chapter 5). **File Name** appears only if the sound is linked (rather than fully imported); you can click it to locate or change the linked file. Note the **Play** button that you can use to test-hear the sound.

To assign a sound to a cell in a Sound channel, you can drag from the sound's cast member. Alternatively, with a cell selected in either Sound channel, you can use Score, Set Sound (or you can double-click the sound cell). This displays a listing of all the sounds in (or linked to) the movie. You can then select from the list to assign a sound to the cell. There is also a Play button, providing a handy central location for testing any sound that's in your movie.

Once a sound is assigned to a cell, you can halt the movie until the sound finishes. As with digital videos, you do that by using the Tempo channel to open Score, Set Tempo (or equivalent). Then you turn on the Wait For Sound1 To Finish button (or Sound2, as applicable).

Rather than having the movie pause while your sound plays, you can select continuous sound cells and use Score, Set Sound to assign the sound to the cells. Or you can assign a sound to one cell and then use in-betweening to assign it to other cells.

As with digital video, if a sound is assigned to a continuous string of adjacent cells in the same channel, it will begin playing and play for the length of the string. Interrupting the string, with an empty cell, for example, causes the sound to start from the beginning of the new string. If a sound (in either sound channel or associated with a digital video) is playing, it will play until it is completed before another sound can start.

As follows, add sound to the typewriter text effect you created in the previous chapter:

> **Import the \director\clips\sounds\mdown.wav file as a cast member.**
>
> **In sound channel 1, assign the new cast member to each frame in about the middle of the sequence that creates each letter in the "Office Supplies" text, as shown in Figure 6.2.**

As usual, your cast and frame numbers needn't match those in the figure. For a short click it's not necessary to use the Tempo channel to have the movie wait until the sound is finished.

> **Play these frames of the movie.**

➡ *Reminder*: You can turn off the sound for the current session of Director as discussed in Chapter 2. To do this, you use Edit, Disable Sounds or equivalent.

LINGO

Importing media in Director allows you to create a sophisticated movie by controlling and coordinating a variety of files. However, the ultimate instrument for controlling most aspects of the movie itself is Lingo, Director's programming language. You can assign Lingo scripts to the entire movie as well as to a variety of movie elements, such as frames, cast members (except sounds), buttons, text, and sprites. We can only touch on the many uses of Lingo, but we'll examine some useful applications.

Buttons

One very important job for Lingo is to make buttons operate. You use the Tools window, discussed in Chapter 4, to create a button on the stage. However, to have a button do something when the user clicks it, you must program the button by providing it with a script. For example, let's create a Start Over button that shows throughout most of the movie. We'll have it begin after the first part of the movie (after the rising balloons), appearing at frame 35.

> Go to the appropriate frame and use the Tools window's **Round Button** tool, shown in Figure 6.3, to create a button in the bottom-left corner.

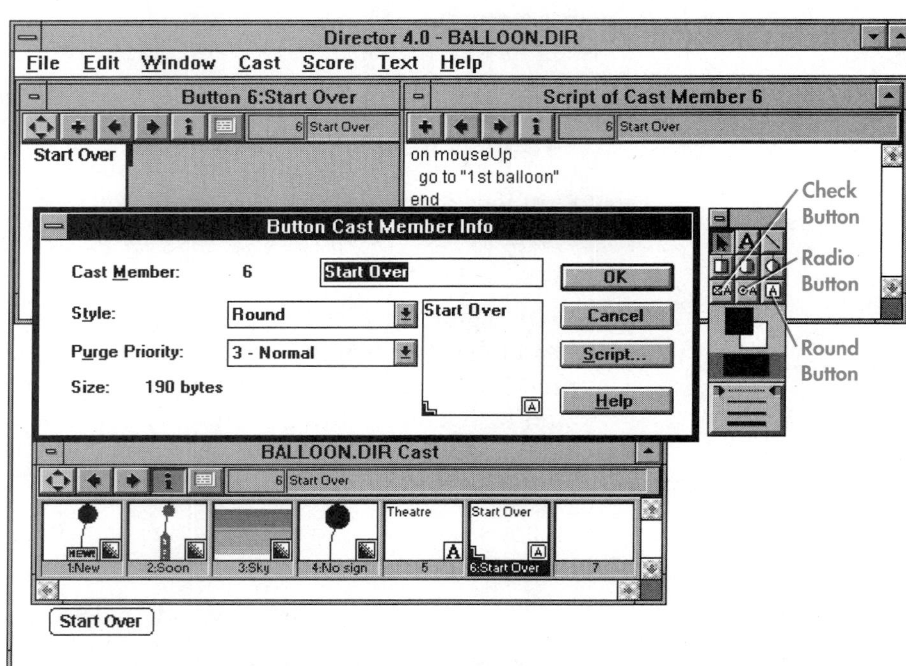

6.3
Button Text window, Script window, and Button Cast Member Info dialog box

The button this tool creates is actually a rectangular one with rounded corners. However, Director refers to it as a round button.

> Enter the button's label, **Start Over**, either on the button itself or by using the button's Text window (shown at the top left).

> Open this cast member's script by using **Window, Script** to open the Script window or by displaying and clicking either Script button shown in color in Figure 6.3.

In the window you'll see the beginnings of programming for the button—specifically, the first and third line of the script you see in the Script window in Figure 6.3 (labeled "Script of Cast Member 6" in the figure). The cursor stands poised in line 2, ready for you to enter script.

> Add the second line of script as shown in the Script window in Figure 6.3.

The resulting script means that when the user clicks and then releases the mouse *(on mouseUp)*, Director should go to the frame with the marker "1st balloon." As you may recall, this is the marker we assigned to the first frame of the movie.

Once a script is assigned to a cast member, an L-shaped bracket (L for Lingo) appears in its bottom-left corner in the Cast window. You can see one such indicator for the Start Over cast member in Figure 6.3.

> Use in-betweening to copy the button to all frames from the current one to the end of the movie.
>
> Play the movie and test the button.

Now consider info for the button.

> With the button's cast member selected, open the **Cast** menu and select **Cast Member Info** or press Ctrl+I or use the Info (i) button.

The Button Cast Member Info dialog box shown in the figure appears.

> Assign the cast member the name **Start Over**.

Style can be used to change the button to a different type: Round, Check, or Radio. Notice that the dialog box has a **Script** button, which provides yet another route for reaching the button's Script window.

Lingo Utensils

Now that you've created your first script, consider some utensils that assist in creating scripts.

- **Help, Contents, Lingo menu** Help for Lingo, with Lingo items listed alphabetically.
- **Lingo menu** Available when the Script window is opened, it features alphabetical lists of the dozens of elements used by Lingo. You can select an item from a list to insert into scripts.
- **Window, Script or Ctrl+0** Displays, activates, or removes the Script window. If the window is visible you can also activate it by clicking its Title bar.
- **Window, Duplicate Window** With Script window opened and active, this command creates a second Script window. You can also use the Alt key to open a duplicate window as discussed for the Digital Video window earlier in this chapter.
- **Cast, Open Script or Ctrl+'** (Ctrl with the "' key) Opens the Script window for the selected cast member. If a Script window is already open, Alt+Cast, Alt+Open Script opens a new Script window for the current cast member.
- **Edit, Disable Lingo** Turns off Lingo scripts so they don't execute when you play the movie. This is a useful implement for ***debugging*** (troubleshooting problems that occur), as it can narrow down the problem by showing whether it is related to scripts.
- **Text, Comment or Ctrl+Shift+>** (Ctrl and Shift with the >. key) A ***comment*** is a line that documents the program with a remark at its

location; it serves no purpose when the program is running. This command changes selected lines in the Script window to comment lines by adding double hyphens (--) at the beginning of each line. Alternatively, you can simply type in double hyphens at the beginning of any line to make it a comment line; using this command allows you to change multiple lines at one time. Changing lines to comments can be useful when you are debugging.

- **Text, Uncomment; Ctrl+Shift<** (Ctrl and Shift with the <, key) Changes selected comment lines in the Script window to standard lines, by removing double hyphens (--) from the beginning of each line. Alternatively, you can simply delete double hyphens from the beginning of an individual line; using this command allows you to change multiple lines at one time.
- **Text, Recompile Script or Ctrl+Shift+R** Converts the script for use. Director will prompt you when it becomes necessary to use this command or the next one.
- **Text, Recompile All Scripts or Ctrl+Alt+R** Converts all scripts for use.
- **Window, Message or Ctrl+M** Displays, activates, or takes away the Message window. With this window you can enter a Lingo command, which Director will execute immediately. In your movie, for example, you could type

  ```
  go to "1st balloon"
  ```

  and press the Enter key. Whether or not the movie is playing, Director will immediately display the movie's first frame.
- **Message window's Trace check box** Turning on this check box causes Director to display scripts as they are executed. It also shows the various messages that Director sends to elements in the movie in order to control them.
- **File, Preferences (or Ctrl+Alt+U), Using Message Window Recompiles Scripts** Normally turned on, this check box causes Director to automatically deal with scripts as necessary when you use the Message window to enter Lingo commands. If this check box is turned off, you must use Text, Recompile All Scripts (or Ctrl+Alt+R) before using the Message window to enter Lingo commands.
- **Score window's Script channel** This channel's cells hold Score Script cast members. These scripts are executed when the playback head reaches the cell's frame. This item and the next three (all related to the Score window) were introduced in Chapter 4.
- **Score window's Script pop-up menu** Shows the score script assigned to a cell selected in the Script channel and allows you to select a different script.
- **Score window's Script Preview button** Displays the first two lines of the selected cell in the Script channel. Clicking this area causes the Script window to display that script.
- **Score window's Script button** Displays and takes away the Score window's Script pop-up area and Script Preview area.

- **File, Movie Info (or Ctrl+U), Allow Outdated Lingo** Makes the movie honor Lingo commands used by previous versions of Director.

Looping Frames

You can use looping of frames to make Director play the same portion of a movie repeatedly. We can use looping to have Director keep showing the first section of the movie, with balloons rising, so that the user has as much time as necessary to drag the cloud out of the way, change text, or perform other operations. Of course, there must be some kind of button provided so the user can continue with the rest of the movie when ready to do so.

Figure 6.4 shows the cast members and scripts you can use to accomplish this task. As usual your cast numbers needn't agree.

6.4
Cast member and scripts for looping

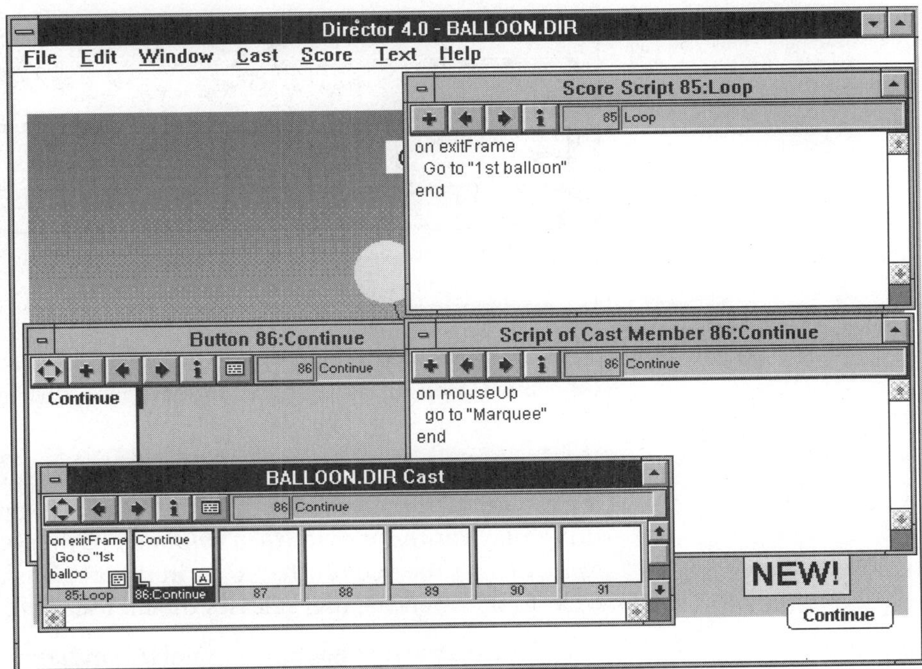

Create the script as shown in the window labeled **Score Script 85:Loop** and place it in the Script channel at the end of the first section (frame 30).

This will cause the movie to restart on reaching that frame.

Create the **Continue** button, shown in the bottom-right corner of the figure, in the first frame. Assign its cast member the **Continue** script shown in the figure, and in-between the cell to the other frames in this section (through frame 30).

Add the cloud back in the movie, as well as its instructional text ("Drag away the cloud to see the exciting announcement").

Test the movie.

Start/Stop Button

Another button that's useful in controlling a movie is a Start/Stop button. While the movie is playing, a user can click this button to make the movie pause. Once the movie is paused, clicking the button causes the movie to start again. Such a button is shown in Figure 6.5. Add it to the sequences following the first section (from frame 30 on).

6.5

Cast member and script for Start/Stop button

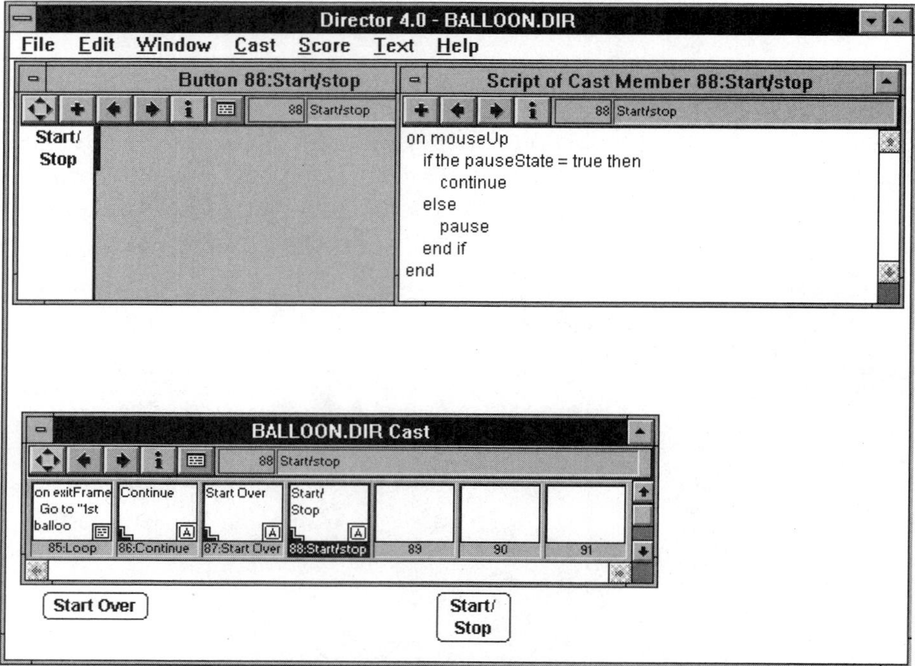

Create the Start/Stop button in the first frame, assign its cast member the Start/Stop script as shown in the figure, and in-between the cell to the other frames in the movie.

To paraphrase this script, it tells Director, "When the user clicks and releases the mouse button *(on mouseUp)*, if the movie is paused *(pauseState = true)*, continue playing the movie *(then continue)*. Otherwise, pause the movie *(else pause)*. That's the end of what to do in this circumstance *(end if)* and the end of what to do when the user releases the mouse *(end)*."

Play the movie and test your Start/Stop button.

Hypertext

Hypertext is text you can click to display material related to that text. Once you finish reading or otherwise viewing the material, you can click to return to the screen with the hypertext.

Director doesn't provide a direct way to automatically create hypertext. However, with scripts and tools, you can create hypertext rather easily.

Let's say, for example, that you are concerned some users will not understand the term "Drag" in the first section. ("Drag away the cloud to see the exciting announcement.") You can highlight the word "Drag" and place an invisible button in front of the word. Then you can assign a script to the invisible button that causes a special frame to appear, which provides a definition of "Drag." This special frame occurs at some point after the movie will end, so it's not otherwise seen.

Figure 6.6 shows the scripts and other items with which this can be accomplished.

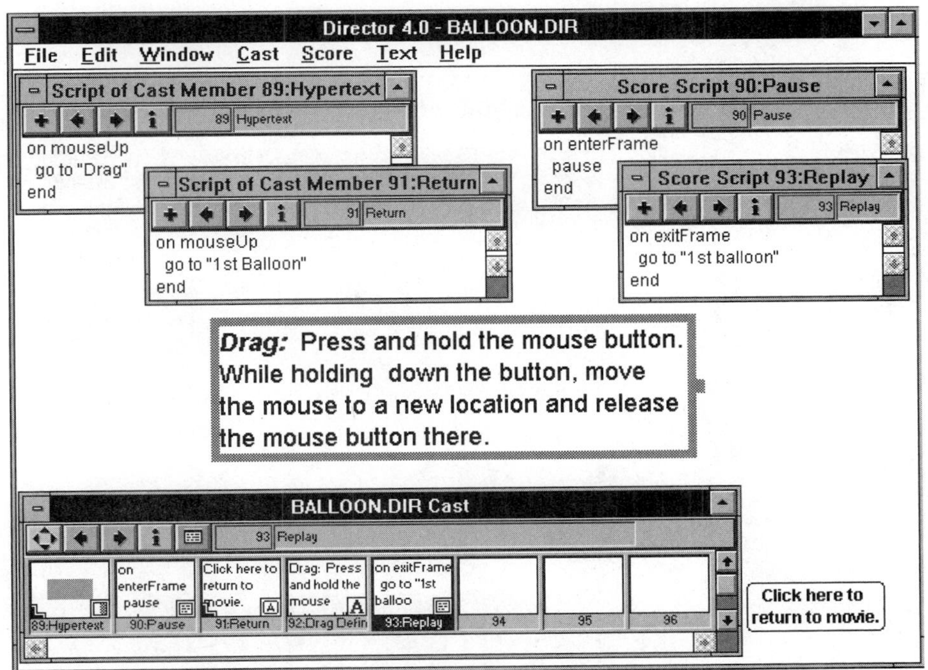

6.6

Cast members and scripts for hypertext

Use the Tools window's **Rectangle** tool to create a color cover for the text, assigning **Lightest** ink effect to the sprite and replicating it over the first 30 frames.

This color is for alerting the user that these words are hypertext. In a real situation, it would be advisable to inform the user in early frames that text in that color can be clicked for additional information.

Open the rectangle cast member's Script window, assigning it the **Hypertext** script in the figure and replicating it over the first 30 frames.

Go to the end of the movie and assign the **Replay** script in the figure to the (currently) final frame in movie.

This will cause the movie to go back to the beginning once it reaches this frame, thereby avoiding the special frame with the "Drag" definition.

In a frame after this one, use the Tools window's **Text** tool to create the **Drag** definition you see in the center of the figure.

Label this frame with the marker **Drag**.

At this frame, in **Script** channel, assign the **Pause** script you see in the figure.

Add the button shown in the bottom-right corner, labeling it as shown.

This button will provide users with a means of returning to where they were.

Assign this button the **Return** script shown in the figure.

Test your hypertext.

Custom Menus

You can also use Lingo to create custom menus. Figure 6.7, for example, shows a menu you can create for your movie.

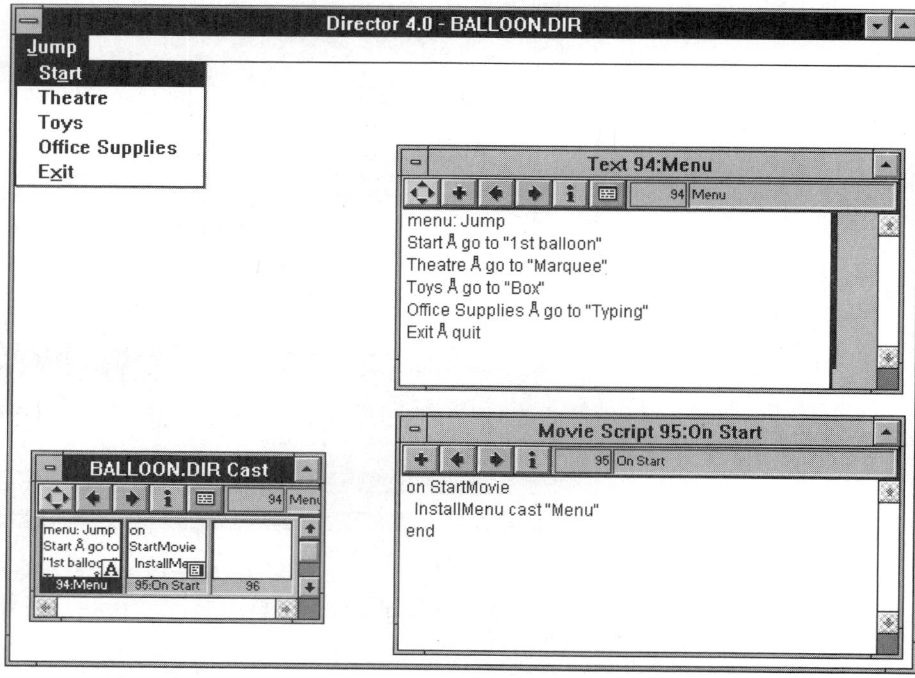

6.7

Cast members and scripts for making a menu

Open the Text window.

You use the Text window to construct the menu. Then you use Lingo to install the menu. This makes the menu you've created replace Director's standard menus and thus it becomes available to the user.

Assign the marker names shown in quotes in the Text window in Figure 6.7 to appropriate frames in the score: 1st balloon at the beginning of the movie, Marquee where the marquee first appears, Box where the box of toys appears, Typing where the typing animation for office supplies appears.

Making a menu requires use of the ≈ or » character (or, with some versions, the Å character). They are created similarly; which one appears will depend on the font. To create the character, you press the Alt key and, still holding down Alt, you use the keypad to enter 0187 (or, for the Å character with some versions, 0197).

Following these guidelines, create the Menu text shown in the Text window in the figure.

The first line (*menu:Jump*) dictates the name of the menu that appears at the top of the menu, as you see at the top left of the figure (Jump). Below that, the words at the left on each line indicate the items that will appear on the menu (such as *Start*). Following each menu item is the special character. After that character is the Lingo statement you want Director to execute when the menu item is selected *(go to "1st balloon").*

You could create additional menus that would appear to the right of this one. To do that you would simply add another line after the last item, making it like the first line. That is, it would say "menu" with a colon (:) and be followed by the name you want at the top of the next menu. Then, on lines that follow, you would provide menu items to select and Lingo statements to execute.

Now to specify when the menu should appear. We want the menu to appear at the beginning of the movie. To accomplish that, we create a ***movie script***. Such a script is not specific to any one item in the movie, such as a particular frame or cast member. Rather, it applies to the movie as a whole.

In the **Cast** window, select an empty cast member.

Use **Window, Script** or equivalent to open the Script window.

The Script window appears, labeled "Movie Script" with the number of the frame you selected.

Add and name the script you see in the figure ("On Start").

When you play the movie you can use the Esc key to stop it and redisplay the standard menu bar. The last item in our new menu (Exit) causes Director to end; you don't want to lose your work should this occur.

Save the movie.

Play the movie and test the menu.

Note that Director sets the accelerator (underlined) character and you cannot change it. The character used may differ from that in the figure.

USING FIND/CHANGE TO HANDLE LARGER MOVIES

Finally, as your movies grow larger and larger, it may become increasingly difficult for you to locate material. However, Director provides various means of finding things and optionally changing them once they are found.

One such item is the Text menu's Find/Change dialog box (Figure 6.8), also available with Ctrl+F. This is used to find and change text in Script and Text windows. One of these two types of windows must be active for this dialog box to be available. It operates in a similar way to features you would find in word processing and other programs. It's also like features available in Windows Write via the Find menu, so you may be familiar with its operation through study of Windows. Basically, it makes the cursor search for your text from the cursor's present position forward through the current window.

To find text, you enter it in the **Find** box and click the **Find** button (or press Enter). If you provide **Change To** text, Director will search for and replace the text when you use the **Change** button (to change only the next instance found) or the **Change All** button (to change all instances). The **Wrap-Around Search** check box, if turned on, causes Director, on reaching the end of the window, to then search from the beginning. Turn on the **Search All Cast Members** check box to have Director search all cast members of the same type as the current one.

Here are other implements that are helpful for finding and changing.

- **Text, Find Again or Ctrl+G** Once you've initiated a search as just described, the dialog box in Figure 6.8 goes away. You can use this

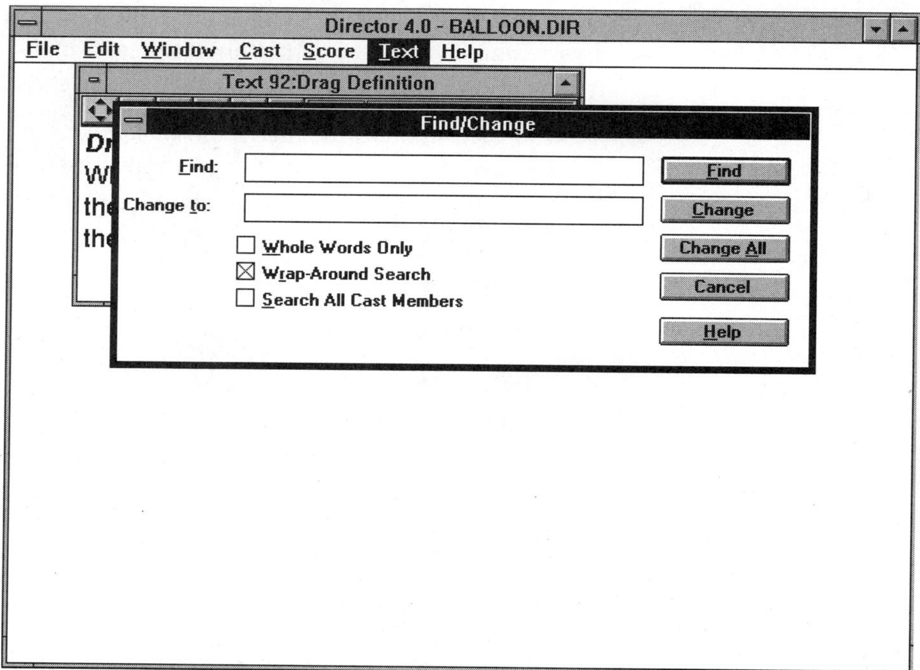

6.8
Text menu's Find/Change dialog box

command to have Director again perform the search, without displaying the dialog box.

- **Text, Change Again or Ctrl+T** This command makes Director automatically both find and change the next instance, also without the dialog box.
- **Text, Find Selection or Ctrl+H** You can highlight text in the Script or Text window and then use this command to make Director search for that highlighted text. Director follows the settings of the check boxes as set in the Find/Change dialog box.
- **Text, Find Handler or Ctrl+Shift+:** (Ctrl with Shift and the :; key) No particular window has to be showing for this command to be available. It displays a dialog box like that shown in Figure 6.9. You use it to find ***handlers***, the various portions of programming that tell Director what to do when a specific action occurs (that is, how to handle that action). This includes the various "on such-and-such" scripts you've been working with, such as "on mouseUp" and "on exitFrame." These actions in your movie appear along the left edge of the list in this dialog box. Following them are the cast number and name associated with the handler. You can use the buttons at the bottom of the box to sort this list **By Name** (alphabetically by cast name) or **By Order** (by cast number and the order in which handlers occur in their scripts). To find an item, you can select the item on the list, then click the **Find** button, or you can combine these two steps by double-clicking the item on the list.
- **Cast, Find Cast Members or Ctrl+;** (Ctrl with the :; key) Use this to find and select one or more cast members throughout the movie. This command displays a dialog box like that appearing in Figure 6.10. The **Whose Type Is** button is normally set for *All* but you can change it so that Director looks for only a particular type of cast member, such as sounds, shapes, or scripts. The **Whose Name Begins With** button can

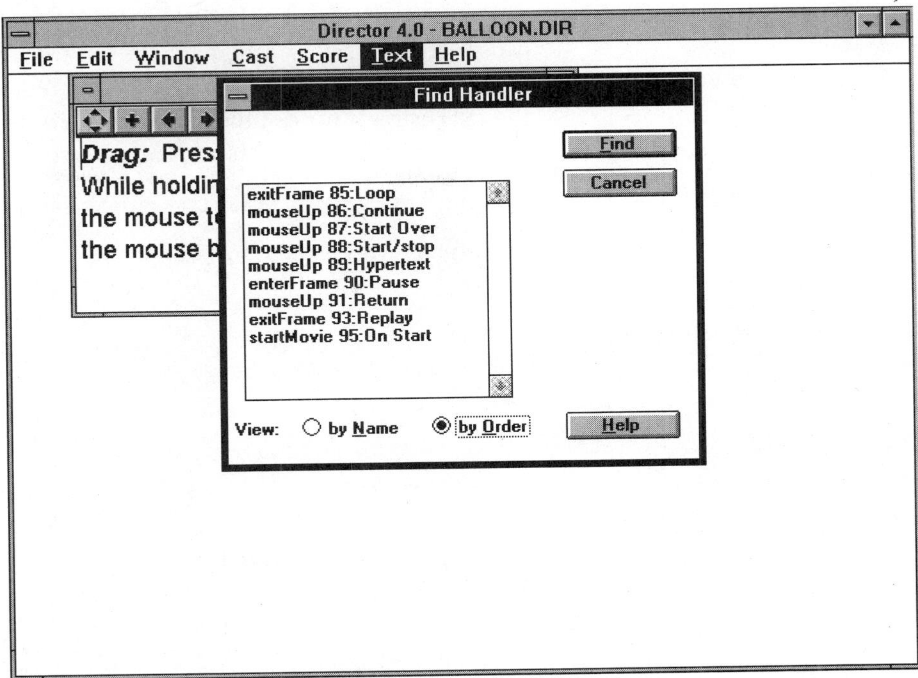

6.9

Text menu's Find Handler dialog box

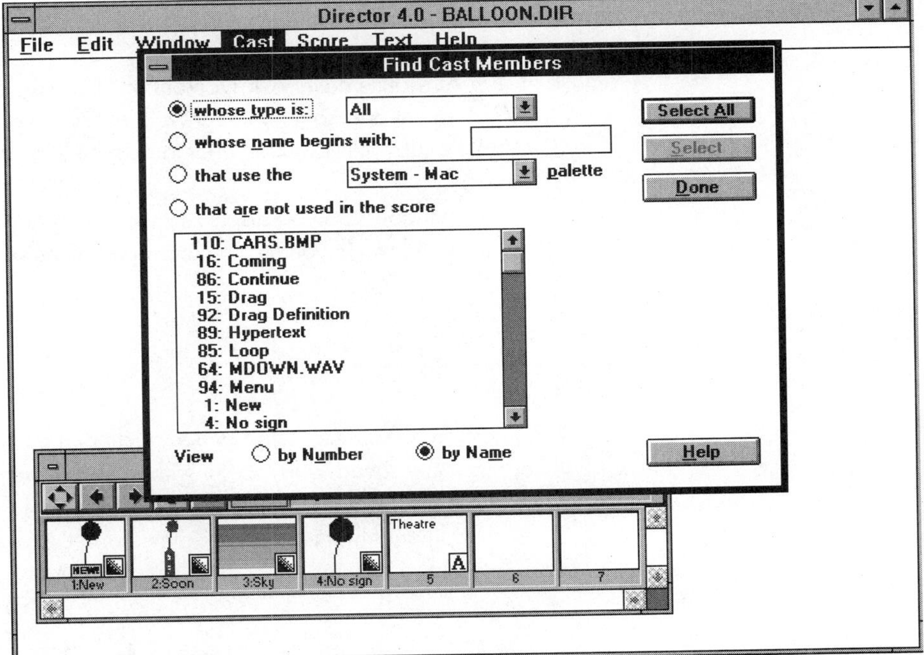

6.10

Cast menu's Find Cast Members dialog box

be especially helpful with the right naming strategy: If you begin similar cast members with the same name, you can use this box to find and select them. For example, Sky blue, Sky pink, and Sky gray could all be selected with Sky. Use the **That Use The** button to limit the list to cast members sharing a particular palette. With the **That Are Not Used In The Score** button you can check that all cast members have been assigned to the score. Use it to find cast members not in use so they can be eliminated or so you can assign them to the score. The list shows cast numbers and names according to the radio button that is selected above. Their order is determined by the radio button that is selected below, **By**

Number or **By Name**. The **Select All** button is always available; using it causes all the cast members on the list to be selected. The **Select** button becomes available once you've highlighted one of the cast members on the list; using it (or double-clicking one of the cast members on the list) causes the cast member to appear, selected, in the Cast window.

Test out these various means of finding items in your movie.

Good luck in creating bigger and better movies!

CHAPTER REVIEW

KEY TERMS

Lingo
controller
cropping
debugging
comment
hypertext
movie script
handlers

REVIEW QUESTIONS

1. **T F** All videos have VCR-type buttons that can be used to control them.
2. Which menu and command can you use to see a list of all of a movie's sounds?
3. What handler tells Director what to do when the user clicks and then releases the mouse?
4. Which window can you display to see scripts appear as they are executed?
5. Which window do you use to construct a menu?

PROJECTS

1. Import the c:\director\clips\video\mchnry.mov video into your movie, add an appropriate sound, and label it with animated text.
2. Add another hypertext example to your movie.
3. Add additional markers to your movie and create a second menu.

Appendix: Fast Reference Tools for Director 4.0

Actual tempo Control Panel, Actual display (Chapter 4)

Air brushes Paint, Air Brushes; double-click the Air Brush tool (Chapter 3)

Align bitmaps Cast, Align Bitmaps (Chapter 5)

Alignment Text, Alignment (Chapter 4)

Auto animate Score, Auto Animate (Chapter 5)

Auto distort Paint window's Effects menu, Auto Distort (Chapter 5)

Background color Paint window's Background Color chip (Chapter 3); Control Panel, Stage Background Color chip; Tools window's Background Color chip (Chapter 4)

Backward Edit, Step Backward; Ctrl+←; keypad 1; keypad 4; Control Panel, Step Backward button; Ctrl+Alt+← (Ctrl and Alt with the ← key) to step backward 10 frames (Chapter 2)

Banner Score, Auto Animate, Banner (Chapter 5)

Bar chart Score, Auto Animate, Bar Chart (Chapter 5)

Bitmap, convert to Cast, Convert To Bitmap (Chapter 4)

Bitmaps, align Cast, Align Bitmaps (Chapter 5)

Blend Score, Set Sprite Blend; Ctrl+Alt+B (Chapter 4)

Bold Text, Style, Bold (Chapter 3)

Borders Text, Border (Chapter 4)

Brush shapes Paint, Brush Shapes; double-click the Paintbrush tool; Paint, Air Brushes; double-click the Air Brush tool (Chapter 3)

Bullet chart Score, Auto Animate, Bullet Chart (Chapter 5)

Buttons Tools window's Button tools (Chapter 6)

Cast Cast menu; Cast window (Chapter 3)

Cast member, edit Cast, Edit Cast Member; cast member double-click; cast member Ctrl+↓; reverse with Ctrl+↑; double-click cell, triple-click, if multiple cells selected (Chapter 3)

Cast member info Cast, Cast Member Info; Ctrl+I; Info (i) button; point to cast member or stage sprite and click right (Chapter 3)

Cast to time Cast, Cast To Time; Alt-drag from Cast window (Chapter 5)

Cast window Window, Cast; Ctrl+3; click Cast window's Title bar (Chapters 1 and 3)

Center alignment Text, Alignment, Center (Chapter 4)

Change Text, Find/Change; Ctrl+F; Text, Change Again; Ctrl+T (Chapter 6)

Clear Edit, Clear; Backspace; Delete key (Chapter 3)

Close window File, Close Window; Ctrl+W; to close all windows, Alt+File, Alt+Close Window; Ctrl+Alt+W (Chapter 1)

Color Palettes window Window, Color Palettes; Ctrl+8; click Color Palette's Title bar (Chapter 1)

Color resolution Cast, Transform Bitmap; double-click the Paint window's Color Resolution indicator (Chapter 3)

Colors, invert Paint window's Effects menu, Invert Colors (Chapter 3)

Colors, switch Paint window's Effects menu, Switch Colors (Chapter 3)

Comment Text, Comment; Ctrl+Shift+> (Ctrl and Shift with the >. key); Text, Uncomment; Ctrl+Shift+< (Ctrl and Shift with the <, key) (Chapter 6)

Compact movie File, Save And Compact; Ctrl+Alt+S; File, Update Movies (Chapter 5)

Control panel Window, Control Panel; Ctrl+2; click Control Panel's Title bar (Chapters 1 and 2)

Convert to bitmap Cast, Convert To Bitmap (Chapter 4)

Copy Edit, Copy; Ctrl+C (Chapter 3)

Credits Score, Auto Animate, Credits (Chapter 5)

Cut Edit, Cut; Ctrl+X (Chapter 3)

Darken Paint window's Effects menu, Darken (Chapter 3)

Delete Edit, Clear; Backspace; Delete key (Chapter 3)

Delete frame Score, Delete Frame; Ctrl+[(Chapter 4)

Delete sprites Score, Delete Sprites; Ctrl+Backspace (Chapter 4)

Destination color Paint window's Destination Color chip (Chapter 3)

Digital video window Window, Digital Video; Ctrl+9; click Video window's Title bar (Chapter 1)

Disable Lingo Edit, Disable Lingo (Chapter 6)

Disable sounds Edit, Disable Sounds; Ctrl+` (Ctrl with the ~` key); Ctrl+~ (Ctrl and Shift with the ~` key); keypad 7; Control Panel, Disable Sounds button (Chapter 2)

Distort Paint window's Effects menu, Distort (Chapter 3)

Duplicate cast member Cast, Duplicate Cast Member; Ctrl+D (Chapter 3)

Duplicate window Window, Duplicate Window; Alt+Window, then Alt+Text, Alt+Digital Video, or Alt+Script (Chapter 6)

Edit cast member Cast, Edit Cast Member; cast member double-click; cast member Ctrl+↓; reverse with Ctrl+↑; double-click cell, triple-click, if multiple cells selected (Chapter 3)

Edit operations Edit menu

Editable Score, Editable check box (Chapter 4)

Effects Paint window's Effects menu (Chapter 3); Score, Auto Animate, Text Effects (Chapter 5)

Exit File, Exit; Ctrl+Q (Chapter 1)

Export File, Export; Ctrl+Shift+E (Chapter 5)

Files File menu (Chapters 1 and 5)

Fill Paint window's Effects menu, Fill (Chapter 3)

Find Text, Find/Change; Ctrl+F; Text, Find Again; Ctrl+G; Text, Find Selection; Ctrl+H; Text, Find Handler; Ctrl+Shift+: (Ctrl and Shift with the :; key); Cast, Find Cast Members; Ctrl+; (Ctrl with the :; key) (Chapter 6)

Flip Paint window's Effects menu, Flip Horizontal; Paint window's Effects menu, Flip Vertical (Chapter 4)

Font Text, Font (Chapter 4)

Foreground color Paint window's Foreground Color chip (Chapter 3); Tools window's Foreground Color chip (Chapter 4)

Forward Edit, Step Forward; Ctrl+→; keypad 3; keypad 6; Control Panel, Step Forward button; Ctrl+Alt+→ (Ctrl and Alt with the → key) to step forward 10 frames (Chapter 2)

Frame durations, lock Edit, Lock Frame Durations; Control Panel's Lock button (Chapter 2)

Frame, change Control Panel, Frame counter (Chapter 4)

Frame, delete Score, Delete Frame; Ctrl+[(Chapter 4)

Frame, insert Score, Insert Frame; Ctrl+] (Chapter 4)

Gradients Paint, Gradients; double-click a Shape tool on the shaded side (Chapter 3)

Help Help menu; Ctrl+? (Ctrl with the ?/ key); Alt+Shift (Chapter 1)

Import File, Import; Ctrl+J (Chapters 5 and 6)

In-between Score, In-Between Linear; Ctrl+B (Chapter 1); Score, In-Between Special; Ctrl+Shift+B (Chapter 5)

Info File, Movie Info; Ctrl+U (Chapter 5); Cast, Cast Member Info; Ctrl+I; Info (i) button (Chapter 3); Score, Sprite Info; Ctrl+K (Chapter 4)

Ink effects for Paint Paint window's Ink pop-up menu (Chapter 3)

Ink effects for Score Score window's Ink pop-up menu (Chapter 4)

Insert frame Score, Insert Frame; Ctrl+] (Chapter 4)

Invert colors Paint window's Effects menu, Invert Colors (Chapter 3)

Italic Text, Style, Italic (Chapters 4 and 5)

Jump to selected cell Score's Jump button (Chapter 4)

Jump to top of score Score's Jump To Top button (Chapter 4)

Left alignment Text, Alignment, Left (Chapters 4 and 5)

Letter slide Score, Auto Animate, Text Effects, Effect, Letter slide (Chapter 5)

Lighten Paint window's Effects menu, Lighten (Chapter 3)

Line Paint window's Line tool (Chapter 3); Tools window's Line tool (Chapter 4)

Line width Paint window's Line Width selector (Chapter 3); Tools window's Line Width selector (Chapter 4)

Lingo, Disable Edit, Disable Lingo (Chapter 6)

Lock frame durations Edit, Lock Frame Durations; Control Panel's Lock button (Chapter 2)

Loop Edit, Loop; Ctrl+L; keypad 8; Control Panel's Loop button (Chapter 2)

Margin Text, Margin (Chapter 4)

Markers window Window, Markers; Ctrl+Shift+M (Chapter 4)

Message window Window, Message; Ctrl+M; click Message window's Title bar (Chapter 1)

Moveable Score Window's Moveable check box (Chapter 4)

Movie Info File, Movie Info; Ctrl+U (Chapter 5)

New movie File, New; Ctrl+N (Chapter 1)

Next cast member Next button; Ctrl+Shift+→ (Ctrl and Shift with the → key) (Chapter 3)

Open movie File, Open; Ctrl+O (Chapter 1)

Open script Cast, Open Script; Ctrl+' (Ctrl with the "' key); Alt+Cast, Alt+Open Script opens new script window for current cast member (Chapter 6)

Options Cast, Cast Window Options (Chapter 3); Paint, Paint Window Options (Chapter 3); Score, Score Window Options (Chapter 4)

Paint window Window, Paint; Ctrl+5; click Paint window's Title bar (Chapters 1 and 3)

Palette, color Score, Set Palette; double-click Score's Palettes channel (Chapter 4); Window, Color Palettes; Ctrl+8; click Color Palette's Title bar (Chapter 1)

Paste Edit, Paste; Ctrl+V; Score, Paste Relative; Ctrl+Shift+V (Chapter 3)

Pattern Paint window's Pattern chip; Paint window's Paint menu, Patterns; double-click the Pattern chip (Chapter 3); Tools window's Pattern chip (Chapter 4)

Perspective Paint window's Effects menu, Perspective (Chapter 3)

Place cast member Place button (Chapter 4)

Play Edit, Play; Ctrl+P; keypad + (the + key on the keypad); keypad Enter toggles Play/Stop; Shift+keypad Enter (Shift with Enter on the keypad) clears and plays; Control Panel, Play button (Chapter 1)

Play selected frames Edit, Selected Frames Only; Ctrl+\ (Ctrl with the |\ key); Control Panel, Selected Frames Only button (Chapter 2)

Preferences File, Preferences; Ctrl+Alt+U (Chapter 1)

Previous cast member Previous button; Ctrl+Shift+← (Ctrl and Shift with the ← key) (Chapter 3)

Print File, Print; Ctrl+Alt+P; File, Print Setup (Chapter 2)

Projector File, Create Projector (Chapter 5)

Quit File, Exit; Ctrl+Q (Chapter 1)

Recompile scripts Text, Recompile Script; Ctrl+Shift+R; Text, Recompile All Scripts; Ctrl+Alt+R (Chapter 6)

Repeat effect Paint window's Effects menu, Repeat Effect; Ctrl+Y (Chapter 3)

Resolution, color Cast, Transform Bitmap; double-click the Paint window's Color Resolution indicator (Chapter 3)

Reverse sequence Score, Reverse Sequence (Chapter 5)

Revert to previous saved movie File, Revert (Chapter 4)

Rewind Edit, Rewind; Ctrl+R; keypad 0; Control Panel, Rewind button (Chapter 2)

Right alignment Text, Alignment, Right (Chapter 4)

Rotate Paint window's Effects menu, Rotate Left/Rotate Right/Free Rotate (Chapter 3)

Rulers Paint, Show/Hide Rulers (or Show/Hide Rulers depending on whether Paint Tools is on or off); Ctrl+Shift+K (Chapter 3)

Save movie File, Save; Ctrl+S (Chapter 1); File, Save As; Ctrl+Shift+S (Chapters 1 and 4); File, Save And Compact; Ctrl+Alt+S (Chapter 5)

Score Score menu; Score window (Chapter 4)

Score window Window, Score; Ctrl+4; click Score window's Title bar (Chapters 1 and 4)

Script window Window, Script; Ctrl+0; click Script window's Title bar; Script button; double-click Score's Script channel (Chapters 1 and 6)

Script, assign Score's Script pop-up menu (Chapter 4)

Script, open Cast, Open Script; Ctrl+' (Ctrl with the "' key); Alt+Cast, Alt+Open Script opens new script window for current cast member (Chapter 6)

Script, preview Score's Script Preview button (Chapters 4 and 6)

Scripts, recompile Text, Recompile Script; Ctrl+Shift+R; Text, Recompile All Scripts; Ctrl+Alt+R (Chapter 6)

Select Edit, Select All; Ctrl+A (Chapter 3)

Selected frames Edit, Selected Frames Only; Ctrl+\ (Ctrl with the |\ key); Control Panel, Selected Frames Only button (Chapter 2)

Setup, print File, Print Setup (Chapter 2)

Shadow Text, Text Shadow (Chapters 3 and 4)

Shapes Paint window's Shape tools (Chapter 3); Tools window's Shape tools (Chapter 4)

Shuffle backward Score's Shuffle Backward button; Ctrl+Shift+↑ (Chapter 4)

Shuffle forward Score's Shuffle Forward button; Ctrl+Shift+↓ (Chapter 4)

Size Text, Size (Chapters 3 and 4)

Slant Paint window's Effects menu, Slant (Chapter 3)

Smooth Paint window's Effects menu, Smooth (Chapter 3)

Sort cast members Cast, Sort Cast Members (Chapter 3)

Sound Score, Set Sound (Chapter 6)

Sounds, disable Edit, Disable Sounds; Ctrl+` (Ctrl with the ~` key); Ctrl+~ (Ctrl and Shift with the ~` key); keypad 7; Control Panel, Disable Sounds button (Chapter 2)

Space to time Score, Space To Time (Chapter 5)

Sparkle Score, Auto Animate, Text Effects, Effect, Sparkle (Chapter 5)

Sprite blend Score, Set Sprite Blend; Ctrl+Alt+B (Chapter 4)

Sprite info Score, Sprite Info; Ctrl+K (Chapter 4)

Sprites, delete Score, Delete Sprites; Ctrl+Backspace (Chapter 4)

Stage window Window, Stage; Ctrl+1 (Chapters 1 and 4)

Step Backward Edit, Step Backward; Ctrl+←; keypad 1; keypad 4; Control Panel, Step Backward button; Ctrl+Alt+← (Ctrl and Alt with the ← key) to step backward 10 frames (Chapter 2)

Step Forward Edit, Step Forward; Ctrl+→; keypad 3; keypad 6; Control Panel, Step Forward button; Ctrl+Alt+→ (Ctrl and Alt with the → key) to step forward 10 frames (Chapter 2)

Stop Edit, Stop; Ctrl+(Ctrl with the >. key); keypad 2; keypad 5; keypad . (the .Del key on the keypad); keypad Enter toggles Play/Stop; Control Panel, Stop button (Chapter 1)

Style Text, Style (Chapters 3 and 4)

Switch cast members Score, Switch Cast Members; Ctrl+E (Chapter 4)

Switch colors Paint window's Effects menu, Switch Colors (Chapter 3)

Tempo Control Panel, Tempo display; Score, Set Tempo; double-click Score's Tempo channel (Chapter 4)

Text Text menu; Paint window's Text tool (Chapter 3); Tools window's Text tool (Chapter 4)

Text effects Score, Auto Animate, Text Effects (Chapter 5)

Text window Window, Text; Ctrl+6; click Text window's Title bar (Chapters 1 and 4)

Tiles Paint, Tiles (Chapter 3)

Tools window Window, Tools; Ctrl+7; click Tools window's Title bar (Chapters 1 and 4)

Tools, Paint window Paint, Show/Hide Paint Tools; Ctrl+Shift+J (Chapter 3)

Trace Message window's Trace check box (Chapter 6)

Trace edges Paint window's Effects menu, Trace Edges (Chapter 3)

Trails Score Window's Trails check box (Chapter 4)

Transition Score, Set Transition; double-click Score's Transition channel (Chapter 4)

Tweak window Window, Tweak; Ctrl+Shift+T; click Tweak window's Title bar (Chapters 1 and 4)

Typewriter Score, Auto Animate, Text Effects, Effect, Typewriter (Chapter 5)

Uncomment Text, Uncomment; Ctrl+Shift+< (Ctrl and Shift with the <, key) (Chapter 6)

Underline Text, Style, Underline (Chapters 3 and 4)

Undo Edit, Undo; Ctrl+Z (Chapter 3)

Update movie File, Update Movies (Chapter 5)

Window operations Window menu

Zoom Paint window Paint, Zoom In; Ctrl++ (Ctrl with the += key); Paint, Zoom Out; Ctrl+- (Ctrl with the _- key) (Chapter 3)

Zoom text Score, Auto Animate, Zoom Text (Chapter 5)

Glossary: Shoptalk for Director 4.0

Accelerate To speed up animation (Chapter 5).

Actual display Section of the Control Panel that displays the actual duration of each frame when it was played (Chapter 2).

Air Brush tool Tool in the Paint window's Tool palette that is used to apply paint according to the air brush's shape (Chapter 3).

Author Individual who creates movies with which users can interact on the computer to gain information and knowledge (Chapter 1).

Auto animate Commands for automatically creating a variety of text effects and items that are useful in presentations (Chapter 5).

Auto distort Method of automatically creating cast members that uses an existing cast member you modify with one of several specific effects. Each new cast member reflects a progression from the original shape to the modified shape. You can then assign the new cast members to the score and thereby create animation that changes the shape of an image on the screen (Chapter 5).

Bounding box White box around a sprite that indicates its perimeter. Sometimes called a *selection box* (Chapter 2).

Cast members Graphics and other items, including sounds, text, movies, and palettes, that are the fundamental building blocks for making a movie. Cast members appear in the Cast window, where each is assigned a number and optionally a name (Chapter 1).

Cell Position where a frame and channel intersect. Cells are used to hold sprites (Chapter 1).

Channel button Button in each of the score's channels. Clicking this button turns off the corresponding channel so its contents won't appear as you run the movie. Turning off is temporary; it's not saved with the movie or once you quit Director (Chapter 4).

Channels Rows of cells in the score, numbered along the left edge. The first six channels are specially designated for effects (Tempo, Palettes, Transitions, Sounds 1 and 2, and Script); the numbered channels are available for sprites (Chapter 1).

Comment Line that documents a program with a remark at its location. It serves no purpose when the program is running (Chapter 6).

Compacting Process of saving a movie in its most compact form to create the smallest possible size for the file. Its use is recommended before distributing a movie (Chapter 5).

Control Panel Window with a set of VCR-type buttons and other controls used to play and otherwise operate movies (Chapter 1).

Controller Strip at the bottom of the Digital Video window with a sound button, a slider switch, and some VCR-type controls. The controller is available only with MOV files, not AVI files. If available, the controller can be displayed as a movie plays, thereby allowing the user to operate it and so control the video (Chapter 6).

Cropping Process of clipping away part of an image (Chapter 6).

Debugging Trouble-shooting problems that occur, typically, during the running of a program (Chapter 6).

Decelerate To slow down animation (Chapter 5).

Dithering The process of mixing pixels of different colors to create a new color. In a gradient, dithering can give the impression of subtle changes in color. Without dithering, colors are limited to those on the palette and color changes are more abrupt (Chapter 3).

Editable text Specifically designated text that can be changed by a user while the movie is playing (Chapter 4).

Effects channels Special channels that are positioned above channel 1 in the score. They include the Tempo, Palette, Transition, Sound, and Script channels (Chapter 4).

Eraser tool Block-shaped tool in the Paint window's Tool palette that you can use to erase art (Chapter 3).

Export To create a new file with the frames of a movie. You can export as a series of bitmap files or in Video for Windows (.AVI) format (Chapter 5).

Film log Animated sequence assigned to a single cast member (Chapter 5).

FPS Abbreviation for frames per second, a unit of speed for a movie (Chapter 2).

Frame counter Section of the Control Panel that shows the number of the frame that's currently displayed. Thus it always corresponds to the frame indicated by the playback head. You can also use the Frame counter to make Director display a particular frame (Chapter 2). Also a box in the Score window, showing the correct frame number, that appears when you drag the horizontal scroll bar (Chapter 4).

Gradient The mixture of paint resulting from a process that creates changes from one color to another (Chapter 3).

Hand tool Hand-shaped tool in the Paint window's Tool palette that you can use to move the entire graphic in the window (Chapter 3).

Handlers Various portions of programming that tell Director what to do when a specific action occurs—that is, how to handle that action (Chapter 6).

Hypertext Text you can click to display material related to that text. Once you finish reading or otherwise viewing the material, you can click to return to the screen with the hypertext (Chapter 6).

Import To bring various files into Director. For example, you can bring in sounds, graphics, video, and other Director movies (Chapter 5).

In-betweening Process of automatically generating intervening sprites between two existing sprites in order to create animation (Chapter 1).

Ink effects Effects you can assign to various Paint tools in the Paint window or to sprites in the score. An ink effect changes the way an ink looks or the way two inks affect each other. Not all ink effects are available for all tools (Chapter 3).

Interface Dialog boxes, menus, and other aspects of Director's display (Chapter 2).

Jump button Button in the score that, when clicked, positions the score so that the selected cell is again visible in the Score window (Chapter 4).

Jump To Top button Button in the score. When the score isn't in its original location (that is, with the Script channel and channel 1 at the top), you can click this button one time to reposition the score there. When the score is in its original position, clicking this button repositions the score with the effects channels displayed (Chapter 4).

Lasso tool Tool at the top of the Paint window's Tool palette that you can use for selecting. With it, you drag a line around the item you want to select and, when you release, the line connects, selecting what is within it. Edges of an item selected with the Lasso tool blink (Chapter 3).

Linear Occurring in a straight line. With linear in-betweening you create the first and final sprites; Director generates the intervening sprites in a straight line (Chapter 5).

Lingo Director's programming language. With Lingo you can program buttons, control movie playback, create menus, and more (Chapter 6).

Linked files Files associated with a movie that are not part of the movie. The movie remembers their location on disk, so that it can refer to such files as necessary (Chapter 5).

Locking Method of freezing the duration of all frames at their speed when last played (Chapter 2).

Looping Repeated playing of a movie or portion of a movie, immediately and endlessly until stopped (Chapter 2).

Marker Implement for documenting the appearance of sprites and other activities that occur in the score. To create a marker you use the **marker well**, an item in the score that provides a supply of markers you can use by dragging into position (Chapter 4).

Moveable sprites Sprites that the user can drag around the stage while the movie is running; they are created by turning on the Moveable check box (Chapter 4).

Movie script Script that is not specific to any one item in the movie, such as a particular frame or cast member. Rather, it applies to the movie as a whole (Chapter 6).

Movies Director files (also called titles or applications) with which users interact on the computer to gain information and knowledge (Chapter 1).

Nudging Process for fine-tuning placement of a sprite with the arrow keys. Pressing an arrow key moves the selected sprite(s) by one pixel in the direction of the key. The arrow keys operate in this fashion as long as the Tweak window is not open (Chapter 4).

Paint Bucket tool Bucket-shaped tool in the Paint window's Tool palette that you can use to pour color. It uses the current foreground color to pour paint into an area, as indicated by the Foreground Color chip (Chapter 3).

Paintbrush tool Brush-shaped tool in the Paint window's Tool palette that is used to apply paint according to the paintbrush's shape (Chapter 3).

Pixel Picture element or screen dot, the smallest size available on the screen (Chapter 3).

Playback head Black box that appears in the score in the row marked "Frame," just above the frame numbers. It indicates the movie's current position and the frame currently displayed on the stage (Chapter 1).

Point A typographical unit of measurement equal to 1/72 inch. Standard reading text is typically 12 points in size (Chapter 3).

Projector An executable (.EXE) movie that can be played (but not edited) on any Windows computer, even without Director (Chapter 5).

Real-time recording Process of creating animations by recording your movements as you make them (Chapter 5).

Registration point A position you can set in the Paint window to line up sequential cast members accurately for smooth animation (Chapters 2 and 5).

Score The grid-type structure that Director uses to organize a movie (Chapter 1).

Selection Rectangle Tool at the top of the Paint window's Tool palette that you can use for selecting. With it, you select by dragging diagonally across the area you want to select. As you do, a dotted rectangle appears, which you use to indicate the area you want to include (Chapter 3).

Shuffling Process of moving the contents of one or more cells forward (down) or backward (up) by one channel in the score. To shuffle, you use the Shuffle Backward and Shuffle Forward buttons (Chapter 4).

Special in-betweening In-betweening of sprites for characteristics other than size and linear position (Chapter 5).

SPF Abbreviation for seconds per frame, a unit of speed for a movie (Chapter 2).

Sprite A copy of a cast member that contains additional information as well, such as the sprite's position on the stage (Chapter 1).

Stage The main area of Director that shows the movie as it is played or displays the current frame of the movie when the movie is stopped (Chapter 1).

Step recording Process of creating animations by recording one frame at a time (Chapter 5).

Tempo display Section of the Control Panel that allows you to see and control the speed at which a movie plays (Chapter 2).

Text box A temporary container created by the Text window's Text tool that you can use to type in text (Chapter 3).

Thumbnails Reduced depiction of a cast member as it appears in the Cast Window (Chapter 3).

Trails Sprites with this check box turned on remain on the screen after being displayed, creating trails (although all or part of the sprite could be overlaid in subsequent frames) (Chapter 4).

Transitions Built-in methods for changing the screen from one scene to the next. They are available via the Transition channel and the Set Transition dialog box (Chapter 4).

Tweaking Process that assists in precise placement. It uses the Tweak window, which allows you to move the selected sprite(s) by minute horizontal and vertical amounts, repeatedly if necessary (Chapter 4).

Users Persons who interact with the computer in order to gain information and knowledge (Chapter 1).

Zooming In the Paint window, the process of magnifying art so that you can work on it with greater precision (Chapter 3). Zoom Text is an auto animate effect for making text enlarge and shrink (Chapter 5).

Index